GREEK and LATIN
in
ENGLISH TODAY

by
RICHARD M. KRILL

BOLCHAZY-CARDUCCI PUBLISHERS

Cover by D. Thomas Langdon

© Copyright 1990

BOLCHAZY-CARDUCCI PUBLISHERS

1000 Brown Street, Unit 101

Wauconda, Illinois 60084

Printed in the United States of America

International Standard Book Number

0-86516-241-7

Library of Congress Catalog Number:

90-22993

Library of Congress Cataloging-in-Publication Data

Krill, Richard M.
    Greek and Latin in English Today / by Richard M. Krill
        p.   cm.
    Includes bibliographical references and index.
    ISBN 0-86516-247-7 : $19.00
    1. English language—Foreign elements—Greek. 2. English
language—Foreign elements—Latin. 3.Greek language—Influence
on English. 4. Latin language—Influence on English. 5. English
language—Word formation. 6. English language—Roots. I. Title.
PE1582.G6K7   1990
422'.481--dc20
                                        90-22993
                                        CIP

Preface

That the ancient languages of Greek and Latin have significantly influenced the vocabulary and grammatical structure of English has long been recognized in learned circles. For this reason serious students of language and those whose professional fields require an in depth understanding of a very sophisticated and technical vocabulary have for many generations devoted a portion of their academic programs, either in secondary school or at the college or university level, to the study of these classical languages in the traditional manner. The results of their efforts on the whole have been easy to predict. Latin students as a group (Greek is less commonly taught in secondary schools) have traditionally received the highest verbal scores in standardized national tests, such as the Scholastic Aptitude Test (SAT), over other groups of students studying a different foreign language or no foreign language at all.

With the realization in recent years that too many of today's most gifted students for various reasons have not enrolled in traditional Latin or Greek courses, special efforts have often been made in academic circles to introduce them at least to a concentrated study of important Greek and Latin roots commonly found in English vocabulary and to set forth for their benefit the basic principles upon which new words are coined annually even to this day from these ancient languages. The primary purpose of this text is to assist in these efforts. Admittedly, this is a poor substitute for the traditional courses in a classical language, taught over a period of two or more years, where literature, philosophy, history, and grammar all play so important a part.

In this vocabulary-building text the author has made every effort to expose students to as much Greek and Latin as possible. The Greek vocabularies, for example, are presented in letters of the Greek alphabet. This helps students to understand strange combinations of letters in English words of Greek origin. In the long run, it also assists them in remembering which roots come from which language and hence in recognizing more natural root combinations. Thousands of students have found this limited exposure to the Greek alphabet a most fascinating and enjoyable experience. On the other hand, for Latin the inclusion of hundreds of short phrases, commonly assumed *in toto* into English, is intended to promote a broader interest in the language itself than what the mere combining of roots can generally produce. A second feature of this text is the rendering of Greek and Latin words in their complete, natural form. Some texts in use today give only word *roots* with no endings and, moreover, furnish no indication of language origin. Since, however, many words from Greek and Latin form their plural by following the rules unique to their original language, it is important for students to obtain some familiarity with word endings too. In this respect it should be pointed out that the complete Greek or Latin word (base and ending), not merely that word's root, traditionally appears in the etymology listing of English dictionaries. A third feature of this text is the inclusion of a separate section (Part III) with more detailed vocabularies of selected fields. Although not intended to be complete in and of themselves, these lists give students an opportunity to observe and work with technical language in an area that may be closer to their major or intended profession. Since those likely to employ this book will share a wide range of career goals, special assignments can be given in this section that are more suited to individual interests.

Most important in this type of text, however, is the need to provide students with numerous examples of English word derivatives in such a way that they can more easily become acquainted with the process of recognizing Greek and Latin roots and hence be in a position to recognize the meanings of unfamiliar words. Each year more new words enter the English language from these language sources than from any other language. In this respect ancient Greek and Latin can hardly be said to be "dead languages," for they have in fact assumed a dominant role over our English vocabulary. Moreover, this process is likely to continue for years to come. Clearly, many young students studying this process today will be in a position at some future date to contribute new words of their own and thereby will further this centuries-old tradition.

This text was originally designed for use by classicists (teachers of Greek and Latin) for a college-level course on derivatives from Greek and Latin where the focus was not to be limited to one or two subject fields. It might also be employed as a vocabulary supplement in a traditional Greek or Latin course. The author welcomes suggestions for future editions.

R.M.K.

About the Author

Richard M. Krill received the degrees of A.B. and A.M. from John Carroll University and Ph.D. from St. Louis University. He has taught classics at LeMoyne College (Syracuse) and the University of Missouri-Columbia. His present position is that of Professor of Classics and Humanities at The University of Toledo, Toledo, OH 43606.

———————————

This book is dedicated to my family:
to my wife Mary Louise and
my three daughters Regina, Michelle and Helen;
to my father Dr. Carl E. Krill, Sr. who to this day remains
for me an inspiration to intellectual pursuits;
to my late father-in-law Prof. William C. Korfmacher
who originally instilled a love of the classics in me; and
of course to my mother Helen and mother-in-law Louise,
both now departed, whose encouragement and love
so deeply enriched my life.

Divisions of Geologic Time

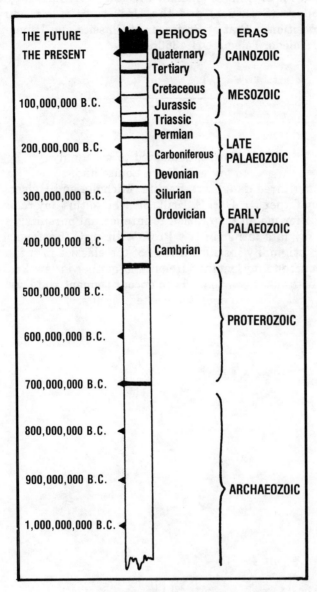

	PERIODS	ERAS
THE FUTURE		
THE PRESENT	Quaternary	CAINOZOIC
	Tertiary	
	Cretaceous	MESOZOIC
100,000,000 B.C.	Jurassic	
	Triassic	
	Permian	LATE PALAEOZOIC
200,000,000 B.C.	Carboniferous	
	Devonian	
300,000,000 B.C.	Silurian	
	Ordovician	EARLY PALAEOZOIC
400,000,000 B.C.	Cambrian	
500,000,000 B.C.		
		PROTEROZOIC
600,000,000 B.C.		
700,000,000 B.C.		
800,000,000 B.C.		
900,000,000 B.C.		ARCHAEOZOIC
1,000,000,000 B.C.		

The names of these sequential time periods contain Greek and Latin roots and suffixes. Can you identify and distinguish them?

Contents

Part III. DERIVATIVES/PHRASES IN SELECTED FIELDS

SPECIAL TOPICS
(Chapters 1-20)

Introduction

Our Language Family

Language can be defined as the expression of thoughts or emotions between or among humans. It is the principal tool of communication for the powers of speech and hearing. Sometimes it is regarded more narrowly as the vocabulary we employ to communicate. In this setting so long as the words spoken remain mutually understandable in a gathering of people, we maintain that the *same* language is being spoken. In situations where only minor variations of expression exist, we acknowledge the presence of *dialects* of the same language.

Many factors account for the development of new languages and dialects. Foremost among them must be man's own imprecise and inconsistent use of verbal communication. Migrations for whatever reasons and isolation, brought on by natural obstructions such as mountains, seas and deserts, certainly have also contributed to the process in the past. Moreover, climatic conditions so variously affect different regions of the world as to produce unique resources and specimens of life in isolated areas wherever man has settled. For these and similar reasons separate vocabularies and languages have developed and spread throughout the earth. Today one can only wonder in retrospect how much less language change would have taken place in antiquity if mankind possessed then the fantastic technological devices of radio, television and space communication satellites which we commonly use today.

The study of the origins of language and the relationship of languages to one another is called *linguistics*. Scholars engaged in this work over the past few centuries have determined which languages are more closely related to one another and which show no kinship at all. Their conclusions are usually based upon the study of thousands of similar-sounding words which identify similar things in the different languages. Words that specify the designation of family relationships, such as "mother," "father," "brother" and "sister," as well as numbers frequently provide sound clues. Basing their conclusions upon such studies, nearly all linguists accept the premise that in the distant past a certain few "mother" tongues predominated and that in the passage of time these languages, at different rates, produced "daughter" languages with the process repeating itself over

1

Indo-European Family of Languages

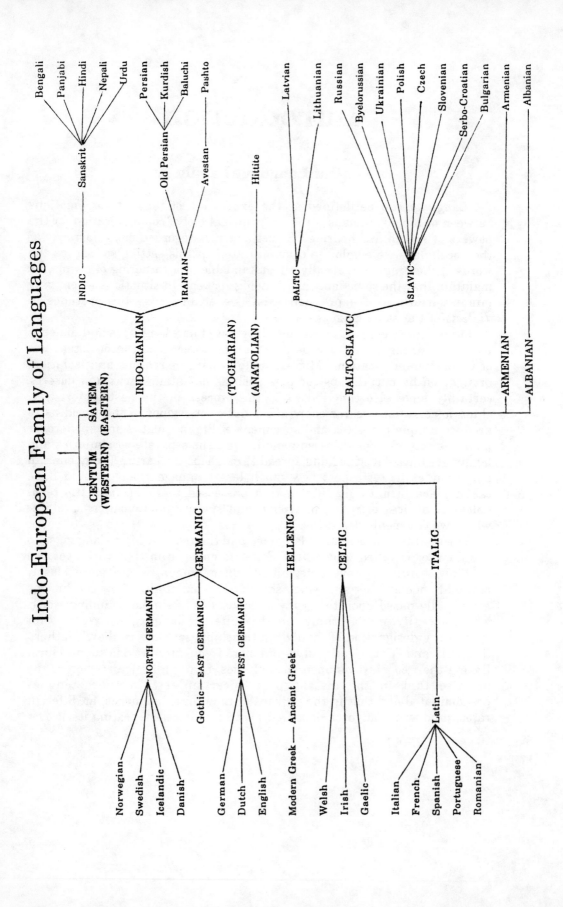

and over again up to the present time. Indeed within this framework some daughter languages were quite prolific with respect to the number of their offspring, while others remained more constant or dwindled to the point of extinction. Those languages which demonstrate a closer kinship to one another are said to belong to the same language *family.* The family of greatest importance to western civilization, if for no other reason than the sheer multitude of its speakers, is the *Indo-European* (later referred to in abbreviated form as IE) family of languages. It is spoken today in one or another of its descendent languages by approximately half of the world's population. Since it also happens to be the original source of our nation's principal tongue, English, greater attention is given to it here. Examine the language graph on the opposite page for some examples of contemporary languages which belong to this family. Included in each branch are only the major language developments. The first division of this family, you will note, occurs simply as a split between western (*centum*) and eastern (*satem*) groups. The two are so labeled from a common pronunciation difference observable in the initial velar or guttural "k" sound in the word meaning "hundred." Many centuries ago in the western languages a hard "k" sound was more commonly applied, while in the eastern group a softer "s" sound usually prevailed. English and French can therefore both be classified as centum languages. The one appears under the Germanic branch, more particularly, the Western Germanic, while the other is derived from Latin in the Italic branch. Armenian and Russian fall into the satem division. Today not all linguists recognize the twofold split of centum and satem groups. They rather proceed directly to the many sub-groups of this large family. Each of these possesses a unique history. Some of the more interesting facts pertaining to each division follow.

1. **Germanic** This branch is sometimes referred to as *Teutonic* to avoid confusion with the modern language German. *Gothic,* an extinct language today from the eastern section, is known mostly from a fourth century edition of the Bible and is therefore very important as a linguistic tool for understanding early developments in the entire language branch. Our own language *English* is thought to have developed from the western Germanic tribes known as Angles, Saxons and Jutes, all of whom migrated to the British Isles from the mainland around the fifth century A.D. Although its name is derived from only one of these groups, the Angles, most of its earliest surviving texts are of Saxon origin. The other western Germanic languages include principally German and Dutch, but the

student of linguistics should also be aware of *Flemish* (spoken in Belgium) and *Frisian* (employed by some people in the Netherlands). The northern Germanic languages include *Norwegian, Swedish, Icelandic* and *Danish.*

2. **Hellenic** From as far back as the first millennium B.C. many dialects of ancient Greek can be identified. These include *Ionic, Aeolic, Doric* and *Attic.* The last of these, spoken around the cultural metropolis of Athens, dominated in literature. Following the conquest of Asia Minor by Alexander the Great in the latter part of the fourth century B.C., *koine* (common) Greek assumed greater importance throughout the eastern Mediterranean. The Christian Bible, for example, was written for the most part in koine Greek.

3. **Celtic** In antiquity the Celts occupied several areas of western and central Europe before finally settling mostly on the British Isles. Indeed one Celtic segment, the Galatians, migrated in an eastward direction and settled in Anatolia, present-day Turkey. Today, however, in spite of the vast geographical area once occupied by Celtic tribes, relatively few people speak languages from this branch. *Welsh* is spoken in Wales, *Irish Gaelic* in Ireland, and *Scottish Gaelic* in Scotland. A few traces of the nearly extinct language *Manx* may yet be found on the Isle of Man. On the European mainland in Brittany, France, the Celtic language *Breton* is spoken today, the result of a migration back from England following the Anglo-Saxon invasion in the fifth century.

4. **Italic** In antiquity several Italic languages were spoken on the Italian peninsula. Foremost among them were *Latin, Oscan* and *Umbrian.* On the other hand, a highly civilized and powerful people known as *Etruscans* occupied central Italy just north of Rome in the first millennium B.C. These people of unknown origin spoke a non-Indo-European language which to this date, in spite of its survival in numerous extant writings, has not been fully deciphered. As the political power of Rome expanded, the language of its speakers, Latin, assumed a dominant position among the city's conquered neighbors. In time these subjugated tribes suffered a complete displacement of their native tongue. Beyond Italy the same thing occurred as the mighty Roman forces exerted their influence during the late Republic and early Empire. Indeed the strong centralized government at Rome employed Latin as the official language for all its western provinces (from Britain and Germany to North Africa) and Greek for its eastern bloc subordinates. Throughout so vast an area and over a period of time lasting

several centuries, it was only natural for the Latin language itself to suffer a similar breakdown. The name given to colloquial Latin speech in its many corrupted forms, prior to its finding a new identity in several distinct modern languages, is *Vulgar Latin.* The word *vulgus* in Latin, like *koine* in Greek, means "common," and in both instances refers to the language as spoken by the common people. As might be expected, Jerome's Latin edition of the Bible, known as the *Vulgate,* is so called because it was written in the common man's tongue. The languages descendent from Latin are known as the *Romance Languages.* Emerging first simply as dialectical variants of Latin, they later developed into *Italian, French, Spanish, Portuguese,* and *Romanian.* Included in this same category, but not listed on the IE graph, are *Catalan* (in northeastern Spain) and *Provencal* (in southeastern France).

5. *Indo-Iranian* This family branch is sometimes referred to merely as *Aryan* and, as its name suggests, is geographically located in the areas of India and Iran today. Classical *Sanskrit,* one of the most important of all ancient IE languages, developed in this branch. Standardized for literary purposes in the fourth century B.C. by a grammarian named Panini, it was employed continuously down into the Middle Ages. Among the Indic languages, however, Sanskrit was preceded in time by an even older *Vedic* language which provided hymns similar in length to the Greek poet Homer's epics, the *Iliad* and *Odyssey.* Several of India's principal languages, including *Hindi, Urdu, Bengali,* and *Panjabi,* belong to this family branch, and all can be traced from Sanskrit. On the other hand, several languages in the souther portion of the Indian peninsula are not part of this family at all. To the Iranian portion of this branch belong *Farsi (Modern Persian), Kurdish, Baluchi, Tajiki, Pashto* and the ancient *Persian* and *Avestan,* all geographically located between eastern Turkey and northern India.

6. *Tocharian* and ***Hittite*** Two separate IE language groups in Asia, known from antiquity but extinct today, are Tocharian and Hittite. Not much can be said with certainty in either case except that both appear to be clearly distinct from the other Indo-Iranian languages of the area. While Hittite is readily identified historically with the great empire which flourished in Asia Minor from 1400 to 1200 B.C., Tocharian is noteworthy for having been traced even to the western frontiers of China.

7. ***Balto-Slavic*** This language group spans the broad geographical area of much of eastern Europe and western Asia. From the northern Baltic area come *Latvian* and *Lithuanian.* Located below these districts, a bit toward the east, are *Russian, Ukrainian* and *Byelorussian.* In the western portion are *Czech, Slovak* and *Polish,* while in the south are *Bulgarian, Macedonian, Slovenian* and *Serbo-Croatian.* One has to be careful not to include in this sub-group languages spoken in neighboring areas, such as Hungarian, Romanian and German (in Austria).

8. ***Albanian*** and ***Armenian*** These two language branches are extraordinary for developing in antiquity but not breaking down into sub-groups. Today *Albanian* is spoken in the country bearing that name and in its surrounding areas. *Armenian* originated east of the Black Sea in areas today under Soviet and Turkish rule.

Theories abound about where the first speakers of Indo-European were located several millennia ago. Some would place them in central Europe, others in the southwestern corner of the Soviet Union before migrations dispersed them in various directions. Not only is the location a matter of debate. Many scholars have criticized the very name "Indo-European" as a label inappropriately applied to this family. To them the greatest problem stems from the implication that all the languages in India are members of this family, which indeed is not the case (*cf.* Indo-Iranian above). The same holds true for the "European" portion of the label because not all the languages in Europe belong to this family either. Non-members in this continent include *Finnish, Hungarian,* and *Basque,* spoken in the western Pyrenees. Also, the earlier-mentioned *Etruscan* language, once spoken by the powerful settlers just north of Rome, is not an IE language either. To date, however, a more satisfactory name has not been found so Indo-European, as imperfect as the label is, remains as the preferred name of this group.

OTHER LANGUAGE FAMILIES	Languages/(Locations)
I. SINO-TIBETAN	Chinese,Burmese, Thai
II. SEMITIC-HAMITIC	Arabic, Hebrew, Berber, Ethiopic, Sudanic
III.URAL-ALTAIC	Finnish, Magyar (Hungarian), Turkish

IV. JAPANESE   Japanese, Korean

V. DRAVIDIAN   (Southern India)

VI. MALAY-POLYNESIAN   (Pacific Islands, Indonesia)

VII. AFRICAN NEGRO   (Central & Southern Africa)

VIII. AMERICAN INDIAN   (North & South America)

In addition to the large Indo-European family of languages, there are several other language families. These are listed in the graph above on the left, with examples in some cases of modern languages that belong to each class on the right.

It has been pointed out earlier in this introduction that the daughter languages of Indo-European possess a kindred relationship to one another. For this reason they are said to be *cognate* languages. The Latin word *cognatus,* from which this term comes, means "sprung from the same stock," hence "related." In similar fashion words themselves among the various cognate languages are said to be *cognates*. Some examples of cognate words follow.

English	Greek	Latin	Russian	Sanskrit
mother	meter	mater	mat'	matar
brother	phrater	frater	brat'	bhratar
is	esti	est	jest'	asti

These words are similar because they derive from a common parent source. For example, the reconstructed Indo-European root for "mother," given in most etymological dictionaries, is *mater.*[1] The conjecture for this and most other IE roots is based strictly on examples surviving in the descendent languages. Proof for the working of this backward, reconstructive process can be no more convincingly demonstrated than in the case of the

---

[1] Since no actual words from the ancient Indo-European language survive, reconstructed roots are usually identified in printed form with an asterisk placed before them.

Language Graph Showing Cognates & Word Derivatives

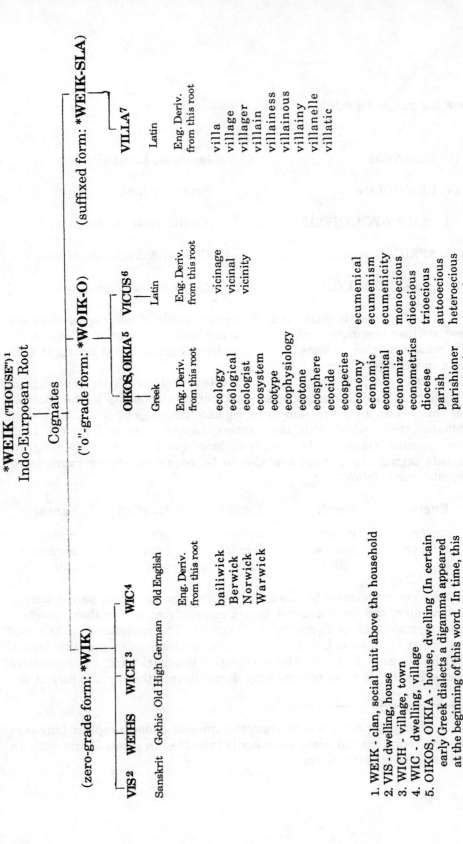

*WEIK ("HOUSE")[1]
Indo-Eurpoean Root

Cognates

(zero-grade form: *WIK)

VIS[2]	WEIHS	WICH[3]	WIC[4]
Sanskrit	Gothic	Old High German	Old English

Eng. Deriv.
from this root

bailiwick
Berwick
Norwick
Warwick

("o"-grade form: *WOIK-O)

OIKOS, OIKIA[5]
Greek

Eng. Deriv.
from this root

ecology
ecological
ecologist
ecosystem
ecotype
ecophysiology
ecotone
ecosphere
ecocide
ecospecies
economy
economic
economical
economize
econometrics
diocese
parish
parishioner
parochial
parochialism
ecesis
ecestics

VICUS[6]
Latin

Eng. Deriv.
from this root

vicinage
vicinal
vicinity

ecumenical
ecumenism
ecumenicity
monoecious
dioecious
trioecious
autooecious
heteroecious
paroecious
perioecious
androecious
gynoecious

(suffixed form: *WEIK-SLA)

VILLA[7]
Latin

Eng. Deriv.
from this root

villa
village
villager
villain
villainess
villainous
villainy
villanelle
villatic

1. WEIK - clan, social unit above the household
2. VIS - dwelling, house
3. WICH - village, town
4. WIC - dwelling, village
5. OIKOS, OIKIA - house, dwelling (In certain early Greek dialects a digamma appeared at the beginning of this word. In time, this letter, which had the sound of a "w," simply disappeared.)
6. VICUS - village, hamlet, quarter of a city
7. VILLA - countryhouse, farm

Romance languages with Latin where we can actually take thousands of parallel words from the modern languages, reconstruct a parent form and then actually see that form in Latin. The parent language may be a "dead" language in that it is no longer spoken, but it nevertheless can be read in thousands of pages of text that survive. Check the samples that follow. It does not matter whether one works backward from the existing modern languages to the parent or from the parent language to its descendent offspring.

Latin:	Italian	Spanish	French	(Meaning)
mater:	madre	madre	mere	(mother)
manus:	mano	mano	main	(hand)
tempus:	tempo	tiempo	temps	(time)

Theories about word relationships or linguistics in general can nearly always be verified by scholars by comparing examples from the Romance languages with the parent word in Latin.

In spite of the presence of cognates among the various related languages, all of which came into existence quite naturally in the early development of each language, another linguistic process played an important role in the enhancement of English vocabulary. This phenomenon is known simply as *word borrowing*. In this situation words existing in one language are simply brought over directly into another with little or no change. All languages throughout the world are continuously being modified by enrichment of this sort. The only requirement is usually a strong contact with speakers of different languages. In the case of English, word borrowing has taken place on all fronts with the result that hundreds of French, Spanish, American Indian, Japanese and Chinese words have been incorporated into our vocabulary by this process. The combined strength of all these sources taken together, however, reveals only a small fraction of our indebtedness to word borrowing from other languages. This is not the situation with Greek and Latin from which sources literally tens of thousands of words have been directly borrowed. So extensive has the process become of coining English words from these two ancient languages that a novice paging through a standard English dictionary, upon first glance at sample word etymologies, might well suspect that the entire English language was a direct offshoot from either Greek or Latin. It is in recognition of this extraordinary phenomenon that numerous attempts have been made in recent years to familiarize students with the basic vocabularies of these two classical languages. By learning a few hundred Greek and Latin words and the process by which they enter English in word borrowing, the meanings of thousands of less familiar words can often be understood today. Moreover, since these roots often tend to be recognized from their appearance in more familiar English words, vocabulary enrichment is not all that difficult. Understanding this process is important not just because it gives us a better perspective about the past development of our language. It is also important for dealing with the formation of future words. Judging from the hundreds of word entries admitted into English in the past few years, it seems that Greek and Latin will continue to be the primary word borrowing sources in the creation of words for decades to come.

Exercise[2]

A. Name the five principal Romance Languages. From what language are they commonly descended?

B. Name three languages spoken in Europe today that are not derived from Indo-European.

C. Which of the following languages belong to the Indo-European Family of languages and which do not?

1. Danish	*3. Arabic*	*5. Polish*	*7. Romanian*
2. Czech	*4. Chinese*	*6. Hebrew*	*8. Albanian*

D. Using Your Dictionary.

1. Give the *abbreviations* used by your dictionary to identify the following languages:

1. Gaelic	*3. French*	*5. Greek*	*7. Portuguese*
2. Russian	*4. Danish*	*6. Persian*	*8. Japanese*

2. Which languages are indicated by the following abbreviations?

1. G	*3. LL*	*5. ME*	*7. ON*
2. Skt	*4. OHG*	*6. ML*	*8. LG*

---

2 It is recommended that students record their answers in a notebook for the exercises below and for those in the chapters that follow.

3. Identify from which Indo-European language each of the following English words are derived. Usually this is explained in the etymology section near the word's definition.

1. *bonanza*	6. *maestro*	11. *scathe*	16. *mayonnaise*
2. *slogan*	7. *magi*	12. *ski*	17. *babushka*
3. *garage*	8. *shawl*	13. *sulfur*	18. *rathskeller*
4. *pizza*	9. *kilt*	14. *mascot*	19. *dynamic*
5. *cobra*	10. *khaki*	15. *martyr*	20. *bankrupt*

4. Identify from which non-Indo-European language or language family the following English words are derived.

1. *algebra*	5. *tea*	9. *typhoon*	13. *admiral*
2. *saffron*	6. *opossum*	10. *manna*	14. *kimono*
3. *ginkgo*	7. *sherbet*	11. *maize*	15. *moccasin*
4. *taboo*	8. *alcohol*	12. *shekel*	16. *coffee*

E. Study the language graph for the IE word *weik* on p. 8 and explain how the general meaning of "house" appears in any ten English word borrowings that come from the Greek root "(o)ec-."

F. Study a map of Europe and western Asia and then identify the principal languages spoken in the numbered areas on the map below.

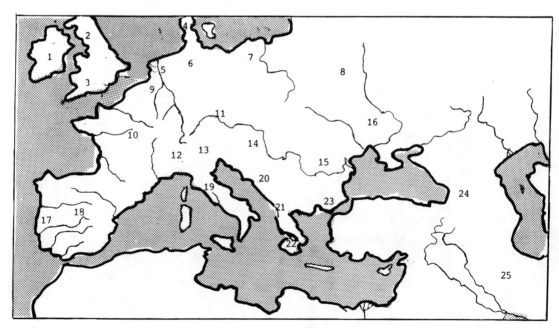

Subatomic Particles

Particle	Symbol	Mass	Lifetime in Seconds
PHOTON	γ	0	Stable
NEUTRINO	ν	0	Stable
ANTI-NEUTRINO	$\bar{\nu}$	0	Stable
ELECTRON	e^-	1	Stable
POSITRON	e^+	1	Stable
PROTON	p	1836	Stable
ANTI-PROTON	$\bar{p}$	1836	Stable
NEUTRON	n	1839	1010
ANTI-NEUTRON	$\bar{n}$	1839	1010
MU MESONS	μ^- μ^+	206	2.22×10^{-6}
PI MESONS	π^- π^+	273	2.56×10^{-8}
NEUTRAL PI MESON	π°	264	$<10^{-15}$
K MESONS	K^- K^+	967	1.2×10^{-8}
NEUTRAL K MESON$_1$	K_1°	~ 973	10^{-10}
NEUTRAL K MESON$_2$	K_2°	~ 973	$\sim 8 \times 10^{-8}$

	Particle	Symbol	Mass	Lifetime in Seconds
HYPERONS	LAMBDA	Λ°	2182	2.6×10^{-10}
	ANTI-LAMBDA	$\bar{\Lambda}^\circ$	2182	2.6×10^{-10}
	SIGMA POSITIVE	Σ^+	2328	$\sim 8 \times 10^{-11}$
	ANTI-SIGMA POSITIVE	$\bar{\Sigma}^+$	2328	$\sim 8 \times 10^{-11}$
	SIGMA NEGATIVE	Σ^-	2342	1.7×10^{-10}
	ANTI-SIGMA NEGATIVE	$\bar{\Sigma}^-$	2342	1.7×10^{-10}
	NEUTRAL SIGMA	Σ°	2326	$<10^{-11}$
	NEUTRAL ANTI-SIGMA	$\bar{\Sigma}^\circ$	2326	$<10^{-11}$
	XI NEGATIVE	Ξ^-	2585	$\sim 10^{-10}$
	ANTI-XI NEGATIVE	$\bar{\Xi}^-$	2585	$\sim 10^{-10}$
	XI NEUTRAL	Ξ°	....	....
	ANTI-XI NEUTRAL	$\bar{\Xi}^\circ$	....	....

Modern physics also is heavily indebted to Greek root words, prefixes and suffixes to form new technical terms. In this list the key terms are entirely Greek, with Latin adjectives as modifiers when required.

Part I
Derivatives from Greek

Μνημοσύνη μήτηρ Μουσάων
Memory, the mother of the Muses.[1]

Chapter One
The Greek Alphabet & Transliteration

<u>History of the Alphabet</u>

The subject of writing in antiquity is indeed a fascinating topic and one of relative importance for those studying English vocabulary from Greek and Latin words. Although many types of picture drawings, commonly known as *pictographs*, can be examined from prehistoric times, only those developments leading more directly to the alphabet, and more specifically the Greek alphabet, are treated in this text. The English alphabet we employ today is basically the same as that used in antiquity by the Romans. Therefore, in the chapters ahead it will be necessary to learn only one new writing script and that will be for words of Greek origin.

Two important writing systems were in use in the eastern Mediterranean area *prior* to the arrival of the Greek alphabet and for this reason deserve special mentioned here. They are *cuneiform* and *hieroglyphics*. The first of these received its name from the "wedge-shaped" look of its characters produced by the tip of a stylus upon a soft material such as clay. The Latin word *cuneus* means "wedge." Cuneiform was in use throughout much of Asia Minor from approximately 3000 B.C. until the start of the Christian era. Having first appeared in the valley of the Tigris and Euphrates Rivers, this unusual script was first employed by the Sumerians and later by their conquerors, the Assyrians. Over the centuries it came to be employed by people of many different languages, some Semitic, some Indo-

---

[1] Hymn to Hermes, 429-430.

European, including Hittite. Initially cuneiform was quite complex. The Sumerians, for example, are believed to have used as many as 600 characters. The later Hittites had about 350, the Elamites about 200, and finally the Persians fewer than 40.

An example of cuneiform script

Throughout most of the Christian era until the nineteenth century little attention had been paid to surviving documents of cuneiform writing. To be sure, the problem of deciphering the script required at least some knowledge of the languages involved and, after a lapse of many centuries, some of these had become completely extinct. It was in the early nineteenth century during a period of high intellectual interest in the Near East that scholars eventually found success with this script. Working with an inscription carved into the side of a steep cliff, known as the *Behistun Rock* from its location at Behistun, Iran, G. Grotefend, a German, and later H. Rawlinson, an Englishman, broke through the mysterious writing system. At this site in 518 B.C. the Persian king Darius once published an account of his magnificent accomplishments in the three official languages of his empire: Old Persian, Elamite and Babylonian. The first clues that led to deciphering the strange writing came about from a series of guesses based upon the proper identification of members of the royal Persian family in a section thought to contain a genealogical listing. Since such a list was already well known from Herodotus' *Histories,* written in ancient Greek, the puzzling script finally became intelligible to scholars of modern times. From the moment of this discovery a far greater understanding of the early history of Asia Minor was possible. Indeed a vast new literature became available to study and appreciate. Included in this manner of writing is the famous *Law Code* of the Babylonian king Hammurabi from approximately 1800 B.C. Other literature in cuneiform treats the subjects of religion, astronomy, mathematics and the deeds and decrees of kings. The recent discovery in the mid-1970s at Ebla in Syria of as many as 15,000 documents written in classical Sumerian cuneiform will soon provide us with an even greater understanding of events in the third millennium B.C.

The familiar and more pictorial hieroglyphic system of writing can likewise be dated as far back as Sumerian cuneiform, *i.e.,* prior to 3000 B.C. Although its use can be traced to speakers of more than one language, it in no way traversed as broad a spectrum as its Eastern counterpart. Certainly the best known examples come from Egypt; however, similar versions can be found in Crete, in Asia Minor among the Hittites, and even in America among early Indians. Labelled by the Greeks of later times as "*hieroglyphics*," that is, "sacred carvings" (from *hieros* - "holy" and *glyphein* - "to carve"), this system of writing is believed to have been employed by Egyptian priests who carved the signs into stone monuments under the direction of their rulers. Over a period of several centuries they were found to be too awkward to be used as a routine means of transcription, so a less elaborate cursive form, known as *hieratic,* eventually came into existence. This too was replaced in time by an even easier script called *demotic*, due to its extensive use by the "people." Hieroglyphics have interesting characteristics. As a non-alphabetic script, its signs or markings were of three types: ideograms, phonetic symbols and determinatives. The pictographic ideograms make sense in and of themselves even to a person unfamiliar with the language because they represent concepts and not the spoken sounds. The phonetic symbols on the other hand represent the spoken sounds, often in groups of two or more consonants. Vowels were not generally considered in their writing; consequently a symbol might represent a single consonant, an entire syllable, or even several syllables. To eliminate any remaining confusion from the combination of ideograms and phonetic symbols, the Egyptian priests usually added determinatives (an eye, a tree, a woman, etc.), which although seemingly not pronounced with the other parts further identified the context of a combination that might otherwise have been interpreted in a couple different ways.

eye	*sun*	*bread*	*to cry*	*to go*

r	*p*	*t*	*jn*	*mn*

Some hieroglyphic ideograms and phonetic symbols

The story of the deciphering of hieroglyphics is no less amazing than that of cuneiform. Once again it resulted from an inscription written in three formats. At the western mouth of the Nile River in Egypt, near Rosetta, some French soldiers of Napoleon Bonaparte in 1799 discovered a stone tablet upon which Egyptian hieroglyphics, the later demotic, and ancient Greek were written. Seized by the British in Cairo a couple years later, it was taken to London and placed in the British Museum, where it is located to this day. A few years after its relocation a French scholar named F. Champollion deciphered the enigmatic hieroglyphics with the help of the ancient Greek. From this work on the *Rosetta Stone* it soon became possible to understand hieroglyphics in other settings.

Early Alphabets Compared

Old Semitic (Hebrew)			Early Greek		
Form	Letter	Equiv.	Form	Letter	Equiv.
∢	aleph	'	∠	alpha	a
9	beth	b, bh	8	beta	b
∧	gimel	g, gh	7	gamma	g
△	daleph	d, dh	△	delta	d
⇥	he	h	⇥	epsilon	e
Y	waw	w	7	digamma	w, v
I	zayin	z	I	zeta	z
日	heth	ḥ	日	eta	ē
⊕	teth	ṭ	⊕	theta	th
Z	yod	y	7	iota	i
Ϗ	kaph	k, kh	Ϗ	kappa	k
L	lamed	l	L	lambda	l
7	mem	m	⋎	mu	m
7	nun	n	Ч	nu	n
⇴	samech	s	Ⅰ	xi	x
•	ayin	'	O	omicron	o
7	pe	p	7	pi	p
⋏	sadhe	ṣ	M	sampi	s
φ	qoph	q	φ	koppa	k
4	resh	r	4	rho	r
W	sin	ś	3	sigma	s
✝	taw	t, th	T	tau	t

The Greek Alphabet

Capital	Small	Name	Transliteration Equivalent	Pronunciation in Antiquity
A	α	alpha	a	*about* (short)
			ā	*father* (long)
B	β	beta	b	*baby*
Γ	γ	gamma	g	*gate*
Δ	δ	delta	d	*dog*
E	ε	epsilon	e	*bed*
Z	ζ	zeta	z (ds)*	*zone*
H	η	eta	ē	*prey*
Θ	θ	theta	th**	*think*
I	ι	iota	i	*hit* (short)
			ī	*machine* (long)
K	κ	kappa	k	*king*
Λ	λ	lambda	l	*leg*
M	μ	mu	m	*me*
N	ν	nu	n	*north*
Ξ	ξ	xi	x (ks)*	*fox*
O	ο	omicron	o	*hot*
Π	π	pi	p	*pot*
P	ρ	rho	r	*rim*
Σ	σ, ς	sigma	s	*song*
T	τ	tau	t	*toy*
Υ	υ	upsilon	y, u	Fr. *tu* (short)
			y	Fr. *sur* (long)
Φ	φ	phi	ph**	*phone*
X	χ	chi	ch**	*chorus*
Ψ	ψ	psi	ps*	*tips*
Ω	ω	omega	ō	*hope*

* - double consonants
** - aspirated consonants

Like cuneiform, Egyptian hieroglyphics have brought us a vast literature and better understanding of the past. It is now possible to read royal proclamations, religious stories, medical treatises and even short "epic" poems. Not all hieroglyphic writing, however, has been deciphered. The work continues. Hittite hieroglyphics, for example, became readable to scholars of modern times only in the mid-twentieth century, this time through a bilingual document which included Phoenician.

Somewhere in Asia Minor in the midst of the Egyptian, Hittite and Assyrian (Babylonian) spheres of influence, the alphabet was born. Considered by many to be of Semitic origin, various forms spread quickly in the early part of the first millennium B.C. In the north the Phoenician and Aramaic branches eventually gave rise to the Hebrew, the Hellenic (Greek), and even, although down the road a bit, the Roman alphabet which we use in English today. Toward the south there developed many other types of alphabetic script, including Ethiopic and Indian versions. With this brief background let us turn now to the Greek alphabet on the previous page.

Study the names and shapes of each Greek letter then cover the chart and read them on the following line, repeating their individual Greek names as you go.

Α Β Γ Δ Ε Ζ Η Θ Ι Κ Λ Μ Ν Ξ Ο Π Ρ Σ Τ Υ Φ Χ Ψ Ω

It should be somewhat comforting to observe that many of the capital letters possess the same shape as their English letter counterparts. Moreover, others may be familiar from the names of Greek fraternities and sororities or certain academic honor societies. Unfortunately, however, we shall be using the lower case or small letters more frequently in the chapters ahead. Since that is so, review them once again in the alphabet chart and then repeat their names as you look at the line that follows.

α β γ δ ε ζ η θ ι κ λ μ ν ξ ο π ρ σ τ υ φ χ ψ ω

With regard to the *pronunciation* given to letters in antiquity, as suggested in the chart, it must be admitted that there is no universal agreement about how *ancient* Greek was pronounced. Certainly it must have undergone change over the centuries as indeed pronunciation in most modern languages has. You should know, however, that the sound equivalents given here are not those used for Modern Greek but rather those generally employed today in English-speaking countries for classical Greek.

Transliteration

If you check in your standard English dictionary any word of Greek derivation, such as the word *telephone,* you will note that the explanation for the etymology does not employ the Greek script but rather the English equivalent letters. It will probably read something like *tēle* *"from afar"* and *phōnē* *"voice, sound."* It might more properly have looked like this: τῆλε *"from afar"* and φωνή *"voice, sound."* The change in format was no doubt brought about because few English-speaking people today can read the Greek letters. The study of these characters, however, can be very beneficial because by it we can possess a greater understanding why some words of Greek origin are spelled correctly (orthographically, that is) the way they are. More specifically, a knowledge of the Greek letters will sometimes help you understand the complex grouping of certain consonants occuring in many English words of Greek origin, *e.g.*, *"-phth-"* (φθ) in *ophthalmology*. One can also better understand some acceptable spelling variations with vowels in certain English words, such as the *"ae/e"* (αι) in *encyclopaedia* or *encyclopedia*.

Throughout much of this book we shall employ the terms *etymology* and *derivatives* because they have much to do with the study of linguistics. The first is employed with reference to the *true* or *literal meaning* of a word usually as determined from an examination of its origin or root parts. The etymology of the word "metropolis," for instance, is "mother city" from its roots. *Word borrowings* or *derivatives* on the other hand are simply those words that have come into existence today as a result of earlier words or roots in another language. The English word "paternal" is ultimately a derivative of the Latin word *pater* which means "father." To facilitate our study of thousands of such derivatives in the English language, we shall first study a couple hundred of the most common Greek and Latin vocabulary words.

Transliteration is the process of rendering words written in one alphabet (in this case Greek) into the script of another. It is a helpful exercise toward gaining a better acquaintance with an unfamiliar alphabet. Furthermore, it serves an important role in the recognition of Greek roots in English words. In most instances the equivalents represented in the alphabet chart that appeared earlier in this chapter apply for transliteration. In other words, β equals "b," λ equals "l," and π equals "p." However, some additional observations should be noted.

1. The Seven Vowels

Although the English alphabet employs *five* vowels, ancient Greek had *seven*. The difference, as you can see, arises from the fact that Greek had two "e"s (ε and η) and two "o"s (o and ω). Generally, in pointing out the origin of a Greek root with one or more of these letters, English dictionaries will identify the long vowels, *eta* and *omega* by placing a *macron* ($\bar{e}$ or $\bar{o}$) above their corresponding transliterated letter. Similarly, the appearance of either of these letters in transliteration *without* a macron (*e* or *o*) in an etymology would show that the original Greek root had only the short Greek vowels *epsilon* or *omicron*. The other three Greek vowels (α, ι, and υ), could be either long or short.

2. Diphthongs

Greek employed *eight* diphthongs originally in antiquity. Since *two* do not appear in English derivatives, they are not presented in this text. The other *six* are as follows:

Greek	Transliteration	Pronunciation in Antiquity
αι	ai	"ai" of *aisle*
ει	ei	"ei" of *reign*
οι	oi	"oi" of *toil*
αυ	au	"ow" of *now*
ευ	eu	short "e" and short "u"
ου	ou	"ou" of *soup*

Note that upsilon *in a Greek diphthong* remains as a "*u*" in transliteration. As a vowel *by itself* it always transliterates as a "*y*." Remember also that the transliterated form will regularly be found only in the etymological portion of a word's entry in your dictionary. Often in actual derivatives in English these diphthongs suffer additional orthographic changes due to Latinization (*cf.* #5 below).

3. The "h" Sound

Although the ancient Greek alphabet possessed the symbol "H," that shape did not carry the "h" sound or form in English transliteration. Instead, it represented only the long "$\bar{e}$." The Greek alphabet that predominated in the eastern Mediterranean contained no independent symbol for "h" alone. Since this sound can already be picked up in the three aspirate consonants (θ, φ, and χ) in Greek, the only problem that remains to be discussed is how to define the "h" separately from the "t," "p," "c" or any other letter. Most commonly this will occur only at the beginning of a word that would otherwise start with a vowel. In such cases the Greeks employed a *rough breathing mark* (') above the initial vowel to show the presence of the initial "h" sound. In all other instances, *i.e.*, where this sound was not to be included with initial vowels, a *smooth breathing mark* (') would be placed above the initial vowel. It was the Etruscans and western Greeks in Italy who seem to have been the initiators of an actual separate "letter" (h) to represent the "h" sound.

Two special situations warrant further comment on the rough breathing mark at the beginning of words. First, an *initial upsilon* always takes the rough breathing mark. Secondly, a rough breathing mark is always placed over the *consonant rho* when it appears in the initial position. In this case the transliteration produced is the combination *"rh"* not *"hr."* For example, the word ὑπερ produces "hyper" and ῥις, ῥινος (nose) gives us the derivative "rhinitis."

Finally, concerning the placement of either breathing mark, the general rule is that it goes directly over the initial vowel (or rho). However, if that letter is capital, the mark is moved slightly to the left. If the initial vowel is part of a diphthong, the mark goes directly over the *second* vowel. Study these examples:

Greek	Transliteration	Derivative
ὑποκριτής	hypokrites	*hypocrite*
ῥυθμός	rhythmos	*rhythm*
Αἴσωπος	Aisopos	*Aesop*
Ἡρόδοτος	Herodotos	*Herodotus*
ἀγορά	agora	*agora*

4. Special Letters

The Greek gamma (γ) in antiquity always possessed the hard "g" sound, as in *"get."* It was never softened to the "g" of *"George."* When, however, it appeared in combination before another palatal consonant, *i.e.*, before a γ, κ, ξ, or χ, it suffered a pronunciation change and took the sound of "n." In such cases, although we still transcribe a gamma in Greek, we should transliterate this letter as an "n" because this was the likely sound it had in antiquity (as indicated from cognates in other languages) and this spelling is given to it in all English derivatives. Note these examples:

Greek	Transliteration	Derivative
δίφθογγος	diphthongos	*diphthong*
λάρυγξ	larynx	*larynx*
βρόγχος	bronchos	*bronchus*

Note the difference between the two Greek letters ξ (xi) and χ (chi). The former produces the "x" in transliteration, the latter, a "ch." Finally, the small sigma is commonly written in Greek in the form "σ" when it takes the initial or medial position in a word. It appears as "ς" in the final position. Study the following:

Greek	Transliteration	Derivative
σκηνή	skene	*scene*
ἄσβεστος	asbestos	*asbestos*

5. Latinization

Before entering the English language, most words of Greek origin first passed through Latin, *i.e.*, they were *Latinized*. This was a process in which they assumed a Latin spelling that resulted in a still a few orthographic changes that have not previously been described. The following are the most common examples:

Greek	Latin/English	Examples
αι	ae, e	*Egypt* (Αἴγυπτος)
		Aeschylus (Αἰσχύλος)
κ	c	*cardiac* (καρδία)
ου	u	*Uranus* (Οὐρανός)
ει	e, i	*Museum* (Μουσεῖον)
		icon (εἰκών)
οι	oe, e	*amoeba* (ἀμοιβή)
		Oedipus (Οἰδίπους)
		cenobite (κοινόβιος)

6. Accents

Ancient Greek employed three accents, an acute (΄), a grave (΅) and a circumflex (^). Most classical scholars believe that these marks, placed above certain vowels or diphthongs, represented in classical Greek a raised *pitch* rather than an increased stress. In time, however, contact with the Latin-speaking world brought about a switch to a stress accent system, as is employed today in English and most other modern languages. To show something of the complicated nature of how Greek accents worked in antiquity, consider this. A typical Greek noun with an acute accent when used as the subject of a sentence, might quite properly take either of the other two accents when employed in a different grammatical setting (as for example, object of the sentence). Moreover, these accents might be placed on a syllable different from their original location.

Not only do the matters noted above pose a problem for most English words derived from Greek. Another more fundamental set of rules comes into play in the process of determining present-day word accent. Today we apply the rules for *Latin* accent to determine where to put the stress on the word in English. The end result is that we totally ignore the location of the original Greek accent. Therefore, although you might see a Greek accent over one syllable in a proper name (*e.g.,* Σωκράτης), you will often find the accent on a different syllable of the word as it is said in English today (*'Sak-re-tez*). Briefly, as a reminder for those who once studied the other classical language, the chief rules regarding accent for Latin are as follows:

1. A word of two syllables is always accented on the penult (second last syllable) and never on the last.

2. On words of three or more syllables, the accent also falls on the penult if that syllable is long, otherwise on the antepenult (third last syllable).

3. A long vowel, a diphthong, or a group of two or more consonants following a short vowel all make a syllable long for purposes of accent.

In the study of word derivations one certainly can question the need for learning the very complicated set of rules governing ancient Greek accents. They are printed here because that is the way they appeared in antiquity. In any case you are cautioned to be aware of the fact that with respect to word accent the accepted English pronunciation for certain Greek words will very often change due to the Latin influence. If you are not sure about the correct accented syllable for new words in English, consult your dictionary. Check the examples below.

Οἰδίπους	Oedipus
Εὐριπίδης	Euripides
Σοφοκλῆς	Sophocles

Review the Greek alphabet once again and the rules for transliteration, then complete the exercises for this chapter that follow.

Exercises

A. Explain briefly why the name *cuneiform* was appropriately given to the ancient form of writing that it represents. Under what circumstances and by whom was it deciphered in modern times?

B. What is the Rosetta Stone and what role did it play in deciphering another ancient form of writing? Where is it located today?

C. Identify the following upper case letters of the Greek alphabet by writing both their name and their usual transliterated equivalent.

1. Γ	*3.* Π	*5.* Ξ	*7.* Ψ
2. H	*4.* X	*6.* Ω	*8.* P

D. Identify the following lower case letters of the Greek alphabet by writing both their name and their usual transliterated equivalent.

1. ν	*3.* σ	*5.* θ	*7.* η
2. φ	*4.* ξ	*6.* ς	*8.* ζ

E. Name the three double consonants (those that include the "s" sound).

F. Name the three aspirated consonants (those that include the "h" sound).

G. Name the seven Greek vowels.

H. Through the process of transliteration identify the following *proper names* from Greek history and mythology. Write their names as they might be found in English today.

1. Σωκράτης	4. Ζεύς	7. ᾽Αθήνη	10. ῎Ολυμπος
2. Δημοσθένης	5. Ποσειδῶν	8. ῾Ηρόδοτος	11. Αἰσχύλος
3. Κῦρος	6. ᾽Αφροδίτη	9. ᾽Οδυσσεύς	12. ῞Ηφαιστος

I. **Transliteration.** Transliterate the following Greek words by following the rules for transliteration given in this chapter. Then write an appropriate English derivative. Note that in the transliteration you must provide the exact letter equivalents, while in the derivative spelling changes affected by Latinization and the dropping of word endings can occur. Observe the differences in the following example:

Greek	Transliteration	Derivative
ζωδιακός	*zodiakos*	*zodiac*

1. αἰθήρ
2. αὐστηρός
3. ῥυθμός
4. χαρακτήρ
5. λαβύρινθος

6. ῥινοκέρως
7. ἔκλειψις
8. θέατρον
9. σφίγξ
10. ἄσβεστος

11. οὐρανός
12. Μουσεῖον
13. φιλοσοφία
14. δρᾶμα
15. ληθαργία

16. μητρόπολις
17. ὑποκριτής
18. ῥοδόδενδρον
19. ἐπιτομή
20. ἀλφάβητος

σκηνὴ πᾶς ὁ βίος.
All life is a stage.[1]

Chapter Two
First Declension Feminine Nouns

As we direct our study to the learning of Greek vocabulary, it is important that you first take notice of the structure in which the material is organized both here in this chapter and in the chapters that follow. For example, nouns are presented in the first few chapters before other parts of speech. This is due to the fact that frequently they can stand by themselves as loan words in English. Even though this is the case, however, you will soon discover that *combinations* of more than one root are equally common occurrences in English vocabulary. Generally, if one root is of Greek origin, the accompanying second and third roots are Greek too. In words with multiple roots different parts of speech may be linked together. A noun, for instance, may be accompanied by an adjective (possibly a number or color), a prepositional-type prefix, or a verb. In other cases two noun roots may be joined together to form a single word in English. Check these examples.

English Word	Greek Word(s)	Part(s) of Speech
angel	angelos (messenger)	noun
acropolis	akros (high); polis (city)	adj. + noun
epitaph	epi (upon); taphos (tomb)	prep. + noun
lithotomy	lithos (stone); temnein (to cut)	noun + verb
hippopotamus	hippos (horse); potamos (river)	noun + noun

In a typical structural approach to the study of Greek and Latin, nouns (and adjectives) are learned in groups according to the unique patterns of inflected endings that each group possesses. Collectively, these groups are known as *declensions* and ancient Greek had three of them. Examine briefly the Greek words in the vocabulary list of this lesson. There you will note, for instance, that all nouns of this group, or declension, end in either an alpha (-α) or an eta (-η). The selection here represents only a small

---

[1] From the Greek Anthology.

sampling of hundreds of nouns that possess this uniqueness. The nouns of subsequent lessons, on the other hand, will possess a different set of endings and will consequently belong to a different declension. First declension nouns are usually feminine in gender even though they commonly do not reflect anything "female" in our sense of gender.[2]

As you proceed to the task of memorizing vocabulary lists, it is normal to ask precisely what should be learned in this activity. Actually, several items demand your attention. First, you should learn the original Greek vocabulary word itself. The reason for this is simply that your English dictionary will usually refer to it *in its full but transliterated form* when it presents the etymology[3] of a word. For example, if you check a word such as "hemisphere" in your dictionary, you should find in its etymology the notation that it comes from two Greek roots: *hemi* ("half") and *sphaira* ("ball"). As you already learned in the last lesson, however, the Greek roots are given in transliterated form. For this reason the vocabulary list in this and subsequent chapters will include the boldfaced transliterated form immediately following the word printed in Greek letters.

A second important element you should want to learn from each vocabulary list is how to distinguish the *root* or *base* of a word from its *ending*. This is due to the fact that, while the ending may often disappear or change slightly in an English derivative, each letter of the base generally must be accounted for. As mentioned before, the endings for first declension nouns are either "-*a*" or "-*e*." The base of these nouns consists of every letter preceding the ending. For example, the Greek words τροφή ("nourishment") and γλῶσσα ("tongue," "language") should be analyzed as follows:

base	ending
troph	-*e*
gloss	-*a*

---

[2] A few masculine nouns in this declension end in "-ας" or "-ης," but they do not provide us with many derivatives in English. Consequently they are not presented in this text.

[3] The etymology of a word is its history as seen through an analysis of its elements. The Greek word ἔτυμον means "true" or "literal" according to the meaning of its root(s).

Any of four things might happen to the *ending* of a first declension Greek noun as it enters the English language.

1) It may enter unchanged.[4]   (*Nike*)
2) It may be Latinized, *i.e.*,
    put in the Latin equivalent form.[5]   (*amoeba*)
3) It may become a silent "-e."[6]   (*phone, scene*)
4) It may drop completely.   (*nymph*)

In derivatives composed of two or more Greek roots, the ending of the first root is usually dropped and a *connecting vowel* (usually an "-o-") is inserted between the roots. For example, the initial roots in the words "petrology" and "psychotherapy" are shortened in this manner and the letter "o" is inserted before the second root begins.

petr- + o + log-   + y
psych- + o + therap- + y

More will be said about combining roots later.

Perhaps most fundamental in your study of vocabulary is the learning of the definition or meaning of the original Greek word, for it furnishes the primary key to understanding English word borrowings today. If you know, for instance, that the word "heliotrope" contains the elements *helios* (sun) and *trepein* (to turn), you should have little difficulty in understanding and remembering its definition ("any plant which *turns* toward the *sun*"). In conclusion therefore in the vocabulary below and in subsequent lessons you should learn the following things: *the complete vocabulary word, the proper transliterated form, the base and ending of each word and, most importantly, its English meaning.* You should also be able to locate these words as roots in derivatives.

---

4 If the final syllable is an "eta" (-η), it is pronounced as a long "e" in English.

5 First declension nouns in Latin have only one ending, namely, "-*a*." Some Greek nouns ending in "eta" will therefore show up in English with the Latinized ending of "-*a*."

6 The silent "-e" ending is simply one that is not pronounced.

Vocabulary

Greek	Transliteration	Meaning	Derivative
ἀγορά	**agora**	marketplace	*agora*
ἀμοιβή	**amoibe**	change	*amoeba*
ἀράχνη	**arachne**	spider	*arachnoid*
βοτανή	**botane**	plant, herb	*botany*
γῆ	**ge**	earth	*geology*
γλῶσσα, γλῦττα	**glossa, glotta**	tongue, language	*polyglot*
δόξα	**doxa**	opinion, glory	*doxology*
ἡδονή	**hedone**	pleasure	*hedonism*
ἡμέρα	**hemera**	day	*ephemeral*
θάλασσα, θάλαττα	**thalassa**	sea	*thalassic*
καρδία	**kardia**	heart	*cardiac*
κεφαλή	**kephale**	head	*cephalic*
λήθη	**lethe**	forgetfulness	*lethal*
μορφή	**morphe**	shape, form	*morphology*
νίκη	**nike**	victory	*nike*
νύμφη	**nymphe**	bride, young woman	*nymph*
ὀδύνη	**odyne**	pain	*osteodynia*
πέτρα	**petra**	rock, boulder	*petrology*
σκηνή	**skene**	tent	*scene*
σφαῖρα	**sphaira**	ball	*sphere*
σχολή	**schole**	leisure, lecture	*scholar*
τέχνη	**techne**	skill, craft	*technology*
τροφή	**trophe**	nourishment	*atrophy*
φωνή	**phone**	voice, sound	*phone*

| χολή | **chole** | bile, gall | *cholic* |
| ψυχή | **psyche** | soul, mind | *psyche* |

It has already been pointed out that the vocabulary of Greek and Latin has long been used to shape the professional terminology of numerous subject fields in English. To provide a good variety of examples to demonstrate this phenomenon, a broad-based vocabulary has been selected for study in each chapter of the first two parts of this text. They cover such fields as law, government, literature, psychology, medicine, and several sciences. Each word in the vocabulary list will be encountered at least once as a derivative in the Derivative Study section that follows. In no way are the examples intended to be all-inclusive. The samples chosen have been divided into two levels of difficulty due to the possibility of great differences in the reader's educational background or academic experiences. A second reason for this division would no doubt be the reader's purpose or goal in studying this subject. For some the simpler words in Group A would be sufficient while for others the more difficult selections in Group B would be more proper. Whether or not all examples are studied, great satisfaction can be gained from discovering the same root in the vocabulary of different subjects. For example, the Greek word φωνή ("voice," "sound") occurs in such words as *telephone, microphone, euphony, dysphonia, homophone,* and *phonogram*. In some of these examples the word borrowings are well known (even though the root elements may never have been previously considered). Even in the cases where the example may not be familiar, however, you can be fairly certain that the word's meaning is somehow related to "voice" or "sound." Examine the words in the Derivative Study section below and find the Greek roots in them from the vocabulary list above. If necessary, consult your dictionary for the meanings of the accompanying roots and for each word's definition.

Derivative Study

Level A

scholastic	*technique*
petrous	*geography*
technical	*telephone*
George	*geometry*
glossary	*thalassocracy*

cardiology
symphony
spheroid
cholera
school
petroleum
botanical
nymphomaniac
arachnophobia
metamorphosis
epiglottis

Peter
psychology
dystrophy
agoraphobia
microphone
scenic
hemisphere
cardiodynia
hedonistic
acephalous
orthodox

<u>*Level B*</u>
technocracy
dysphonia
amoebocyte
melancholy
hedonics
myocardium
antiphon
anthropomorphic
heterodox
hemerocallis
chololith
pericardium
euphony
psychedelic
ionosphere
geocentric
cholesterol
petroglyph
odynophobia
geothermic
lethologica

amoebiasis
pedotrophy
botanize
geotropic
thalassography
anhedonia
atmosphere
encephalitis
cephalodynia
hypertrophy
hypoglossal
nympholepsy
homophone
microcephalic
arachnid
biotechnology
psychodynamic
tachycardia
glossitis
xylophone
apogee

Special Topics: Common Short Suffixes

At this point it is fitting to say a few words about suffixes. Some word endings add much to the meaning of a word, and for this reason they will be examined in detail later. Others, usually consisting of only two or three letters, are important not for their meaning but only because they help us bring about a desired change in a word's part of speech (from adjective to noun or verb, or the like). For example, the words *evangelical, evangelist, evangelism,* and *evangelize* all come from the Greek roots *"eu"* (good) and *"angelos"* (messenger). When two or more similar words possess the same main roots and differ only in their suffixes, English dictionaries often provide the etymology only once, either in the first entry of such words or in its most commonly known form. You are expected to understand that the same roots carry through in all the related entries. In addition to providing the purely grammatical function described above, some short suffixes possess the additional characteristic of helping to make a word into an abstract noun (*technology*) or into a noun agent (*technologist*)). The meanings and/or functions of some of the most common short suffixes are given here so you can more readily recognize them in the sample words we are studying.

Suffix	Meaning/Function	Example
-al	"pertaining to" (forms adjective)	*glossal*
-an (-ian)	"having to do with" (forms noun)	*utopia*
-ia (-y)	"quality of," "act of" (forms noun)	*phobia*
-ic (-ac after "i")	"pertaining to" (forms adjective)	*cardiac*
-ics	"study of," "science of" (forms noun)	*phonics*
-ious (-ous)	"pertaining to," "like" (forms adjective)	*amorphous*
-ism	"belief in," "condition of" (forms noun)	*hedonism*
-ist	"one concerned with,""believer in" (forms noun)	*pharmacist*
-sis, (-sia, -sy)	"state of," "act of" (forms noun)	*hypnosis* *aphasia*

Exercise

A. Give two English word borrowings from the Greek word γλῶττα and two from γλῶσσα.

B. Although we have several borrowings from both variant forms for the word above, we do not have them from both θάλασσα and θάλαττα, but rather from only one. Give three examples from that root.

C. Name and explain the spelling variance your dictionary may give for the following words: *amoebic, amoeboid* and *amoebiasis*.

D. Explain how the meaning of the word *lethal* has anything to do with its derivative meaning "forgetfulness." Does your dictionary list any word borrowing where the original root meaning is closer to its present-day meaning?

E. Using your English dictionary, find a Greek first declension noun root in each of the following words. Try to write that noun in Greek according to the rules of transliteration before giving the meaning of the root. Example: *stoic* fr. στοά "porch"

1. *selenography*	3. *zoology*	5. *etiology*	7. *diet*
2. *narcotics*	4. *empirical*	6. *hysteria*	8. *acme*

F. **Matching**. The terms in column one below all contain a root in the vocabulary of this lesson. Match them with their definition in column two.

E.g., hypertrophy ("d")	a. fear of pain
1. *agoraphobia*	b. earthlike
2. *geochronology*	c. carving on a rock
3. *hedonism*	d. excessive growth or development
4. *technocracy*	e. having many shapes
5. *odynophobia*	f. time measurements from earth data
6. *polymorph*	g. fear of the marketplace
7. *phonography*	h. government by craftsmen
8. *orthodoxy*	i. true belief or opinion
9. *petroglyph*	j. recording of sound
10. *geomorphic*	k. pleasure-seeking

G. **Transliteration**. Give the transliterated form and a word borrowing for each of the following Greek words.

1. ἀμαζῶν
2. ὀστρακισμός
3. βλασφημία
4. συμβίωσις

5. αἴνιγμα
6. βαρβαρισμός
7. στωικός
8. δεσπότης

9. ἐτυμολογία
10. ὀρθογραφία
11. τεχνολογία
12. πολυανδρία

ὁ ἰατρὸς λύπης ἀνθρώποις χρόνος.
The healer of pain for humans is time.

Chapter Three
Second Declension Masculine Nouns

In the last chapter you studied feminine nouns of the first declension. The next declension, the second, focuses on both masculine and neuter nouns. Only the masculine are treated in this chapter. These words differ in that they no longer possess an ending in alpha (-α) or eta (-η). Instead, they regularly end in omicron sigma (-ος) while the base includes every letter prior to this ending.

Just as some Greek words of the first declension have entered the English language directly, that is, with no additional roots or endings attached, the same situation exists for second declension nouns. When they do appear in English in this fashion, any of the following things may happen to the "-os" ending.

1) It may enter unchanged.	(*cosmos, Helios*)
2) It may be Latinized, *i.e.*, put in the Latin equivalent form.[1]	(*chorus, estrus*)
3) It may become a silent "e."	(*cycle*)
4) It may drop completely.	(*angel, myth*)

Study the words in the vocabulary list below and then attempt to identify them as roots in the words in the Derivative Study section which follows. If necessary, use an English dictionary to determine the meanings of additional elements accompanying these roots as well as the current definition of each word.

Vocabulary

Greek	Transliteration	Meaning	Derivative
ἄγγελος	**angelos**	messenger	*angel*
ἀδελφός	**adelphos**	brother	*Philadelphia*

---

[1] Second declension masculine nouns in Latin end in "-*us*."

ἄνθρωπος	anthropos	human	*anthropology*
βίος	bios	life	*biology*
γάμος	gamos	marriage	*monogamy*
δάκτυλος	daktylos	finger	*dactylic*
δῆμος	demos	people	*epidemic*
δρόμος	dromos	running, race	*syndrome*
ἥλιος	helios	sun	*helium*
θάνατος	thanatos	death	*thanatophobia*
θεός	theos	god	*theology*
ἰατρός	iatros	healer, physician	*psychiatrist*
ἵππος	hippos	horse	*hippodrome*
κόσμος	kosmos	universe, order	*cosmos*
κύκλος	kyklos	circle, wheel	*cycle*
λίθος	lithos	stone	*monolith*
λόγος	logos	word, speech, study	*logic*
μῦθος	mythos	tale	*myth*
νεκρός	nekros	corpse, dead	*necrosis*
νόμος	nomos	law, science of	*economics*
ξένος	xenos	stranger, foreigner	*xenophobia*
οἶκος	oikos	house	*ecology*
οἶστρος	oistros	sting, gadfly	*estrus*
ὀφθαλμός	ophthalmos	eye	*ophthalmic*
τόπος	topos	place	*topic*
τύραννός	tyrannos	absolute ruler	*tyranny*
ὕπνος	hypnos	sleep	*hypnosis*
φόβος	phobos	fear	*phobia*

χορός	**choros**	singer, dancers	*chorus*
χρόνος	**chronos**	time	*chronometer*
χρυσός	**chrysos**	gold	*chrysanthemum*

Derivative Study

Level A

bicycle	*astronomy*
economy	*hippopotamus*
cosmonaut	*evangelist*
mythology	*polygamy*
amphibious	*atheism*
tyrannicide	*heliocentric*
anthropomorphic	*utopia*
chronological	*philanthropist*
necropolis	*hypnotherapy*
democracy	*cyclical*
cyclone	*ophthalmologist*
neolithic	*cosmopolitan*
pediatrician	*polytheism*
autonomy	*angelic*
choreography	*estrogen*
topography	*necrology*
synchronize	*cosmetic*

Level B

heliotrope	*exogamy*
eolithic	*cyclorama*
xenomorphic	*cosmology*
chryselephantine	*monadelphous*
hypnagogic	*tyrannosaur*
polyestrus	*enophthalmous*
bionomics	*chrysolite*
pandemic	*misanthrope*
syndactyl	*perihelion*
necrophagous	*nephrolith*
xenogamy	*anthropoid*
dactylogram	*ectopic*

paleolithic	*endogamy*
heliolatry	*symbiotic*
anachronism	*lycanthrope*
endemic	*diadelphous*
palindrome	*necroscopy*
pantheism	*hippocampus*
thanatopsis	*monoecious*
mythomania	*chrysalis*
gamete	*polydactylous*
proestrus	*syngamy*
synoecy	*diadromus*

Exercise

A. Explain the transliteration of the "*n*" in the word ἄγγελος in this lesson's vocabulary.

B. Explain how the roots "*estr-*"" and "*ec-*" are determined from the Greek words οἶστρος and οἶκος respectively in the vocabulary of this chapter.

C. Explain the difference between *necrophobia* and *thanatophobia*.

D. Explain why the following phrases qualify as *palindromes*.

   1. Νίψον ἀνόμημα μὴ μόναν ὄψιν. "Wash your sins, not only your face." (on a water font at the former church Hagia Sophia in Istanbul)

   2. A man, a plan, a canal, Panama.

D. **Transliterate.** Write the following proper names from Greek history and mythology as we might find them in English today.

1. Ἄρτεμις	8. Ἀχιλλεύς	15. Θουκυδίδης
2. Πλάτων	9. Βάκχος	16. Αἴσωπος
3. Ἀλέξανδρος	10. Ξενοφῶν	17. Ἀγαμέμνων
4. Ἀριστοφάνης	11. Εὐριπίδης	18. Σόλων
5. Ὅμηρος	12. Ἀριστοτέλης	19. Σοφοκλῆς
6. Φειδίας	13. Ἡρακλῆς	20. Ἐπίκουρος
7. Οἰδίπους	14. Μαραθῶν	

E. Using your English dictionary, find a Greek second declension noun root in each of the following words. Try to write that root in Greek script before giving the meaning of that root.

1. *epitaph*   2. *odometer*   3. *hippopotamus*   4. *polemic*

ἔργον δ᾽ οὐδὲν ὄνειδος, ἀεργίη δέ τ᾽ ὄνειδος.
Work is not a disgrace; laziness is.[1]

Chapter Four
Second Declension Neuter Nouns

A large number of Greek second declension nouns happen not to be masculine in gender like the words you studied in the last lesson. Instead they are neuter and possess an ending in omicron nu (-ον). As might be expected, the base for these words includes every letter prior to this ending. The few words that come directly from this group of nouns will reflect the neuter ending in English in one of the following ways.

1) It may enter unchanged.   *(dendron)*
2) It may be Latinized, *i.e.*,
    put in the Latin equivalent form.[2]   *(phylum)*
3) It may become a silent "e."   *(centre, theatre)*
4) It may drop completely.   *(erg)*

Study the words in the vocabulary list below. Then attempt to identify them as roots in the English words in the Derivative Study section that follows. Use an English dictionary, if necessary, to determine the meanings of additional elements accompanying these roots as well as the current definition of each word.

Vocabulary

Greek	Transliteration	Meaning	Derivative
βιβλίον	**biblion**	book	*Bible*
δένδρον	**dendron**	tree	*dendrology*
ἔργον	**ergon**	work	*energy*
ζυγόν	**zygon**	yoke, pair	*zygomatic*
ζῷον	**zoon**	animal	*zoology*
θεατρόν	**theatron**	viewing place	*theater*

[1] Hesiod, *Works and Days*, 311.
[2] Latin second declension neuter nouns end in "-*um*."

κέντρον	**kentron**	center	*geocentric*
ξύλον	**xylon**	wood	*xylophone*
ὀστέον	**osteon**	bone	*osteology*
πτερόν	**pteron**	feather, wing	*pterodactyl*
φάρμακον	**pharmakon**	remedy, drug	*pharmacy*
φύλλον	**phyllon**	leaf	*chlorophyll*
φῦλον	**phylon**	race, tribe	*phylum*
φυτόν	**phyton**	plant	*phytology*
ᾠόν	**oon**	egg	*oology*

Derivative Study

Level A

helicopter	*amphiteatre*
bibliography	*dendrochronology*
anthropocentric	*ergometer*
osteopathy	*oogenesis*
pharmaceutical	*bibliomania*
dendroid	*dipteral*
zygomorphic	*zoomorphic*
theatrical	*xylography*
egocentric	*diphyllous*
phytogenesis	*phylogeny*
erg	*osteotomy*

Level B

zygodactyl	*pharmacodynamic*
brachypterous	*phyllophagous*
pharmacology	*oogamous*
glottochronology	*philodendron*
ergophobia	*heliocentric*
rhododendron	*bibliotics*
hyperostosis	*zoophilous*
oosphere	*pseudodipteral*
psychopharmacology	*ergonomics*
centrifugal	*bibliophile*
xylotomous	*phyllotaxy*

megalopteran	*pharmacokinetics*
zoophobia	*xylophagous*
pharmacopoeia	*synergy*
zygophyte	*zoophyte*
anergy	*oophyte*
osteoid	*orthopterous*

Special Topics: More Greek Suffixes

Review the suffixes presented in Chapter Two. Due to their simple forms and highly functional nature, little significance is attached to their meanings. There are, on the other hand, several suffixes for which the meaning contributes highly toward understanding an entire word. Such is the case with those listed below. Even in this group you will observe, however, that the same grammatical needs of English are satisfied. Hence to keep the list from becoming too lengthy, some related suffixes which only further qualify the root are placed in parentheses.

Suffix	Meaning	Example
-archy (-arch)	"rule by"	*monarch*
-cracy (-crat)	"rule by," "type of government"	*democracy*
-gram	"something written"	*monogram*
-graphy (-graph)	"writing," "instrument for writing"	*phonograph*
-ician	"specialist in "	*technician*
-itis	"disease of," "inflammation of"	*ecephalitis*
-latry (-lator)	"worship of"	*heliolatry*
-logy (-logist)	"study of," "science of"	*anthropology*
-mania	"madness for," "passion about"	*nymphomania*
-meter (-metry)	"measure"	*chronometer*
-nomy (-nomist)	"science of," "laws governing"	*economy*
-oid	"having the form of," "like"	*hypnoid*
-pathy (-path)	"feeling," "disease/treatment of"	*psychopath*
-phile (-philous)	"lover of"	*bibliophile*

-phobia (-phobe) "fear of"   *agoraphobia*

-scopy (-scope)   "viewing," "instrument for viewing"   *helioscope*

-taxy (-taxis)   "arrangement"   *phyllotaxy*

-tomy (-tomist)   "cutting"   *anatomy*

Exercise

A.   Find a Greek second declension neuter noun root in each of the following words. According to the rules for transliteration try to write it in Greek before giving its meaning.   Since they are not included in the vocabulary list of this lesson, you will have to consult your English dictionary.

    1. *decathlon*   2. *stadium*   3. *emporium*   4. *neurology*

B. **Matching**. Match the term on the left with the definition on the right.

1. *megalopteran*	a. working together
2. *xylophagous*	b. leaf-eating
3. *synergy*	c. yoke-shaped
4. *geocentric*	d. fusion of fingers
5. *phyllophagous*	e. having large wings
6. *zygmorphic*	f. science of work
7. *phytogenesis*	g. resembling an animal
8. *zooid*	h. development of plants
9. *ergonomics*	i. earth-centered
10. *zygodactyly*	j. wood-eating

C. **Fields of Study.** Identify the specific subject or focus of each of the following "*fields of study*" as indicated by the various Greek roots that you have now learned.

1. *anthropology*	10. *chronology*
2. *heliology*	11. *morphology*
3. *geology*	12. *petrology*
4. *mythology*	13. *technology*
5. *ecology*	14. *zoology*
6. *topology*	15. *cardiology*
7. *necrology*	16. *psychology*
8. *phytology*	17. *pharmacology*
9. *oology*	18. *dendrology*

φιλαργυρία μητρόπολις πάντων τῶν κακῶν.
The love of money is the root of all evil.[1]

Chapter Five
Third Declension Nouns

Having studied feminine, masculine and neuter nouns of the first and second declensions as three separate groups, we now can focus our attention on the rather large number of nouns which belong to the third declension in Greek. In this group, however, no special attention will be given to gender.[2]

A glance at the vocabulary list below will show that two forms are commonly given for each word. The first, usually shorter, is the word as it appears in the nominative (subjective) case. The second form, generally longer, is the genitive (possessive) case and commonly ends is "ος." No fixed rule will apply in all instances for determining the complete root for English words derived from the first form; however, the root for the second form consists of every letter prior to the ending "-os." On occasions in the vocabulary list below when the root of the first form tends to match that of the second, the second simply has not been given. Finding examples of derivatives from both roots for all the vocabulary words below may indeed be impossible. Still, you will discover that this process of listing the two roots for nouns of this declension is standard procedure for English dictionaries today. Study the following examples and consult your dictionary, if necessary.

Greek Forms	Deriv. fr. 1st	Deriv. fr. 2nd
γυνή, γυναικός	miso*gyn*ist	*gyne*cology
πούς, ποδός	octo*pus*	*podi*atrist
δέρμα, δέρματος	pachy*derm*	*derma*tology

---

[1] Diogenes in Diogenes Laertius, *Lives* 6.50.

[2] If our primary goal were other than one of learning Greek vocabulary for the purpose of studying derivatives in English words, we might have to undertake this time-consuming task of memorizing the gender for each word. Such would be the case, for instance, if we were planning to read Greek literature. It is for this reason that traditional elementary Greek courses include this important aspect of grammar.

Vocabulary

Greek	Transliteration	Meaning	Derivative
αἷμα, αἵματος	haima, haimatos	blood	*hematology*
ἄλγος	algos	pain	*cardialgia*
ἅλς, ἁλός	hals, halos	salt	*haline*
ἀνήρ, ἀνδρός	aner, andros	man, husband	*polyandry*
ἄνθος	anthos	flower	*anthology*
γάλα, γάλακτος	gala, galaktos	milk	*galactic*
γαστήρ, γαστρός	gaster, gastros	stomach	*gastric*
γένος, γένεος (γένους)	genos, geneos	race, kind	*genus*
γέρων, γέροντος	geron, gerontos	old man	*gerontology*
γυνή, γυναικός	gyne, gynaikos	woman, wife	*gynecology*
δαίμων, δαίμονος	daimon, daimonos	spirit	*demon*
δέρμα, δέρματος	derma, dermatos	skin	*dermatitis*
δύναμις	dynamis	power, force	*dynamic*
ἔθνος	ethnos	nation	*ethnic*
εἰκών, εἰκόνος	eikon, eikonos	image, statue	*icon*
ἔρως, ἔρωτος	eros, erotos	love	*Eros*
ἦθος	ethos	custom, habit	*ethics*
ἰχθύς, ἰχθύος	ichthys, ichthyos	fish	*ichthyology*
κάλλος	kallos	beauty	*calligraphy*
κανών	kanon	rule	*canon*
κρύος	kryos	cold (frost)	*cryostat*
κύων, κυνός	kyon, kynos	dog	*cynical*
μήν	men	month	*menopause*

μήτηρ, μητρός	**meter, metros**	mother	*metropolis*
μῖσος	**misos**	hatred	*misogynist*
νύξ, νυκτός	**nyx, nyktos**	night	*nyctophobia*
ὄνυμα, ὀνύματος	**onyma, onymatos**	name	*synonym*
ὄρνις, ὄρνιθος	**ornis, ornithos**	bird	*ornithology*
παῖς, παιδός	**pais, paidos**	child	*pediatrics*
πατήρ, πατρός	**pater, patros**	father	*patriarch*
πόλις	**polis**	city	*acropolis*
πούς, ποδός	**pous, podos**	foot	*tripod*
πῦρ	**pyr**	fire	*pyre*
ῥίς, ῥινός	**rhis, rhinos**	nose	*rhinoceros*
σάρξ, σαρκός	**sarx, sarkos**	flesh	*sarcophagus*
σθένος	**sthenos**	strength	*calisthenics*
στόμα, στόματος	**stoma, stomatos**	mouth	*stoma*
σῶμα, σώματος	**soma, somatos**	body	*somatic*
ὕδωρ, ὕδατος	**hydor, hydatos**	water	*hydrogen*
φύλαξ, φύλακος	**phylax, phylakos**	guard	*prophylaxis*
φώς, φωτός	**phos, photos**	light	*photograph*
χείρ	**cheir**	hand	*chiropractor*
χρῶμα, χρώματος	**chroma, chromatos**	color	*polychrome*

Derivative Study

Level A

encyclopedia	*photometer*
geriatrics	*ichthyoid*
canonize	*analgesic*
antonym	*phosphorus*
stenohaline	*erotic*
chirography	*monandrous*

patronymic
pyrotechnics
octopus
anemia
dynamite
misogamy
chromatic
stomatic
demoniac
photosynthesis
metronymic
iconic
pyromania
photon
nostalgia
sthenic
gastralgia
ethical
police
philander
hydrant

Level B
ichthyophagous
chromatolysis
cryophilic
dermatophyte
dyne
anaphylactic
pyretic
ethos
polygyny
psychosomatic
androgen
chiromancy
pyrheliometer
epidermis
chromosphere
acronym
polygala

galaxy
hemophilia
gastronomy
cryotherapy
pachyderm
podiatrist
photostat
misanthrope
iconoclast
genealogy
canonical
political
toxemia
generic
pedagogy
ethnocentric
hyperalgia
dynamics
sarcasm
podium
pandemonium

nyctaphonia
demonology
aniseikonia
ethnogeny
patristic
emmenagogue
Calliope
phylactery
thermodynamic
pederasty
asthenia
platypus
amerorrhea
homonym
osteoichthyous
surgeon
halophyte

nyctalopia	hydrophilic
ethnocracy	perianth
misology	cryobiology
pyrogenic	androecium
photochromic	eroticism
cynocephalous	ethnography
chromosome	demonolatry
iconography	cynical
sarcoma	erogenous
chriropter	galactose
monostomous	cardiasthenia
ichthyosaur	stomatology
polyanthus	neuralgia
apodal	rhinal
androgynous	gastritis
prophylactic	dermatology
cryonics	cosmopolitan
nyctohemeral	pyrolysis
gerontocracy	cynophobia

Exercise

A. In the etymology of each of the following words find the root with a Greek third declension noun. Employing the rules of trans-literation, try to write that root in Greek before giving its English meaning. Since none are included in the vocabulary list of this lesson, you will have to consult your English dictionary.

    1. *bucolic*   2. *astronomy*   3. *antagonist*   4. *orthodontist*

B. **Matching.** Match the term on the left with its definition on the right.

1. *hydrography*	a. rule by the elderly
2. *toponymy*	b. having an affinity for water
3. *misogamy*	c. sugar in the blood
4. *gerontocracy*	d. study of place names
5. *glycemia*	e. relating to the care of children
6. *misogyny*	f. charting of water
7. *hydrophilic*	g. hatred of women
8. *geomorphology*	h. pain caused by light
9. *pediatric*	i. aversion to marriage
10. *photodynia*	j. study of earth's shape

τῷ σοφῷ ξένον οὐδέν.
To the wise man nothing is foreign.[1]

Chapter Six
Adjectives

In your study of the parts of speech in English several years ago, you no doubt learned that the primary function of adjectives was to *limit* or *qualify* nouns. To students unfamiliar with another foreign language the relationship between an adjective and noun may erroneously be viewed as almost coincidental and arising merely from the customary proximity of one to the other. Frequently, an adjective stands immediately before a noun in what is called the attributive position, as in the sentence:

"The *large* book was taken by the *small* child."

You should also recall that an adjective can likewise appear in the predicate position, as in the examples:

"The book is *large* ," or "The child was *small* ."

Students familiar with almost any European foreign language, however, will immediately recognize a tighter bond between an adjective and the noun it modifies. This closeness appears in the required agreement between them in *gender* (masculine, feminine or neuter), in *number* (singular or plural), and in *case* (subjective, objective, or possessive). Since most adjectives in English possess only *one* single form that satisfies all circumstances, no special attention is usually paid to these matters. For example, in the sentences above the adjectives "large" and "small" would not change spelling or take on a special different ending if we substituted nouns of different gender or number. In most Indo-European languages changes of this sort would commonly take place.

You will recall that nouns in Greek assume gender in a fashion different from those in English. Words such as "stone," "marriage," "victory," and "earth" are neuter in English but masculine or feminine in ancient Greek. Although each noun usually could possess but a single gender, the Greek adjective was required to be adaptable to any of the three

---

1 Antisthenes in Diogenes Laertius, *Lives* 6.12.

genders, depending upon which noun it was modifying. One could express the Greek adjective for the word "narrow" in three different ways (with nouns of three different gender) as follows:

στενὸς δάκτυλος   - narrow finger (masc.)
στενὴ γλῶττα   - narrow tongue (fem.)
στενὸν δένδρον   - narrow tree (neuter)

To indicate the broader aspect of adjectives in the vocabulary that follows, the masculine form, usually given in English dictionaries, will be written out completely. This will then be followed by only the endings for the feminine and neuter genders. Many adjectives will be recognized as belonging to a combination of the first and second declensions since they possess the endings of these declensions with which you are already quite familiar. Such is the case with the word "stenos" above. Most other adjectives represent a combination of the third and first declensions wherein the masculine and neuter belong to the third declension and the feminine belongs to the first. Adjectives in this group assume an appearance as follows:

παχύς, παχεῖα, παχύ - thick

In Greek there existed no rule that a second declension masculine adjective could modify only a second declension masculine noun. What did matter was that masculine agreed with masculine (fem. with fem., *etc.*) apart from any consideration of declension.[2] Study these examples.

παχὺς δάκτυλος   - thick finger (masc.)
παχεῖα γλῶττα   - thick tongue (fem.)
παχὺ δένδρον   - thick tree (neuter)

In earlier lessons it was pointed out that the root of nouns included every letter prior to the ending. The same rule holds for Greek adjectives. One exception should be noted however. Frequently the final upsilon (υ) of third declension adjectives is retained. For example, in word borrowings from the Greek word **tachys, tacheia, tachy** ("swift") the final "-y" is kept in *tachycardia* but lost in *tachometer*.

---

2 The same rules for adjective-noun agreement apply in Latin which will be seen extensively later in many Latin phrases.

If you consult your English dictionary for some examples of English derivatives from the vocabulary words below, you will discover that very few of them exist as separate words in English completely in and of themselves. Instead, the roots of adjectives commonly appear only in combination with nouns. In this single capacity, however, they enrich our language tremendously.

Vocabulary

Greek	Transliteration	Meaning	Derivative
ἄκρος, -α, -ον	akros	high, topmost	acropolis
ἄλλος, -η, -ον	allos	other	allopathy
ἄριστος, -η, -ον	aristos	best	aristocracy
αὐτός, -ή, -όν	autos	self	autonomy
βαρύς, -εῖα, -ύ	barys	heavy	barometer
βραδύς, -εῖα, -ύ	bradys	slow	bradycardia
βραχύς, -εῖα, -ύ	brachys	short	brachycephalic
γλυκύς, -εῖα, -ύ	glykys	sweet	glycerin
γυμνός, -ή, -όν	gymnos	naked	gymnasium
ἕτερος, -α, -ον	heteros	other	heterodox
εὐρύς, -εῖα, -ύ	eurys	wide	euryhaline
θερμός, -ή, -όν	thermos	hot	thermometer
ἱερός, -ά, -όν	hieros	holy	hierarchy
ἴσος -η, -ον	isos	equal	isotope
κακός, -ή, -όν	kakos	bad	cacophonous
κοινός, -ή, -όν	koinos	common	koine
μακρός, -ά, -όν	makros	large	macrocosm
μέγας, μεγάλη, μέγα	megas, megale	great, large	megaphone
μέσος, -η, -ον	mesos	middle	Mesopotamia

μικρός, -ά, -όν	**mikros**	small	*microscope*
μόνος, -η, -ον	**monos**	single, one	*monarchy*
νέος, -α, -ον	**neos**	new	*neolithic*
ὀλίγος, -η, -ον	**oligos**	few	*oligarchy*
ὅλος, -η, -ον	**holos**	whole	*holograph*
ὁμός, -ή, -όν	**homos**	same	*homonym*
ὅμοιος, -α, -ον	**homoios**	similar	*homeopathy*
ὀρθός, -ή, -όν	**orthos**	straight, true	*orthodox*
παλαιός, -ά, -όν	**palaios**	old	*paleography*
πᾶς, πᾶσα, πᾶν	**pas, pan (pant-)**	all	*pantheon*
παχύς, -εῖα, -ύ	**pachys**	thick	*pachyderm*
πλατύς, -εῖα, -ύ	**platys**	flat, broad	*platypus*
πολύς, πολλή, πολύ	**polys (poly)**	many	*polytheism*
σκληρός, -ά, -όν	**skleros**	hard	*sclerosis*
σοφός, -ή, -όν	**sophos**	wise	*sophist*
στενός, -ή, -όν	**stenos**	narrow	*stenographer*
ταχύς, -εῖα, -ύ	**tachys**	swift	*tachometer*
ψευδής, -ές	**pseudes**	false	*pseudonym*

Derivative Study

Level A

microphone	*philosophy*
acrophobia	*monologue*
cacography	*autocracy*
polygamy	*Mesozoic*
thermodynamics	*sclerosis*
sophomore	*heterodox*
megalopolis	*hieroglyphics*
glycogen	*autopsy*

pandemic　　　　　　*thermostat*
isobar　　　　　　　*pandemonium*
neophyte　　　　　　*Paleolithic*
pachysandra　　　　*allotropic*
panorama　　　　　　*holocaust*
monopoly　　　　　　*barytone*
macron　　　　　　　*stenosis*
autobiography　　　*megalith*
aristocrat　　　　　*monolith*

Level B
hologynic　　　　　　*oligophagous*
pseudoesthesia　　　*aneurysm*
tachytrophism　　　*platyrrhine*
gymnosperm　　　　　*brachypterous*
mesoderm　　　　　　*homograph*
eurythermic　　　　*heterogeneous*
homeomorphic　　　　*bradylogia*
stenotopic　　　　　*hyperbaric*
isomerous　　　　　　*orthopedic*
glycemia　　　　　　*autohypnosis*
isodynamic　　　　　*oligochrome*
catholic　　　　　　*platyhelminth*
Pandora　　　　　　　*pseudosoph*
homogeneous　　　　*panchromatic*
tachyphagia　　　　*bradykinesia*
brachydactylia　　*homeostasis*
homophone　　　　　　*stenohaline*
sophistry　　　　　　*isosceles*
cenesthesia　　　　*monotheism*
micrometer　　　　　*macrocephaly*
autogamy　　　　　　*barograph*
isobar　　　　　　　*acrodynia*
heterochromatic　　*Akron*
glycosuria　　　　　*autocephalous*
cacodemon　　　　　　*cenobite*
megalomania　　　　*neophobia*
thermotaxis　　　　*allophane*
scleroderma　　　　*Paleozoic*

pansophic	*euryhaline*
mesosphere	*pseudomorph*
isogamous	*amphibrach*
sclerotic	*panacea*
heterotopia	*thermoanesthesia*
heterophyllous	*homogamous*
holograph	*aristotype*
allomorph	*holandric*
mesophyte	*heterotaxis*
tachyphylaxis	*acromegaly*
platyopia	*antipodal*
microbiology	*autogamy*
heterocyclic	*perigynous*
heteromorphous	*paraplegia*

Exercise

A. **Matching**. Match the word on the left with its proper definition on the right.

1. *bradyglossia*		a.	bad handwriting
2. *heterogamous*		b.	slowness of speech
3. *homochromatic*		c.	having a slow heart
4. *pseudomorph*		d.	sun worship
5. *eurythermic*		e.	equal before the law
6. *cacography*		f.	union of unlike gametes
7. *heliolatry*		g.	having a wide range of heat
8. *isonomy*		h.	rule by a few
9. *bradycardia*		i.	having the same color
10. *oligarchy*		j.	having a deceptive form

B. **Phobias**. Identify the object of fear in each of the following words by providing the meaning of the accompanying Greek root. As a challenge to other students, list ten additional "fears," including roots not previously studied.

1. *gamophobia*	6. *cynophobia*
2. *hypnophobia*	7. *hydrophobia*
3. *odynophobia*	8. *acrophobia*
4. *neophobia*	9. *gynephobia*
5. *gymnophobia*	10. *pan(t)ophobia*

C. **Antonyms.** Many English words possess an antonym (opposite) by reason of a change of the Greek adjective preceeding the same Greek noun as, for example, *bradycardia* and *tachycardia*. Form antonyms of the following words by switching each adjective with its opposite in the vocabulary list of this lesson. You can verify your answers in your dictionary.

1. *neolithic*		8. *oligochromatic*
2. *stenothermic*		9. *microcosm*
3. *heterogenous*		10. *homosexual*
4. *anisochromatic*		11. *cryostat*
5. *brachycephalic*		12. *tachylogia*
6. *atheistic*		13. *allokinetic*
7. *orthodox*		14. *polychromatic*

D. **Similarities or likenesses.** Words referring to similarities are created when the suffix "*-oid*" is attached to a Greek root, as *hypnoid* means "resembling sleep." Identify what each of the following words "resembles" from the root preceeding the suffix "*-oid*." You may have to check some in your English dictionary. Can you list a few other examples of English words with the same suffix?

1. *anthropoid*		6. *android*
2. *hematoid*		7. *deltoid*
3. *osteoid*		8. *spheroid*
4. *hyoid*		9. *hydroid*
5. *mastoid*		10. *geoid*

Chapter Seven
Colors and Numbers

Having considered nouns and adjectives in previous chapters, we might suppose that we are now ready to look to other parts of speech from which we assume Greek words into English, but that is not the case. Colors and numbers are usually adjectives too. Indeed they could have been included in the vocabulary of the preceding chapter, but that list, you recall, was already quite extensive without them. They therefore are grouped separately below.

Colors

Greek	Transliteration	Meaning	Derivative
ἄργυρος	**argyros**	silver	*argyrism*
γλαυκός	**glaukos**	blue-green, gray	*glaucoma*
ἐρυθρός	**erythros**	red	*erythrism*
κύανος	**kyanos**	blue	*cyanide*
λευκός	**leukos**	white	*leukemia*
μέλας, μέλανος	**melas, melanos**	black	*melanin*
ξανθός	**xanthos**	yellow	*xanthine*
πορφύρα	**porphyra**	purple	*porphyry*
χλωρός	**chloros**	light green	*chlorine*
χρυσός	**chrysos**	gold	*chrysolite*

The following list on numbers contains the most common *cardinal* numbers (one, two, three, *etc.*) in Greek. Some are found with great

---

1 Protagoras.

frequency in English derivatives, others are not. Likewise included are a
few *ordinal* numbers (first, second, third, *etc.*) and some *adverbial*
numbers (once, twice, *etc.*) too. Between the transliterated form and the
English meaning a special column has been added in which the most
common root in English derivatives is presented in parentheses. Finally,
also included in this chapter are a few Greek nouns that happen to appear
with Greek numbers in English words. Some were presented in earlier
chapters but are given here with additional meanings; others are being
introduced for the first time.

Numbers

Greek	Translit.	Common Root	Meaning	Derivative
ἥμισυς	hemisus	(HEMI-)	half	*hemisphere*
ἕν (μόνος)	hen (monos)	(HEN-, MON-)	one, single	*henotheism* *monarchy*
πρῶτος	protos	(PROT-)	first	*prototype*
δύο (δίς)	dyo, dis	(DY-, DI-)	two (twice)	*dyad* *dipteral*
δίχα	dicha	(DICH-)	in two	*dichotomy*
δεύτερος	deuteros	(DEUTER-)	second	*Deuteronomy*
τρεῖς (τρίς)	treis, tris	(TRI-)	three (thrice)	*trilogy*
τέσσαρες τέτταρες	tessares tettares	(TETRA-)	four	*tetrapod*
πέντε	pente	(PENT-)	five	*pentathlon*
ἕξ	hex	(HEX-)	six	*hexagon*
ἑπτά	hepta	(HEPT-)	seven	*heptagonal*
ὀκτώ	okto	(OCT-)	eight	*octopus*
ἐννέα	ennea	(ENNEA-)	nine	*enneaphyllous*
δέκα	deka	(DEC-)	ten	*decathlon*
ἑκατόν	hekaton	(HECT-)	hundred	*hectograph*
χίλιοι	chilioi	(KIL-)	thousand	*kilogram*

Related Vocabulary

Greek	Translit.	Meaning	Derivative
ἆθλον	**athlon**	contest	*triathlon*
γωνία	**gonia**	angle, corner	*hexagonal*
ἕδρα	**hedra**	seat; base, side	*tetrahedron*
λόγος	**logos**	writing, speech, study	*trilogy*
μέρος	**meros**	part	*heptamerous*
μέτρον	**metron**	measure	*pentameter*
στίχος	**stichos**	verse, line, row	*hemistich*
τεῦχος	**teuchos**	book; tool	*Pentateuch*

Derivative Study

Level A

chrysanthemum	*glaucous*
kilometer	*octogon*
dichromatic	*monogamy*
melancholy	*leukocyte*
tetrology	*hyphen*
monarch	*tricycle*
protocol	*chlorophyll*
triagonal	*monotheism*
monotony	*xanthoderma*
tetrarch	*Decalogue*

Level B

erythrocyte	*Melanesia*
deuterogamy	*hexadactylism*
monocarpic	*diphyllous*
anthocyanin	*hypochlorous*
cyanosis	*argyrophil*
chryselephantine	*tetrapterous*
protophyte	*heptamerous*

protozoa   hexameter
triad   decamerous
dioecious   protagonist
hectoliter   chloranthy
erythrophobia   hypoxanthine
deuterium   chrysalis
pseudodipteral   tribrach
tetrastich   Decameron
protolithic   chloropsia
xanthophyll   acrocyanosis
decapod   triskaidekaphobia
triglyph   tetrachloride

Exercises

A. **Matching.** Match the term on the left with its proper phrase on the right.

1. *triathlon*   a. having two pairs of limbs
2. *Penteteuch*   b. consisting of three contests
3. *glauconite*   c. five books of the Bible
4. *acrocyanosis*   d. yellow-leafed
5. *xanthophyll*   e. deficient skin pigmentation
6. *melanism*   f. black skin pigmentation
7. *tetrapod*   g. having bluish extremities
8. *Deuteronomy*   h. containing the second law
9. *ennead*   i. dull-green mineral
10. *leukoderma*   j. having nine parts

B. **Word-Formation.** Starting with the definition or principal elements, form an English word using the Greek roots you have studied. Check your answers in a dictionary.

1. having four parts
2. semicircular
3. having five measures or metrical feet
4. making 1,000 circles (per second)
5. having redness in the skin

Chapter Eight
Prefixes

Prepositions were employed in ancient Greek in much the same way as they occur in English today, that is, they always introduce a phrase. In our language we say, for example, "*in* the street," "*on* the table," "*through* the circle," or "*above* the house." A different way many of these same prepositions could be used in ancient Greek, however, was as *prefixes*. As such, they assisted in the formation of single new words in compound form. You have already encountered many examples of this practice in the derivative study sections of earlier chapters. They are even more common with verbs that are yet to be studied. Examples of prepositions as prefixes are: "*anti*thesis," "*hyp*othesis," and "*syn*thesis." Similarly, a few common adverbs are also employed in this fashion and therefore are included in the vocabulary list below.

Three matters deserve special attention as you study the prefixes in this chapter. First, prepositions ending with a vowel often lose that vowel before roots beginning with a vowel. Second, prepositions ending in a consonant often have that consonant modified before roots beginning with certain consonants. Finally, on occasion certain prefixes assume *no special meaning*. In such cases, the meaning of the root to which they happened to be attached is intensified. The few prefixes occasionally used in this manner are identified below by the words "*intensive use*" under the meaning.

This scene from a Greek vase painting shows a sculptor at work on a herm. The text reads: ΗΙΠΑΡΧΟΣ ΚΑΛΟΣ (Handsome Hiparchus).

---

[1] Attributed to Caesar Augustus in Suetonius' *Vita Aug.*, 25.

Vocabulary

Greek	Regular Form	Before Vowel	Meanings	Examples
ἀ-	a-	an-	not, without	*atheist*
				anarchy
ἀμφί	amphi-	amph-	around, both	*amphibious*
ἀνά	ana-	an-	back, again, up	*anamnesis*
			intensive use	*aneurysm*
ἀντί	anti-	ant-	opposite,	*antarctic*
			against	*antibiotic*
ἀπό	apo-	ap-	away from	*apogee*
διά	dia-	di-	through, across	*diameter*
δυς-	dys-	dys-	bad, difficult	*dysphoria*
ἐν	en- (em-)	en-	in, on	*endemic*
ἔνδον	endo-	end-	within	*endogamy*
ἐκ	ek-	ex-	out, out of	*eccentric*
ἔξω	exo-	ex-	outside, outer	*exogamy*
ἐπί	epi-	ep-	upon	*epidemic*
εὐ-	eu-	ev-	well, good	*euphony*
κατά	kata-	kat-	down	*catastrophe*
			intensive use	*catholic*
μετά	meta-	met-	after, change	*metamorphosis*
			beyond	*metacarpal*
παρά	para-	par-	beside, against	*parallel*
			almost	*paramedic*
περί	peri-	peri-	around, near	*periscope*
προ	pro-	pro-	before	*prophet*
συν	syn- (sym-)	syn-	with, together	*synchronize*
ὑπέρ	hyper-	hyper-	over, above,	*hypertrophy*
			excessive	
ὑπό	hypo-	hyp-	under, below	*hypogeal*

Derivative Study

Level A

atom	synthesis
diagonal	antidote
hypodermic	endemic
ecstasy	epitaph
analysis	catalogue
anemia	symposium
epidermis	prognosis
antiseptic	apodal
symphony	encephalitis

Level B

hypochondriac	peristyle
apostate	prophylactic
amphibrach	metaphysics
parentheses	anatomy
dyslexia	euthanasia
hypertrophy	dyspepsia
evangelist	catalysis
hypertension	periphery
euphemism	diaphanous
apocryphal	euphotic
paragraph	aniseikonia
dyspnea	epigeous
anaphylaxis	amphiprostyle
anestrous	catatonia
epicardium	anorexia
anonymous	metempsychosis
dystrophy	hypoglossal
symbiotic	anachronism
perigee	synergy
perihelion	antonym
tetrastichous	hexateuch
distich	azygous

Exercise

A. **Matching.** Match the term on the left with its proper phrase on the right.

1. *euphotic*	a. possessing no pain
2. *hypertrophy*	b. subterranean
3. *analgesic*	c. marriage within a group
4. *prophylactic*	d. preventing beforehand
5. *hypogeal*	e. excessive nourishment
6. *hyperbaric*	f. having two colors
7. *anabiosis*	g. having good light
8. *dichromic*	h. using excessive air pressure
9. *dichromatic*	i. returning to life
10. *endogamy*	j. extending through time

B. **Forming Antonyms.** Using the prefixes in the vocabulary of this lesson, form opposites of the following words. Check your answers in a dictionary.

1. *perihelion*	6. *catadromous*
2. *euphonia*	7. *apogee*
3. *hypocinesia*	8. *hyperphonia*
4. *atrophy*	9. *perimeter*
5. *exogamy*	10. *pantheism*

Chapter Nine
Verbs

In English verbs are studied according to principal parts, that is, according to the few forms from which all other inflected forms are derived. These principal parts are three in number and consist of the following:

1) the present infinitive   (*to walk, to sing*)
2) the past tense   (*walked, sang*)
3) the past participle   (*walked, sung*)

In ancient Greek the situation for verbs was similar but more complex. For instance, due to the large number of possible inflected forms, it is necessary for students attempting to read the literature of this language to learn "six" principal parts of most verbs. As with the verb "to sing" above, Greek verb roots could also change completely in orthography as one moved from one principal part to another.

For those whose primary interest is not the reading of Greek literature in the original but only the recognition and understanding of Greek roots in English words, special effort has been made to make the learning process of the complicated structure of the Greek verb easier but beneficial. On the one hand, no attempt will be made to have students expend a considerable amount of time learning unimportant verb forms. On the other hand, some explanation of the proper format employed by lexicographers in making references to Greek verbs in dictionary etymologies is felt in order. It is that process that is summarized here.

Consult the etymology of the following words in your English dictionary: 1) *synagogue*; 2) *prognosis*; and 3) *aphasia*. All include a Greek verb in the second element. Your notations should look like this:

1) synagogue   (Greek: *syn-* together; *agein-* to lead, bring)
2) prognosis   (Greek: *pro-* before; *gignoskein-* to know)
3) aphasia   (Greek: *a-* not; *phanai-* to speak)

---

[1] Archimedes. (Motto of the state of California)

By way of cross reference each of these Greek verbs can be found in the vocabulary below. In all cases English dictionaries make identification of the verb based upon its present infinitive ("to lead," "to know," and "to speak"). In Greek the most common infinitive ending is "-ειν," and the root for it includes every letter prior to this ending. Different infinitive endings that you may encounter in dictionaries are: "-ναι" or "-εσθαι." These come from deponent[2] or irregular verbs. The fact that *"agogue"* in *synagogue* does not match the root of its infinitive *"ag-"* or that *"gno-"* in *prognosis* does not agree with its infinitive root *"gignosk-"* should pose no serious problem to you if you understand that English words are often derived from different principal parts of the Greek verb and that many of these principal parts have strange-looking roots that show little resemblance to the root of the present infinitive. To make allowance for this phenomenon affecting the verb, the format for the vocabulary list below has been modified slightly. Instead of giving a transliteration for each present infinitive, which you should easily be able to provide at a mere glance at this point in your study, the second column has been set aside to list the most common roots of the Greek verb found in English derivatives. It is suggested that you memorize these forms as you study the vocabulary. Remember that although the Greek "kappa" is retained as a "k" in the spelling for the Common Root, it can frequently be found as a "c" in English words due to Latinization.

Vocabulary

Infinitive	Common Roots	Meaning	Derivative
ἄγειν	AGOG-, AGOGUE-	to lead, bring	*synagogue*
αἰσθάνεσθαι	AISTHE-, ESTHE-	to feel, perceive	*esthetic*
ἀκούειν	AKOU-	to hear	*acoustics*
βάλλειν	BALL-, BOL-	to throw	*symbol*
γίγνεσθαι	GON-, GEN-	to be born, become	*genetic*
γιγνώσκειν	GNO-	to know	*agnostic*

---

2 Deponent verbs have only passive endings in Greek for the most part for their active meanings.

γλύφειν	GLYPH-	to carve	*triglyph*
γράφειν	GRAPH-, GRAM-	to write	*telegraph*
διδόναι	DO-	to give	*antidote*
ἱστάναι	STA-	to stand, set	*thermostat*
κινεῖν	KINE-	to move, set in motion	*kinetic*
κλέπτειν	KLEP-	to steal	*kleptomania*
κρίνειν	KRI-	to judge	*critical*
κρύπτειν	KRYPT-, KRYPH-	to hide	*crypt*
λύειν	LY-	to loosen, dissolve	*analysis*
μαίνεσθαι	MAN-	to be mad	*mania*
μνᾶσθαι	MNE-, MNES-	to remember	*amnesia*
ὁρᾶν	OPT-, OR-, OP-	to see	*optical cyclorama*
πάσχειν	PATH-, PATHE-	to feel, suffer	*sympathy*
ποιεῖν	POIE-, POET-	to do, make	*poetic*
ῥεῖν	RHE-, -RRHE-	to flow	*pyorrhea*
σκέπτεσθαι	SKEP-, SKOP-	to examine	*skeptical*
στρέφειν	STROPH-, STREP-	to turn, twist	*strophe*
σχίζειν	SCHIS-, SCHIZ-	to split	*schism*
τάσσειν	TAK-, TAX-	to arrange	*syntax*
τέμνειν	TOM-	to cut	*atom*
τιθέναι	THE-	to put, place	*thesis*
τρέπειν	TROP-	to turn	*tropism*
τρέφειν	TROPH-	to nourish	*atrophy*
φαγεῖν	PHAG-	to eat	*aphagia*
φαίνειν	PHA-, PHAN-	to show	*epiphany*

φάναι	PHAS-, PHE-	to speak, say	*aphasia*
φέρειν	PHER-, PHOR-	to bear, carry	*phosphorous*
φιλεῖν	PHIL-	to love	*philosophy*

Derivative Study

Level A

tactics	*pedagogy*
schizophrenia	*apathy*
amnesty	*hieroglyphics*
hypothesis	*euphemism*
sarcophagus	*optometrist*
phonograph	*hypercritical*
dystrophy	*psychopath*
heliotrope	*bibliography*
diagnosis	*apostate*
periscope	*diarrhea*

Level B

taxonomy	*cyanophil*
geotropism	*amblyacousia*
streptococcus	*geostrophic*
otoscope	*anecdote*
esophagus	*demagogue*
cryptogram	*kinesiotherapy*
lithotomy	*metathesis*
metastasis	*otorrhea*
ballistics	*petroglyph*
diaphanous	*anamnesis*
phyllotaxy	*autotrophic*
chromatophore	*cryptanthous*
schizotrichia	*hypnagogic*
anthropophagous	*pharmacopoeia*
onomatopoetic	*xylophagous*
hyperesthesia	*mystagogue*
apocryphal	*ecstasy*
catalysis	*paralysis*

hemostat   *dialysis*
apostrophe   *antipathy*
rheotrope   *anesthesia*
galactagogue   *hydrogen*
anacusia   *metaphor*
hemopoiesis   *hemolysis*
diacritical   *isotropic*
boustrophedon   *troposphere*
hydrolysis   *paramnesia*
antistrophe   *anastrophe*
anatropous   *prothesis*
hypostasis   *prostomium*
hypotaxis   *phanerogam*
anaphora   *apogamy*
anagogic   *embolism*
schizoid   *synopsis*
periphery   *paramnesia*
synesthesia

Special Topics: Greek Plural Forms in English

Most nouns in English are made plural by the simple addition of the suffix "*-s*" or "*-es*." Many words of ancient Greek origin, however, are made plural according to the rules governing the formation of plurals for either Greek or Latin nouns in antiquity. Most Greek nouns follow the second route, that is, they enter the English language having first been Latinized. In such cases a specific Greek word initially assumes the singular Latin form corresponding in declension to that which it possessed in ancient Greek. It then is made plural according to the Latin rules for that declension and gender. Although some examples of this phenomenon are given below, Latin plurals will be discussed more in detail in the next division of this text.

There are many instances in which Greek nouns have entered the English language directly and are made plural according to Greek rules. Study the examples below. You will note that this occurs most commonly with second declension neuter nouns and all third declension nouns. Greek words that yield to the "Latin" plural are placed in parentheses.

Declension (gender):

GREEK		LATIN	
Sing.	Plur.	Sing.	Plur.

First (f.) *-a,-e* | *-ai* | *-a* | *-ae* |

| *(amoibe)* | *(amoibai)* | *amoeba* | *amoebae* |

Second (m.) *-os* | *-oi* | *-us* | *-i* |

(bronchos)	*(bronchoi)*	*bronchus*	*bronchi*
(daktylos)	*(daktyloi)*	*dactylus*	*dactyli*
(embolos)	*(emboloi)*	*embolus*	*emboli*
(kolossos)	*(kolossoi)*	*colossus*	*colossi*
(obelos)	*(obeloi)*	*obelus*	*obeli*
(pyloros)	*(pyloroi)*	*pylorus*	*pylori*
(thalamos)	*(thalamoi)*	*thalamus*	*thalami*
(thallos)	*(thalloi)*	*thallus*	*thalli*
(thesauros)	*(thesauroi)*	*thesaurus*	*thesauri*

Second (n.) *-on* | *-a* | *-um* | *-a* |

(bakterion)	*(bakteria)*	*bacterium*	*bacteria*
criterion	*criteria*		
(encomion)	*(encomia)*	*encomium*	*encomia*
(gymnasion)	*(gymnasia)*	*gymnasium*	*gymnasia*
phenomenon	*phenomena*		
prolegomenon	*prolegomena*		
protozoon	*protozoa*		
(pyxidion)	*(pyxidia)*	*pyxidium*	*pyxidia*
(stadion)	*(stadia)*	*stadium*	*stadia*
toxon	*toxa*		
zoon	*zoa*		

Third (m./f.) * | *-es* | * | *-es* |

analysis	*analyses*
basis	*bases*
calyx	*calyces*
catharsis	*catharses*
crisis	*crises*
diaeresis	*diaereses*

diagnosis	diagnoses
diakinesis	diakineses
diaphoresis	diaphoreses
ellipsis	ellipses
emphasis	emphases
exegesis	exegeses
hypostasis	hypostases
hypothesis	hypotheses
larynx	larynges
metamorphosis	metamorphoses
metastasis	metastases
meninx	meninges
paralysis	paralyses
phalanx	phalanges
prognosis	prognoses
prothesis	prostheses
synthesis	syntheses
taxis	taxes
thesis	theses

Third (n.) ***** **-ata** ***** **-a**

adenoma	adenomata
carcinoma	carcinomata
lemma	lemmata
miasma	miasmata
osteoma	osteomata
phantasma	phantasmata
stoma	stomata
trauma	traumata
zygoma	zygomata

*There are many possible third declension singular endings in both Greek and Latin.

Exercise

A. **Matching.** Match the terms on the left with their closest definition on the right.

1. *dysphasia*	a. hidden away
2. *taxonomy*	b. complete memory of the past
3. *apocryphal*	c. extending across earth
4. *euphemism*	d. difficult speaking
5. *hypnagogic*	e. state of well-being
6. *diageotropism*	f. difficulty in swallowing or eating
7. *ichthyophagous*	g. fish-eating
8. *euphoria*	h. good-sounding speech
9. *dysphagia*	i. sleep-bringing
10. *hypermnesia*	j. classification of laws

B. **Review.** Answer the questions below according to the material presented in this or earlier chapters.

1. Explain briefly the difference in spelling for the same Greek root in the words "*anesthetic*" and "*aesthetics.*"

2. Identify the meanings of two Greek roots that appear in English words as "*the.*"

3. Give the difference in meaning for the "*an-*" in the words "*anarchy*" and "*aneurysm.*"

4. According to etymology what is the difference between an *agnostic* and an *atheist*?

5. What is the difference between a *synonym, homonym, antonym* and *eponym*?

6. According to etymology what is the difference between *chromophil* and *chlorophyll*?

A

ἀ-, ἀν- a-, an- "not," "without" (8)
ἄγγελος angelos "messenger" (3)
ἄγειν agein "to lead," "to bring"(9)
ἀγορά agora "marketplace" (2)
ἀγών agon "contest," "struggle"
ἀδελφός adelphos "brother" (3)
ἆθλον athlon "contest" (7)
αἷμα, αἵματος haima, haimatos
    "blood" (5)
αἰσθάνεσθαι aisthanesthai "to feel,"
    "perceive" (9)
αἰτία aitia "cause"
ἀκμή akme "highest point"
ἀκούειν akouein "to hear" (9)
ἄκρος, akros "high," "topmost" (6)
ἄλγος algos "pain" (5)
ἄλλος allos "other" (6)
ἅλς, ἁλός hals, halos "salt" (5)
ἀμοιβή amoibe "change" (2)
ἀμφί amphi "around," "both" (8)

ἀνά ana "back," "up," "again" (8)
ἀνήρ, ἀνδρός aner, andros "man"
    (5)
ἄνθος anthos "flower" (5)
ἄνθρωπος anthropos "human,"
    "man" (5)
ἀντί anti "against," "opposite" (8)
ἀπό apo "from," "away from" (8)
ἀράχνη arachne "spider" (2)
ἄργυρος argyros "silver" (7)
ἄριστος aristos "best" (6)
ἀρχαῖος archaios "old"
ἀστήρ, ἀστέρος aster "star"
αὐτός autos "self" (6)

B

βάλλειν ballein "to throw" (9)
βαρύς barys "heavy" (6)
βιβλίον biblion "book" (4)

---

[1] In this vocabulary list only the nominative, singular is given for nouns, unless there is a change of root, in which case the genitive, singular is also listed. This follows the customary manner of reference in etymologies of most English dictionaries, except that here, of course, the Greek alphabet is employed instead of transliteration. Adjectives likewise are presented in the nominative, singular form but generally only in the masculine gender. Most prepositions are given only in their standard form, not as they sometimes occur as prefixes in words. Verbs are listed in their present, infinitive form. Additional information, especially for verbs, can be found in the lesson (indicated in parentheses) where the word is initially presented for study. The absence of a number, on the other hand, indicates that the entry was not included in the vocabulary list of earlier chapters.

βίος bios "life" (3)
βοτανή botane "plant," "herb" (2)
βοῦς, βόος bous, boos "cow," "ox"
βραδύς bradys "slow" (6)
βραχύς brachys "short" (6)

Γ

γάλα, γάλακτος gala, galactos
   "milk" (5)
γάμος gamos "marriage" (3)
γαστήρ, γαστρός gaster, gastros
   "stomach" (5)
γένος, γένεος genos "race," "kind"
   (5)
γέρων, γέροντος geron, gerontos
   "old man" (5)
γῆ ge "earth" (2)
γίγνεσθαι gignesthai "to be born"
   (9)
γιγνώσκειν gignoskein "to know"
   (9)
γλαυκός glaukos "gray," "blue-
   green" (7)
γλυκύς glykys "sweet" (6)
γλύφειν glyphein "to carve" (9)
γλῶσσα, γλῶττα glossa, glotta
   "tongue," "language" (2)
γράφειν graphein "to write" (9)
γυμνός gymnos "naked" (6)
γυνή, γυναικός gyne, gynaikos
   "woman" (5)
γωνία gonia "angle," "corner" (7)

Δ

δαίμων daimon "spirit" (5)
δάκτυλος daktylos "finger" (3)
δέκα deka "ten" (7)
δένδρον dendron "tree" (4)

δέρμα, δέρματος derma, dermatos
   "skin" (5)
δεύτερος deuteros "second" (7)
δῆμος demos "people" (3)
διά dia "through," "across" (8)
δίαιτα diaita "way of living"
διδόναι didonai "to give" (9)
δίχα dicha "in two" (7)
δολιχός dolichos "long"
δόξα doxa "opinion," "glory" (2)
δρόμος dromos "running," "race"
   (3)
δύναμις dynamis "power," "force"
   (5)
δυσ- dys- "bad," "difficult" (8)

Ε

ἕδρα hedra "seat," "base," "side"
   (7)
ἔθνος ethnos "nation" (5)
εἰκών eikon "image," "statue" (5)
ἐκ ek "out," "out of" (8)
ἑκατόν hekaton "hundred" (7)
ἐμπόριον emporion "trading place
ἐν en "in," "on" (8)
ἕν hen "one" (7)
ἔνδον "within" (7)
ἐννέα ennea "nine" (7)
ἕξ hex "six" (7)
ἔξω exo "outside," "outer" (7)
ἐπί epi "upon" (3)
ἑπτά hepta "seven" (7)
ἔργον ergon "work" (4)
ἔρως, ἔρωτος eros, erotos "love" (5)
ἐρυθρός erythros "red" (7)
ἕτερος heteros "other" (6)
εὖ eu "well," "good" (8)
εὐρύς eurys "wide" (6)

Z

ζυγόν zygon "yoke" (4)
ζωή zoe "life," "animal"
ζῷον zoon "animal" (4)

H

ἡδονή hedone "pleasure" (2)
ἥλιος helios "sun" (3)
ἡμέρα hemera "day" (2)
ἦθος ethos "custom" "character" (5)
ἥμισυς hemisys "half" (7)

Θ

θάλασσα, θαλαττα thalassa "sea" (2)
θάνατος thanatos "death" (3)
θεατρόν theatron "viewing place" (4)
θεός theos "god" (3)
θερμός thermos "hot" (6)

I

ἰατρός "physician" (3)
ἱερός hieros "holy" (6)
ἵππος hippos "horse" (3)
ἴσος isos "equal" (6)
ἱστάναι histanai "to stand" (9)
ἰχθύς ichthys "fish" (5)

K

κακός kakos "bad" (6)
κάλλος kallos "beauty" (5)
καλός kalos "beautiful"
κανών kanon "rule" (5)
καρδία kardia "heart" (2)
κατά kata "down," "according to" (8)
κέντρον kentron "center" (4)
κεφαλή kephale "head" (2)
κινεῖν kinein "to move" (9)

κλέπτειν kleptein "to steal" (9)
κοινός koinos "common" (6)
κόσμος kosmos "universe" (3)
κρίνειν krinein "to judge" (9)
κρύος kryos "cold," "frost" (5)
κρύπτειν kryptein "to hide" (9)
κύκλος kyklos "circle" (3)
κύων, κυνός kyon, kynos "dog" (5)

Λ

λευκός leukos "white" (7)
λήθη lethe "forgetfulness" (2)
λίθος lithos "stone" (3)
λόγος logos "word," "study" (3)
λύειν lyein "to loosen" (9)

M

μακρός makros "large" (6)
μαίνεσθαι mainesthai "to be mad" (9)
μέγας, μεγαλη megas, megale "great" (6)
μέλας, μέλανος melas, melanos "black" (7)
μέρος meros "part" (7)
μέσος mesos "middle" (6)
μετά meta "after," "change" (8)
μέτρον metron "measure" (7)
μῆν men "month" (5)
μήτηρ, μητρός meter, metros "mother" (5)
μικρός mikros "small" (6)
μῖσος misos "hatred" (5)
μνᾶσθαι mnasthai "to remember" (9)
μόνος monos "single," "one" (6)
μορφή morphe "shape," "form" (2)
μῦθος mythos "tale" (3)

N

νάρκη narke "numbness"
νεκρός nekros "corpse," "dead" (3)
νέος neos "new" (6)
νεῦρον neuron "string," "sinew"
νίκη nike "victory" (2)
νόμος nomos "law," "science of"
   (3)
νύξ, νυκτός nyx, nyctos "night" (5)
νύμφη nymphe "bride," "young
   woman" (2)

Ξ

ξανθός xanthos "yellow" (7)
ξένος xenos "stranger" (3)
ξύλον zylon "wood" (4)

Ο

ὁδός (h)odos "way," "road"
ὀδούς, ὀδόντος odontos "tooth"
ὀδύνη odyne "pain" (2)
οἶκος oikos "house" (3)
οἶστρος oistros "sting," "gadfly" (3)
ὀκτώ okto "eight" (7)
ὀλίγος oligos "few" (6)
ὅλος holos "whole" (6)
ὁμός homos "same" (6)
ὅμοιος homoios "similar" (6)
ὀφθαλμός ophthalmos "eye" (3)
ὁρᾶν horan "to see" (9)
ὀρθός orthos "straight," "true" (6)
ὄρνις, ὄρνιθος ornithos "bird" (5)
ὀστέον osteon "bone" (4)
ὄνυμα, ὀνύματος onyma, onymatos
   "name" (5)

Π

παῖς, παιδός paidos "child" (5)

παλαιός palaios "old" (6)
παρά para "beside," "almost" (8)
πᾶς, παντός pas, pantos "all" (6)
πάσχειν paschein "to feel" (9)
πατήρ, πατρός patros "father" (5)
παχύς pachys "thick" (6)
πεῖρα peira "experiment"
πέντε pente "five" (7)
περί peri "around," "near" (8)
πέτρα petra "rock," "boulder" (2)
πλατύς platys "flat," "broad" (6)
ποιεῖν poiein "to make," "do" (9)
πόλις polis "city" (5)
πολύς polys "many" (6)
πορφύρα porphyra "purple" (7)
πόλεμος polemos "war"
ποταμός potamos "river"
πούς, ποδός pous, podos "foot" (5)
προ pro "before" (8)
πρῶτος protos "first" (7)
πτερόν pteron "feather," "wing" (4)
πῦρ pyr "fire" (5)

Ρ

ῥεῖν rhein "to flow" (9)
ῥίς, ῥινός rhinos "nose" (5)

Σ

σάρξ, σαρκός sarkos "flesh" (5)
σελήνη selene "moon"
σθένος sthenos "strength" (5)
σκηνή skene "tent" (2)
σκέπτεσθαι skeptesthai "to
   examine" (9)
σκληρός skleros "hard" (6)
σοφός sophos "wise" (6)
στάδιον stadion "stade" (a length)
στενός stenos "narrow" (6)

στίχος stichos "row," "verse"
στόα stoa "porch," "colonnade"
στόμα, στοματος stoma, stomatos "mouth" (5)
στρέφειν strephein "to turn" (9)
συν syn "with," "together" (8)
σφαῖρα sphaipa "ball" (2)
σχίζειν schizein "to split" (9)
σχολή schole "leisure" (2)
σῶμα, σώματος soma, somatos "body" (9)

Τ

τάλαντον talanton "a weight"
τάσσειν tassein "to arrange" (9)
τάφος taphos "tomb," "grave"
ταχύς tachys "swift" (6)
τέμνειν temneim "to cut" (9)
τέσσαρες tessares "four" (7)
τεῦχος teuchos "book," "tool" (7)
τέχνη techne "skill," "craft" (2)
τῆλε tele "from or at a distance"
τιθέναι tithenai "to place" (9)
τόπος topos "place" (3)
τρεῖς, τρίς treis "three" (7)
τρέπειν trepein "to turn" (9)
τρέφειν trephein "to nourish" (9)
τροφή trophe "nourishment" (2)
τυραννός tyrannos "ruler" (3)

Υ

ὕδωρ, ὕδατος hydor "water" (5)
ὑπέρ hyper "above," "excessive" (8)
ὕπνος hypnos "sleep" (3)
ὑπό hypo "under," "below" (8)
ὑστέρα hystera "womb"

Φ

φαγεῖν phagein "to eat" (9)
φαίνειν phainein "to show" (9)
φάναι phanai "to speak, say" (9)
φάρμακον pharmakon "drug" (4)
φέρειν pherein "to carry" (9)
φιλεῖν philein "to love" (9)
φόβος phobos "fear" (3)
φύλαξ, φύλακος phylax, phylakos "guard" (5)
φύλλον phyllon "leaf" (4)
φῦλον phylon "race," "tribe" (4)
φυτόν phyton "plant" (4)
φωνή phone "voice," "sound" (2)
φώς, φωτός phos, photos "light" (5)

Χ

χείρ cheir "hand" (5)
χίλιοι chilioi "thousand" (7)
χλωρός chloros "light green" (7)
χολή chole "bile," "gall" (2)
χορός choros "singers" (3)
χρόνος chronos "time" (3)
χρυσός chrysos "gold" (3)
χρῶμα, χρώματος chroma, chromatos "color" (5)

Ψ

ψευδής pseudes "false" (6)
ψυχή psyche "soul," "mind" (2)

Ω

ᾠδή ode "poem," "song"
ᾠόν oon "egg" (4)

The Circulatory System

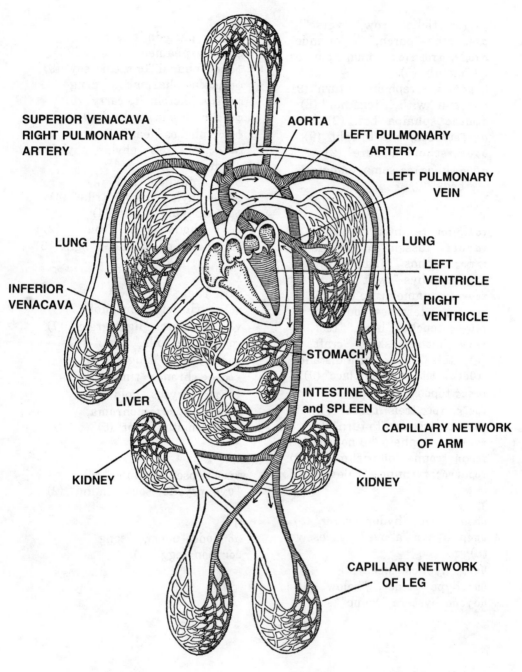

SUPERIOR VENACAVA
RIGHT PULMONARY
ARTERY

AORTA

LEFT PULMONARY
ARTERY

LEFT PULMONARY
VEIN

LUNG

LUNG

LEFT
VENTRICLE

INFERIOR
VENACAVA

RIGHT
VENTRICLE

STOMACH

INTESTINE
and SPLEEN

CAPILLARY NETWORK
OF ARM

LIVER

KIDNEY

KIDNEY

CAPILLARY NETWORK
OF LEG

In the modern science of anatomy, Greek and Latin words and suffixes serve as the basis of the nomenclature system. In this anatomical system, can you identify the influences of ancient terminologies?

Part II
Derivatives from Latin

Tabula rāsa
A blank slate[1]

Chapter Ten
Introduction to Latin

Having completed our study of the vocabulary of classical Greek, we now proceed to Latin, the language of the ancient Romans. From this point you will no longer encounter an unusual foreign script from which you have to make transliterations to understand otherwise strange characters. You probably recall from chapter one that the writing format that we employ for English today is practically the same as that used by the Romans nearly 2,000 years ago. Before turning to the pronunciaton chart for these letters on the next page, you should first note the few differences between the two alphabets. First, the Romans never used the letters "*j*" and "*w*." On the other hand, the letter "*i*" could be used as both a vowel and consonant. As a vowel, it could be long or short. The same holds true for their letter "*v*" which we now express with "*u*," "*v*," or "*w*." However, in this text, as in most modern editions of Latin, the separate letters "*i*" and "*j*" are used to distinguish the vowel and consonant, respectively, as are also the "*u*" and "*v*." Finally, the letters "*x*," "*y*," and "*z*" were introduced rather late into Latin from the Greek letters "*xi*," "*upsilon*," and "*zeta*," respectively, and were only used in Latin words of Greek origin that contained these letters.

Pronunciation

Over the centuries the pronunciation of Latin certainly underwent many changes. The chart on the next page presents the sound equivalents for *standard classical Latin* as it is believed to have been spoken in the late Roman Republic and early Empire, *i.e.*, in the period of the first century before the Christian era and the subsequent 150 years. A second column indicates the chief pronunciation differences often applied in phrases dealing with law and certain other contemporary subjects that developed in Britain over the past few centuries.

---

[1] The mind before receiving outside impressions.

The Roman Alphabet

Latin Letters		Classical Latin Sound	Example	British/Legal/Mod. Lat. Sound	Example
A	ā[2]	ah	*father*	ay	*play*
	a	a (short)	*about*	a (short)	*about*
B	b	b	*boy*	b	*boy*
C	c	c	*can*	c[3]	*can*
D	d	d	*dog*	d	*dog*
E	ē	ey	*prey*	ee	*meet*
	e	e (short)	*met*	e (short)	*met*
F	f	f	*father*	f	*father*
G	g	g	*go*	g[4]	*go*
H	h	h	*hand*	h	*hand*
I	ī	ee	*machine*	i	*kite*
	i	i (short)	*hit*	i (short)	*hit*
I	j	y	*yet*	j	*just*
K	k	k	*kick*	k	*kick*
L	l	l	*lion*	l	*lion*
M	m	m	*man*	m	*man*
N	n	n	*no*	n	*no*
O	ō	o (long)	*hope*	o (long)	*hope*
	o	o (short)	*not*	o	*not*
P	p	p	*poet*	p	*poet*
Q	q(u)	q(u) (kw)	*quick*	q(u) (kw)	*quick*
R	r	r	*rose*	r	*rose*
S	s	s	*say*	s	*say*
T	t	t	*take*	t	*take*
V	ū	u (long)	*rude*	u (long)	*rude*
	u	u (short)	*dull*	u (short)	*dull*
V	v	w	*wine*	v	*vine*

---

[2] Long vowels are marked with a macron (‾) placed above. All other single vowels are consequently presumed to be short.

[3] "C" was pronounced as "ch" before the vowels "e" and "i."

[4] "G" was pronounced soft as in "George" before an "e" or "i."

Diphthongs:

Latin Sound	Classical Latin Example		British/Legal/Mod. Lat. Sound	Example
ae	i (long)	*like*	ay	*play*
au	ou	*house*	ou	*house*
ei	*ei*	*vein*	ei	*vein*
oe	oi	*toil*	oi	*toil*

Particular attention must be given to the pronunciation of Latin since so many phrases in this language are still in use in English today. Not only must attention be focused on the sounds, the proper division of words into syllables and the correct placement of accents should also be learned.

Syllables

The rules listed below apply for dividing Latin words into syllables. Since tens of thousands of English word borrowings from Latin are also divided into syllables following these same guidelines, they are well worth knowing.

1. When a single consonant comes between two vowels, it goes with the vowel that follows.[5] *E.g., casa (ca-sa)* and *cōgitō (cō-gi-tō)*.

2. Two consonants appearing in a medial position between two vowels are split, the first going with the first vowel and the second going with the second. *E.g., tempus (tem-pus)* and *arbor (ar-bor)*.

3. When more than two consonants come between two vowels, the first goes with the preceding vowel and the rest go with the vowel that follows. *E.g., fenestra (fe-nes-tra)* and *mōnstrum (mōn-strum)*.

There are two exceptions to rule three. The first occurs with a *blend*. In this case a consonant group with a liquid consonant ("*l*" or "*r*") in the second position is not split between two syllables but rather is taken as a

---

5 Contiguous vowels or a vowel and a diphthong (those instances where no consonant intervenes) are also divided into separate syllables. *E.g., tua (tu-a)* and *patriae (pa-tri-ae)*.

unit with the second syllable. *E.g.*, *patrēs (pa-trēs)* and *lacrima (la-cri-ma)*. The second exception occurs when a word is composed of *compound elements* that can normally stand by themselves, as when a root is preceded by a prepositional prefix. Here the main elements remain together in their original units, as it were, rather than being separated according to any rule above. *E.g.*, *abest (ab-est)* and *trānsferō (trāns-fe-rō)*.

<u>Accent</u>
    Accent in Latin is the stress placed on a polysyllabic word. In considering the placement of an accent on a word, we always should remember that our concern is over which syllable (not which vowel) receives the stress. The rules for accent in Latin are as follows:[6]

1. Words with only two syllables always receive the accent on the initial syllable, that is, the *penult*. *E.g.*, *térra* and *ámor*.

2. If the word has more than two syllables, the accent goes on the *penult* if that syllable is long. It is long *if* it contains a long vowel or a diphthong. It is also long if it possesses a short vowel that is followed by two or more consonants. *E.g.*, *portāre (por-tā-re)*, *amoenus (a-moé-nus)* and *puella (pu-él-la)*.

3. If the *penult* is short on a word of more than two syllables, the accent falls on the third last syllable, that is, the *antepenult*. *E.g.*, *sanguinis (sán-gui-nis)* and *perpetuum (per-pé-tu-um)*.

Exercise

A. Divide the following Latin words into syllables according to the rules set forth in this lesson. Use slashes or hyphens to indicate the separations.

---

    6 From what follows it might be easier always to count syllables from the *end* of the word. The last syllable is known as the *ultima* (because the Latin word *ultimus* means "last"), the second last is the *penult* (because the Latin word *paenultima* means "almost last"), and the third last syllable is known as the *antepenult* (since *ante* means "before").

1. *dulcitūdo*
2. *parentis*
3. *mediocritas*
4. *testificandum*
5. *populus*
6. *secundum*
7. *arbitrium*
8. *fragmentum*
9. *magister*
10. *contendere*
11. *ūnicornis*
12. *remittere*

B. Place accents on the proper syllables of the Latin words below according to the rules set forth in this lesson. (Usually the accent is placed above the vowel in the syllable.)

1. *incertus*
2. *immortālis*
3. *auxilium*
4. *defendere*
5. *adulēscentia*
6. *argūmentum*
7. *auctōritas*
8. *persuādēre*
9. *requiēscat*
10. *difficultas*
11. *fābula*
12. *sigillum*

C. Practice reading the following Latin phrases according to the classical Latin pronunciation. If necessary, ask your instructor for assistance.

1. *ad astra per aspera*
2. *suī generis*
3. *homō sapiēns*
4. *in mediās rēs*
5. *habeās corpus*
6. *ex officiō*
7. *omnia vincit amor*
8. *sine quā nōn*
9. *in vīnō vēritas*
10. *errāre humānum est*

Fortūna est caeca.
Fortune is blind.[1]

Chapter Eleven
First Declension Nouns

In our approach to the study of Latin vocabulary, nouns are presented first simply because this part of speech has furnished us with thousands of English words that can stand by themselves and are easily recognized due to only slight orthographic modification or possibly to none at all. Centuries ago, grammarians recognized that all Latin nouns could be classified into one of five large groupings called *declensions* due to their common sets of inflectioned endings. Since it is easier to explain a few significant grammatical features pertaining to nouns through this same arrangement, the vocabularies in the next few chapters are set forth in this traditional fashion.

The process by which English words have been created from Latin nouns is the same as that employed for Greek and discussed in the first portion of this text. In fact it is a bit simpler with the elimination of the foreign alphabet and the need for an intermediary step wherein Greek words were first Latinized. Because Latin possesses a closer tie to English than Greek does from a chronological, geographical, and historical viewpoint, it will be beneficial to become better acquainted with certain additional grammatical aspects of the language which were ignored earlier in our treatment of Greek. In this respect the following features should be noted about nouns in general:

1. You should know the *complete Latin form*. Listed first in the vocabularies of this text, this form of the word is in the nominative (subjective) case. In number it is singular. English dictionaries always employ this form when citing the etymology of a word derived from a Latin noun. For example, if you consult your English dictionary for the word "lunar," you will discover that it comes from *luna*, the Latin word for "moon."

2. You should know the *stem* or *base*. This is the main part of the word with the case-ending removed. Generally every letter in this portion of the word is required in word borrowings. For example, the English word "ne-

---

[1] Cicero, *Dē Amicitiā* 15.54.

bulous" contains every letter in the base of its Latin noun predecessor *nebula* (*nebul-*); on the other hand, it does not possess the ending "-*a*."

3. For the various noun declensions you should know the *plural ending* in the nominative case. The reason for this is simply that several English words, directly assumed from Latin, form their plural *according to the Latin rule* instead of following the standard custom in English of adding "-s" or "-es." For example, the preferred plural of our words "*alga*" and "*vertebra*," is "*algae*" and "*vertebrae*," respectively.

4. English words composed of two or more Latin roots often have a connecting vowel, usually an "-*i*-," inserted between the two. Such is the case, for instance, with the words "stelliform" (*stell-i-form*) and "herbivorous" (*herb-i-vorous*). For Greek roots, you may recall, the connecting vowel was usually an "-*o*-." E.g., "philosophy" (*phil-o-sophy*).

5. To some extent, you should know the *gender* of Latin nouns, *i.e.*, whether a word is masculine, feminine or neuter. To understand the scientific binomial naming of plants and animals according to the International Rules of Nomenclature, this is essential because a generic noun is always qualified by an accompanying adjective, and adjectives must always agree with nouns in gender, number and case. Consider the examples: *Ursus americānus* (black bear), *Euphorbia pulcherrima* (poinsettia), and *homō sapiēns* (man). Moreover, many common Latin phrases and mottoes contain nouns with adjectives in agreement such as *persōna nōn grāta, magna charta* and *magnum opus*. The matter of gender in English is quite easy to understand. In this language all nouns are neuter except those which happen to refer specifically to the male or female sex. In ancient Greek, Latin and many modern languages it is quite another matter. In these languages thousands of words are masculine or feminine which have almost no relationship to masculinity or femininity, and some words are neuter which by our standards ought to have been masculine or feminine. Students of these languages must always memorize the gender of each noun and should do it at the time when the word is first encountered.

Having made these observations about nouns in general, let us now turn to some particulars of the first declension. In the vocabulary of this chapter you will note that all words possess a final "-*a*." This letter represents the *ending* for the nominative singular form. The *stem* or *base* therefore includes every letter prior to this ending. In direct word borrowing, any of three things might happen to the ending in this declension, especially if it enters our language with no modifiers attached to it.

1. The ending may enter unchanged.   (*alumna, corona*)

2. It may become a silent "-e."   (*fortune, cause*)

3. It may drop completely.   (*form, herb*)

The nominative plural case ending for first declension nouns is "-*ae.*"
A list of a few English words whose plural form can have this ending is
presented in the Special Topics section at the end of this lesson. The
following pattern, however, applies to all first declension nouns:

Latin Singular	Latin Plural	Word Base
stella (-a)	*stellae (-ae)*	*stell-*
terra (-a)	*terrae (-ae)*	*terr-*

With respect to gender, nearly all first declension nouns are *feminine.*
The single exception to this in the vocabulary list which follows is the word
nauta ("sailor"), which happens to be masculine. Other masculine nouns
of this declension, not included below, are *poeta* ("poet") and *agricola*
("farmer").

While many Latin words exist in English completely in and of
themselves, many do not. They rather appear only as one of two or more
elements in a word of multiple parts. When this happens, the base without
ending is often employed. The secondary elements often appear with full
meaning in their own right and in part of speech might be an adjective,
noun, preposition or verb. Often, on the other hand, the main root is accompanied by little more than a suffix ending that alters the part of speech but
possesses little meaning of its own. A few of these common short suffixes
are presented later in this chapter.

Vocabulary

Latin Form	Meaning	Derivative
alumna	foster-daughter	*alumna*
ancilla	maid-servant	*ancillary*
anima	soul, breath	*animate*
aqua	water	*aqueous*

aquila	eagle	*aquiline*
camera	room, chamber	*camera*
causa	reason, motive	*cause*
cella	store room	*cellar*
copia	abundance	*copious*
corōna	crown	*corona*
culīna	kitchen	*culinary*
culpa	fault, blame	*culpable*
cūra	care	*cure*
fāma	reputation	*fame*
fēmina	woman	*feminine*
fīlia	daughter	*filial*
fōrma	shape	*form*
fortūna	fate	*fortune*
glōria	renown	*glory*
herba	plant, grass	*herb*
īnsula	island	*insular*
lacūna	hole, gap	*lacuna*
lingua	tongue, language	*lingual*
littera	letter	*literal*
lūna	moon	*lunar*
nauta	sailor	*nautical*
nebula	mist, cloud	*nebulous*
patria	fatherland	*patriot*
pecūnia	money	*pecuniary*
penna	feather, wing	*pennant*
persōna	character, mask	*person*

poena	punishment	*penal*
pugna	fight	*pugnacious*
stēlla	star	*stellar*
tabula	table, list	*tabulate*
terra	earth, land	*terrarium*
umbra	shade	*umbrella*
unda	wave	*undulate*
vertebra	joint	*vertebra*
via	way, road	*via*
vīta	life	*vital*

Derivative Study

In each word in the list below find a Latin root from the vocabulary list in this lesson. Consult your dictionary for its current meaning and try to determine how the Latin root of this lesson relates to this meaning. Accompanying roots with which you may not yet be familiar will, of course, also affect the meaning of these words.

Level A

personify	*uniform*
fortunate	*lunatic*
inanimate	*glorify*
herbivorous	*linguistics*
terrestrial	*umbrage*
coronation	*aqueduct*
stelliform	*secure*
conform	*illiterate*
pugnacity	*causative*
inundate	*infamous*
femininity	*lacunar*
cella	*affiliate*
peninsula	*astronaut*

penalize

revitalize

bilingual

territory

Level B

bicameral

sublingual   apolune

aquamarine   terraqueous

invertebrate   exculpate

coroner   defamatory

umbriferous   aquiferous

transform   filicide

adumbrate   nebulize

animism   unicameral

umbrage   herbaceous

misfortune   multilingual

insulin   repugnant

inculpable   curator

penumbra   penniform

extra-terrestrial   perilune

undulatory   insecure

illiteracy   cornucopia

terracotta   aquanaut

One of the earliest Latin transcriptions was written from right to left on this weapon. It reads as follows: *Manios med fhe fhaked Numasioi. (Manios has made me for Numasios.)*

Special Topics

A. The Latin Plural, I

The plural of several English words that were originally first declension Latin nouns is often formed *according to the Latin rule, i.e.,* with the ending "*-ae.*" The following are just a few examples:

ala	*cicada*	*lamella*	*patina*
alga	*cisterna*	*lamina*	*penna*
alumna	*coma*	*larva*	*primipara*
antenna	*corolla*	*libra*	*ruga*
arena	*corona*	*lingua*	*scapula*
areola	*formula*	*lorica*	*theca*
bacca	*gemma*	*macula*	*tibia*
camera	*gutta*	*mina*	*umbra*
cella	*lacuna*	*nebula*	*vertebra*

B. Latin Phrases

Many Latin words in the vocabulary list of this chapter appear in English as part of complete Latin phrases. A few are listed below. Your dictionary should provide you with a literal meaning (often in the etymology portion of the entry) and a current meaning for each.

arbor vītae	*lapsus linguae*
aqua fortis	*lingua franca*
aqua rēgia	*mea culpa*
aqua vītae	*persōna nōn grāta*
camera lūcida	*prō fōrmā*
camera obscūra	*tabula rāsa*
Corōna Austrālis	*terra alba*
Corōna Boreālis	*terra firma*
curriculum vītae	*terra incognita*
dramatis persōnae	*verbātim ac litterātim*
in camera	*via media*

C. Common Short Suffixes

Review the list of Short Suffixes in Greek at the end of chapter two because many of the suffixes in that language appear in Latin as well. Furthermore, just as they tended to possess little special meaning of their own but generally served only a grammatical function, they maintain these same features in Latin too. The part of speech usually formed by each is noted in the list below. Suffixes with more specialized meaning will be presented in a later chapter.

Suffixes

Lat.	Example	Eng.	Example	Part/Speech	Meaning
-ābilis	*culpābilis²* *laudābilis*	**-able, -ible**	*culpable* *laudable*	adj.	"able to (be)," "worthy of"
-ālis	*vītālis* *navālis*	**-al**	*vital* *naval*	adj.	"pertaining to"
-ānus	*urbānus* *mundānus*	**-ane**	*urbane* *mundane*	adj.	"pertaining to"
-āris	*lunāris* *populāris* *vulgāris*	**-ar**	*lunar* *popular* *vulgar*	adj.	"pertaining to"
-ōsus	*copiōsus* *gloriōsus* *verbōsus*	**-ous, -ose**	*copious* *glorious* *verbose*	adj.	"full of"
-tās	*levitās* *libertās*	**-ty**	*levity* *liberty*	n.	"state of," "condition," "quality of"
-tor	*liberātor* *victor*	**-tor**	*liberator* *victor*	n.	"the doer," "the one who"
-tūdo	*magnitūdo* *fortitūdo*	**-tude**	*magnitude* *fortitude*	n.	"quality of"

---

2 Check in the Latin dictionary following lesson twenty to find the ultimate root that was modified with each suffix. *E.g., laudābilis* is from *laudāre* (to praise) and therefore means "worthy of being praised."

Exercise

A. Latin Plurals.   Write both the root meaning and present definition of any *fifteen* words in the list in part "A" of the Special Topics section of this lesson.   You may have to consult both your own English dictionary and the Latin dictionary following lesson twenty.

B. Latin Phrases. Using your English dictionary, translate as many Latin phrases as you can in part "B" of the Special Topics section of this lesson and relate the present-day context in which each is used.

C. Suffix Review. Using Latin words in this or later chapters, give at least *two* additional examples of each suffix in section "C" of the Special Topics of this lesson as they appear in English. Also, give *two different* examples where the Greek suffixes "*-ism*" and "*-ist*" are attached to Latin roots.

D. Identifying additional roots. Using your English dictionary, identify the Latin first declension noun root in each of the following words. These were not included in the vocabulary list of this chapter due to the fact that only one or two word borrowings developed from them.

1. *antenna*	4. *alimony*	7. *riparian*
2. *charter*	5. *gemmologist*	8. *vaccinate*
3. *lachrymal*	6. *colony*	9. *noxious*

E. Matching. Match the term on the left with its closest definition on the right.

1. *magnanimous*	a. crescent-shaped
2. *penology*	b. bring to life again
3. *inculpable*	c. having two chambers
4. *revitalize*	d. plant killer
5. *cosmonaut*	e. sailor of the universe
6. *bicameral*	f. move from the road
7. *herbicide*	g. under the earth
8. *subterranean*	h. having great spirit
9. *deviate*	i. blameless
10. *semilunar*	j. study of prisons

Angustus animus pecūniam amat.
The narrow mind loves money.[1]

Chapter Twelve
Second Declension Masculine Nouns

Latin nouns of the second declension are for the most part either *masculine* or *neuter* in gender. Neuter nouns will be examined in the next lesson. Most masculine nouns, you will note from a cursory view of the vocabulary list below, possess "-*us*" as the ending for the nominative singular form. A few, however, have an ending in "-*er*." While the base for nouns in "-*us*" can be determined by the simple removal of this ending, for nouns in "*er*" it is more properly determined from the genitive (possessive) singular form by the removal of its ending "-*i*." It is for this reason that a second form is sometimes given below for a few vocabulary words.

The following things might happen to the most common ending,"-*us*," when English words are directly coined from second declension nouns:

1. The ending may enter unchanged.   *terminus, focus*

2. It may become a silent "-e."   *mode, nerve*

3. It may drop completely.   *digit, fisc*

The nominative plural for all masculine nouns of this declension is formed by adding the case-ending "-*i*," to the word stem or base. A few examples of English words that have this plural ending are given at the end of this lesson in the Special Topics section. In conclusion, study the following chart for important aspects pertaining to the nouns of this lesson.

Nom. Sing.		Gen. Sing.		Nom. Plur.		Word Base
locus	*(-us)*	*locī*	*(-ī)*	*locī*	*(-ī)*	*loc-*
radius	*(-us)*	*radiī*	*(-ī)*	*radiī*	*(-ī)*	*radi-*
ager	*(-er)*	*agrī*	*(-ī)*	*agrī*	*(-ī)*	*agr-*

---

[1] Cicero, *Dē Officiīs* 1.20.68.

Vocabulary

Latin Form	Meaning	Derivative
ager, agri	field	*agrarian*
alumnus	foster-son	*alumnus*
annus	year	*annual*
circus	ring	*circus*
cuneus	wedge	*cuneiform*
deus	god	*deity*
digitus	finger	*digit*
equus	horse	*equestrian*
fiscus	purse, treasury	*fiscal*
focus	hearth	*focus*
fūmus	smoke	*fume*
gladius	sword	*gladiola*
liber, librī	book	*library*
locus	place	*local*
magister, magistrī	ruler, leader	*magistrate*
medicus	physician	*medical*
modus	measure, method	*mode*
morbus	disease	*morbid*
nervus	cord, sinew	*nerve*
numerus	number	*numeral*
oculus	eye	*ocular*
populus	people	*popular*
racēmus	bunch of grapes	*raceme*
radius	ray, staff	*radius*

rāmus	branch	*ramus*
servus	slave	*servant*
socius	companion, ally	*social*
somnus	sleep	*somnolent*
stimulus	whip, goad	*stimulus*
taurus	bull	*taurine*
terminus	boundary, end	*terminus*
vir, virī	man	*virile*

Derivative Study

Level A

deify	*locality*
nervous	*sociology*
focal	*stimulate*
master	*populous*
oculist	*digital*
society	*virility*
terminal	*fumigate*
dislocate	*numerical*
radiant	*libretto*
gladiator	*ramify*
annuity	*circular*
agriculture	*medicine*
perfume	*modify*
servile	*fisc*

Level B

binoculars	*bifocals*
exterminate	*morbidity*
enumerate	*ramiform*
eradiate	*deification*
superannuate	*somnambulate*
confiscate	*gladiate*
allocate	*biennial*
nervine	*locomotive*
fumitory	*subservient*

digitalis	*racemic*
ramification	*socialistic*
perennial	*agronomy*
equine	*cuneate*
module	*virago*
numerology	*somniferous*
morbific	*digitiform*
Taurus	*enervate*
determinant	*depopulate*
libel	*magistracy*

Special Topics

A. <u>The Latin Plural, II</u>

The plural of several English words originally from Latin second declension nouns is often formed *according to the Latin rule, i.e.,* with the ending "*-i*" added to the word base. Check your dictionary for the following possibilities:

abacus	*coccus*	*malleus*	*rhombus*
alumnus	*colossus*	*modulus*	*rhonchus*
alveolus	*crocus*	*nevus*	*solidus*
annulus	*cumulus*	*nexus*	*stimulus*
bacillus	*discus*	*nimbus*	*stratus*
cactus	*fungus*	*ocellus*	*terminus*
caduceus	*genius*	*oculus*	*thallus*
calculus	*humerus*	*radius*	*thyrsus*
cirrus	*locus*	*ramus*	

B. <u>Latin Phrases</u>

Some Latin phrases with vocabulary words from this lesson are occasionally found in English. Check your dictionary for both the literal and current meanings for each phrase below.

annō Dominī (A.D.)	*ex librīs*
circus maximus	*hōrā somnī (h.s.)*
deus ex māchinā	*in locō parentis*

locus sigillī
modus operandī (m.o.)
modus vīvendī
locō citātō (loc. cit.)
locum tenēns
locus classicus

oculus dexter (o.d.)
oculus sinister (o.s.)
per annum
terminus ā quō
terminus ad quem
toga virīlis

Exercise

A. **Latin Plurals.** Write both the root meaning and present definition of any *fifteen* words in the list in part "A" of the Special Topics section of this lesson. You may have to consult both your own English dictionary and the Latin dictionary following lesson twenty.

B. **Latin Phrases.** Using your English dictionary, translate as many Latin phrases as you can in part "B" of the Special Topics section of this lesson and relate the present-day context in which each is used.

C. **Identifying Additional Roots.** Using your English dictionary, identify the Latin second declension masculine noun root in each of the following words.

1. *mundane*
2. *pork*
3. *cancriform*
4. *horticulture*
5. *capricorn*
6. *diabolic*
7. *dominate*
8. *capillary*

D. **Matching.** Match the term on the left with its closest definition on the right.

1. *dislocate*
2. *enervate*
3. *asocial*
4. *modicum*
5. *racemic*
6. *insomnia*
7. *circulate*
8. *ramify*
9. *terminal*
10. *medicate*

a. appearing in clusters
b. split into branches
c. treat a disease with drugs
d. sleeplessness
e. move in a ring or orbit
f. forming an end
g. solitary
h. reduce mental vigor
i. small measure
j. put out of place

Nec vitia nostra nec remedia tolerāre possumus.
We can tolerate neither our vices nor their remedies.[1]

Chapter Thirteen
Second Declension Neuter Nouns

Latin nouns of the second declension with an ending of "-*um*" for the nominative singular form are neuter. The *base* for words in this category includes every letter prior to the ending. When equivalent English words are formed from nouns in this declension, the ending (-*um*) can have the same possible results by change or lack of change as the endings for other noun groups studied thus far.

1. The ending may enter unchanged.   *folium, odium*

2. It may become a silent "-e."   *vine, lucre*

3. It may drop completely.   *verb, plumb*

The plural of neuter nouns is always formed by adding the ending "-*a*" to the word base. Several instances of this phenomenon occur in English, a few examples of which are given at the end of this lesson in the Special Topics section. Study the following graph which applies to all neuter nouns of this declension:

Neuter Singular	Neuter Plural	Word Base
bellum (-um)	*bella (-a)*	*bell-*
vitium (-um)	*vitia (-a)*	*viti-*

Vocabulary

Latin Form	Meaning	Derivative
argentum	silver	*argenteous*
aurum	gold	*aurous*
bellum	war	*bellicose*

---

1 Livy in the preface (9) to his famous history *Ab Urbe Condita*.

dorsum	back	*dorsal*
exemplum	sample, copy	*example*
ferrum	iron	*ferrous*
folium	leaf	*folium*
grānum	seed	*grain*
imperium	power, rule	*imperial*
jugum	yoke	*jugular*
labium	lip	*labial*
lignum	wood	*lignite*
lucrum	gain, profit	*lucre*
nūntium	message	*enunciate*
odium	hatred	*odium*
officium	duty, service	*official*
ōtium	leisure	*otiose*
ōvum	egg	*ovum*
plumbum	lead	*plumb*
pretium	value, worth	*precious*
saeculum	age, world	*secular*
spatium	distance	*space*
strātum	covering	*stratum*
verbum	word	*verb*
vīnum	wine	*vine*
vitium	flaw, defect	*vice*

Derivative Study

Level A
foliage　　　　　　　　　　*Argentina*
exemplify　　　　　　　　　*imperialistic*

vicious
precious
subjugate
annunciation
stratosphere
ligneous
plumber
vice
belligerent
vitiate
dorsum
ovulate
verbal
otiose
spacious
viniculture
renunciation
aureate
ferroelectric
oval
appreciate
proverb

stratify
oviform
spatial
official
defoliate
rebel
verbatim
vintage
secularize
adverb
lucrative
granular
exemplary
ovoid
vinegar
portfolio
price
endorse
bilabial
odium
substratum
granary

Level B
viniferous
auriferous
argentiferous
plumbiferous
ferriferous
oviparous
verbiage
otioseness
odious
dorsoflect
trifoliate
ovicide
dorsolateral
ferromagnetic
dorsoventral

conjugal
lignify
stratigraphy
aureola
ligniform
officious
conjugation
ferric
secularity
denunciation
ovule
labiodental
belligerency
exfoliate
oviduct

depreciate   *stratocumulus*
verbalization   *rebellious*
vintner   *plumbism*
granulate   *granule*

Special Topics

A. The Latin Plural, III

Several English words derived directly from Latin neuter nouns of the second declension (or from similar forms created from verbs) are made plural according to the Latin rule for such words, *i.e.* they add the nominative plural ending "-*a*" to their word base. Check the following words in your dictionary:

addendum	*cinerarium*	*forum*	*pyxidium*
agendum	*consortium*	*ilium*	*quantum*
atrium	*continuum*	*incunabulum*	*rostrum*
bacterium	*corium*	*jugum*	*septum*
biennium	*curriculum*	*labium*	*serum*
calcaneum	*datum*	*memorandum*	*solum*
capitulum	*desideratum*	*millennium*	*spectrum*
cecum	*dorsum*	*momentum*	*speculum*
cerebellum	*duodenum*	*moratorium*	*stratum*
cerebrum	*erratum*	*omentum*	*tergum*
ciborium	*filum*	*ovum*	*trapezium*
cilium	*folium*	*pudendum*	*vacuum*

B. Latin Phrases

The following Latin phrases, containing a vocabulary word from this lesson, are occasionally found in English. Check your dictionary to find both the literal and current meaning for each expression.

ab ōvō   *labium ōris*
ante bellum   *labium uterī*
cāsus bellī   *lignum vītae*
cum grānō salis   *novus ordo sēclōrum*
ex officiō   *post bellum*
exemplī grātiā (e.g.)   *verbum sat sapienti*
in vīnō vēritas

C. The "-ti-" Letter Combination

The vocabulary list for this lesson happens to include a few words that possess the letter combination "-*ti*-" in the middle. They are: *nūntium, pretium, spatium,* and *vitium*. During the golden age of classical Latin about 2,000 years ago, the "*t*" in this combination is believed to have been pronounced hard, as in "tight." At some point down the road, however, an "*s*" sound crept into the pronunciation resulting in a change from *spa-ti-um,* for example, to something more like *spa-tsi-um*. This phenomenon is confirmed by the fact that a "-*c*-" is regularly substituted for the "-*t*-" in manuscripts of late Latin and in the orthography of various cognates in the Romance languages and in English derivatives. On the other hand, a few English words retain the letter representing the original spelling in classical Latin. Consider the following:

Latin	"-t-" Retained	"-c-" Employed
spatium	*spatial*	*space; spacious*
vitium	*vitiate*	*vice; vicious*

This phenomenon can likewise be detected in conversion of the Greek or Latin abstract noun ending "-*tia*" to "-*ce*" or "-*cy*" in English. Study these examples:

Greek/Latin	"-t" Retained	"-ce"/"-cy" Used
adolēscentia	*adolescent*	*adolescence*
dēmocratia	*democrat*	*democracy*
variātio	*variation*	*variance*

D. Hybrid Words

The English language possesses many composite words whose elements originate in different languages. In linguistics these are known as *hybrids*. In spite of the fact that words of this sort rarely receive enthusiastic support from language purists, they nevertheless often manage to retain a firm place in the vocabulary of a language once they gain initial acceptance. The preface to the first edition of Stedman's *Medical Dictionary* rather eloquently sets forth the lexicographer's negative attitude toward such words. There he writes in part:

The vocabulary of science is founded mainly upon the Greek and to a lesser extent upon the Latin, but has in any case a Latin form, and this unfortunate conjunction has resulted in many barbaric and cacophonic mixtures, painful to the ear and vexatious to the spirit of any one with a sense of linguistic fitness. If it were possible, a moulding of the language of medicine on pure Greek or Latin forms were most desirable, but the speech of man is wilful and cannot be coerced; at most an attempt can be made to guide it, or to point out what is preferable. It is not the function of a lexicographer to deny the right of citizenship to every word that is not constructed upon strict etymological lines, and it would do little good if he did, but he can indicate the correct terms and throw the weight of whatever authority may be accorded him on the right side. This I have endeavored to do. For example, one who consults this dictionary for a definition of *oophorectomy* will be referred to *oothecotomy* and under that title will find the definition. If, however, a barbarous word is in existence, it will be defined, but the correct term will also be given. For example, *ovariotomy* (of mixed Latin and Greek derivation and therefore deplorable) is defined under that title, but a correct synonym, *oothecotomy,* is also given, and the consulter can use the proper term, or can continue in his evil course as he will. Even under *appendicitis,* though with faint hope of the suggestion being adopted, the preferable term, *scolecoiditis,* is indicated.[2]

In coining new words today, scientists of all fields tend to support the precept of avoiding hybrids whenever possible. Greek roots are kept with Greek, and Latin with Latin. In some instances blending will take place with some frequency due to the fact that a desired root in one language must be matched with a popular suffix of the other (*e.g., -phobia* or *-cide*). Finally, the merging of Greek and Latin roots is not the only possible combination for hybrid words in English. There is virtually no limit to the number of possible language combinations. Some examples of hybrids are the following:

---

[2] Taken from the eleventh, revised edition of Thomas L. Stedman's *A Practical Medical Dictionary,* New York: William Wood and Company, 1932, p. v. The dictionary was first published in 1911.

sociology	(*socius* - Lt.; *logos* - Gk.)
petroleum	(*petra* - Gk.; *oleum* - Lt.)
claustrophobia	(*claustrum* - Lt..; *phobia* - Gk.)
ecocide	(*oikos* - Gk.; *caedere* - Lt.)
television	(*tele* - Gk.; *vidēre, vīsus* - Lt.)
automobile	(*autos* - Gk.; *mōbilis* - Lt.)
appendectomy	(*appendix* - Lt.; *ektemnein* - Gk.)
ovariotomy	(*ōvārium* - Lt.; *temnein* - Gk.)
semigloss	(*sēmi* - Lt.; *gloss* - Scand.)
aqualung	(*aqua* - Lt.; *lung* - Ger.)

Exercise

A. Latin Plurals. From the list of words given in part "A" of the Special Topics section of this lesson, write both the root meaning and present definition of any *fifteen* examples. You may have to consult both your own English dictionary and the Latin dictionary following lesson twenty for assistance.

B. Latin Phrases. Using your English dictionary, translate as many Latin phrases as you can in part "B" of the Special Topics section of this lesson and relate the present-day context in which each is used.

C. Matching. Match the term on the left with its closest definition on the right.

1. *ovoid*	a. wine yield
2. *granivorous*	b. join together
3. *lignify*	c. hateful
4. *proverb*	d. egg-shaped
5. *vintage*	e. egg-bearing
6. *conjugate*	f. at leisure
7. *otiose*	g. gold-bearing
8. *odious*	h. word spoken before
9. *auriferous*	i. make into wood
10. *oviparous*	j. seed-eating

D. Identifying Additional Roots. Using your English dictionary, identify the Latin second declension neuter noun root in each of the following words.

1. *auxiliary*
2. *argument*
3. *donation*
4. *venal*

5. *insignia*
6. *pulpit*
7. *damn*
8. *cubicle*

The Latin inscription on the famous Parthenon temple (above) in Rome reads: *M. AGRIPPA L. F. COS. TERTIVM FECIT*. Translated into English, this is "M(arcus) Agrippa, son of Lucius, consul for the third time, made (this)."

Salūs populı suprēma lēx estō.
Let the safety of the people be the highest law.[1]

Chapter Fourteen
Third Declension Nouns

For students not familiar with the many intricacies of the Latin language, nouns of the third declension may offer some difficulties or problems not previously encountered with nouns studied in the last three chapters. This is true for several reasons. First, on the non-technical side, the number of nouns belonging to this declension happens to be very large. Consequently, the Vocabulary List for this group has been divided into two and is presented over two lessons.

A second reason why this declension poses some difficulties is that for the first time all three genders are represented in a single group. The list below will therefore indicate the *gender* of each word, "*m.*" for masculine, "*f.*" for feminine, or "*n.*" for neuter. Knowing the gender of a noun will help in understanding the agreement of adjectives with nouns in certain Latin phrases. It will also serve to make easier an understanding of plurals of certain English words that are formed directly from nouns of this declension.

Another major reason why nouns of this declension present difficulties stems from the fact that often derivatives are formed from two different roots of the same Latin word. Consequently it is necessary to learn two forms of most words. The first of these is the customary *nominative* case, used in Latin when the word functions as subject. Often it is the shorter of the two cases and carries a "*s*" sound in its ending. The second form is the *genitive* (possessive) case which always ends in "*-is.*" The *base* for this second form includes every letter prior to this ending.

Finally, since the Latin plural ending of masculine and feminine nouns is different from the neuter, we can correctly form the English *plural* of words taken directly from nouns of this declension *only* if we know their respective genders and endings. To make the plural of masculine and feminine nouns, the ending "*-ēs*" is added directly to the base of the genitive form. To make the neuter plural, the ending "*-a*" is added to this base. Check the examples in the following table:

---

[1] Motto of the state of Missouri.

Singular (Nom., Gen.)	Gender	Word Base	Plural
cōdex, cōdicis	m.	cōdic-	cōdicēs (-ēs)
corpus, corporis	n.	corpor-	corpora (-a)
os, ossis	n.	oss-	ossa (-a)
rādix, rādīcis	f.	rādīc-	rādīcēs (-ēs)
urbs, urbis	f.	urb-	urbes (-es)

Vocabulary

Latin Form	Gender	Meaning	Derivative
arbor	f.	tree	arboretum
ars, artis	f.	skill, craft	art
cīvis	m., f.	citizen	civic
crīmen, crīminis	n.	accusation, fault	crime
dux, ducis	m., f.	leader	duke
frāter, frātris	m.	brother	fraternal
genus, generis	n.	kind, class, birth	genus
homō, hominis	m.	human being, man	homicide
ignis	m.	fire	ignite
jūdex, jūdicis	m.	judge	judicial
latus, lateris	n.	side, flank	lateral
lēx, lēgis	f.	law	legal
lūx, lūcis	f.	light	lucid
mare, maris	n.	sea	marine
māter, mātris	f.	mother	maternal
mēns, mentis	f.	mind	mental
mors, mortis	f.	death	mortal
nōmen, nōminis	n.	name	nominal
nox, noctis	f.	night	nocturnal

opus, operis	n.	work, labor	*opus*
ōrdō, ōrdinis	m.	order, series	*ordinal*
pater, patris	m.	father	*paternal*
pāx, pācis	f.	peace	*pacify*
rēx, rēgis	m.	king	*regal*
sāl	m.	salt	*saline*
sōl	m.	sun	*solar*
soror	f.	sister	*sorority*
tempus, temporis	n.	time	*temporal*
urbs, urbis	f.	city	*urban*
vōx, vōcis	f.	voice	*vocal*

Derivative Study

Level A

legalize	*cooperate*
general	*salad*
duchess	*criminal*
mentality	*suburb*
contemporary	*equivocal*
judicious	*mortify*
solarium	*civil*
arboreal	*hominid*
bilateral	*regent*
matrimony	*ignition*
vocation	*pacific*
paternity	*maternity*
fraternity	*sororial*
artifact	*legislation*
immortal	*translucent*
civilian	*generous*
igneous	*demented*
Lucifer	*opera*
paternalism	*artistic*
noctilucent	*illegal*

unilateral
mariner
operetta
regiment
prejudice
fraternize

compatriot
equinox
submarine
matron
patriarch
marina

<u>Level B</u>
criminology
ignescent
ducal
nomenclature
generic
arborescence
matrix
regicide
fratricide
quadrilateral
matriarch
arboriculture
parasol
elucidate
vociferous
maritime
confraternity
patrilineal
ignigenous
transmarine
ducat
luciferous
genre
judiciary
noctiphobia
insolate
binomial
equilateral
regalia
incriminate
vocative
artisan
homage

hominoid
saleratus
dementia
adjudicate
urbiculture
artifice
expatriate
denominate
pacifist
illegitimate
mentor
genocide
mortician
repatriate
extemporaneous
matrilineal
sororate
collateral
solstice
civilize
arborization
temporize
incivility
mortuary
inoperable
amortize
noctambulist
homiculture
salifiable
legislator
noctiluca
matricide
lucent

Special Topics

A. The Latin Plural, IV

Review the rules for making Latin third declension nouns plural which were given near the beginning of this chapter and make the following English words plural according to these guidelines. Since the gender will not be known for those words not included in the vocabulary of this lesson, it may be necessary to consult your English dictionary.

apex	*cortex*	*latex*	*radix*
appendix	*crux*	*mare*	*rumen*
arbor	*finis*	*matrix*	*semen*
calyx	*foramen*	*murex*	*vertex*
cervix	*genus*	*nomen*	*vortex*
cicatrix	*helix*	*opus*	

B. Latin Phrases

Each of the following Latin phrases contains a word from the Vocabulary List of this lesson. Since they are sometimes encountered in English today, try to give a correct translation for them and check your answers in a dictionary.

alma māter	*lēx tāliōnis*
ante mortem	*Mare Frīgoris*
arbor vītae	*Mare Tranquilitātis*
ars grātiā artis	*mēns rea*
ars poētica	*nōn compos mentis*
Artium Baccalaure(āt)us (A.B.)	*opere citātō*
Artium Magister (A.M.)	*pater familiās*
causa mortis	*pia māter*
cum grānō salis	*post mortem*
dūra māter	*prō tempore (prō tem.)*
ex tempore	*rigor mortis*
fīat lūx	*sub jūdice*
homō sapiēns	*suī generis*
ignis fatuus	*tempus fugit*
lēx scripta	*vōx populī*

C. The Diminutive Suffix

In Latin a diminutive suffix was commonly added to words to indicate "smallness" of an object. No single spelling was adopted in all instances to obtain this desired effect. Indeed a variety of possibilities existed in Latin itself. You should note two things, however, from the graph and examples which follow. First, the presence of a "-*l*" is contained among all the possible forms of both Latin and English. Secondly, one of the Latin gender endings of the first or second declension (*-us, -a, -um*) regularly completes the diminutive. This ending may appear in English derivatives either unchanged, dropped completely, or modified to an "-*e*." Most English dictionaries give appropriate recognition to the diminutive suffix by citing both the Latin diminutive form and its original root word. You should check some of the examples below to acquaint yourself with the method employed in your dictionary .

Latin Forms	Modified English Forms
-(i)culus, -a, -um	-(i)cle
-ellus , -a, -um	-el
-illus, -a, -um	-il(e)
-olus, -a, -um	-ol(e)
-ulus, -a, -um	-ule

Original Latin	Meaning	Latin Dimin.	English Word
calx, calcis	stone	*calculus*	*calculus*
caput, capitis	head	*capitulum*	*capitulum*
cerēbrum	brain	*cerēbellum**	*cerebellum*
cōdex, cōdicis	book	*cōdicillus*	*codicil*
corpus, corporis	body	*corpusculum*	*corpuscle*
cubīle, cubīlis	bed	*cubiculum*	*cubicle*
fōrma	shape	*formula*	*formula*
gladius	sword	*gladiolus**	*gladiolus*
grānum	grain	*grānulum**	*granule*
liber	book	*libellus*	*libel*
novum	new	*novellum*	*novel*
scalprum	knife	*scapellum**	*scapel*
vacuum	empty	*vacuolum**	*vacuole*
venter	stomach	*ventriculus*	*ventricle*

* - Not common in classical Latin.

Exercise

A. **Latin Plurals.** From the list of words given in part "A" of the Special Topics section of this lesson, write both the root meaning and present definition of any *fifteen* examples. You may have to consult both your own English dictionary and the Latin dictionary following lesson twenty.

B. **Latin Phrases.** Using your English dictionary, translate as many Latin phrases as you can in part "B" of the Special Topics section of this lesson and relate the present-day context in which each is used.

C. **Identifying Additional Roots.** Using your English dictionary, identify the Latin third declension noun root in each of the following words.

1. *ambition*   6. *mercenary*
2. *calamity*   7. *vernal*
3. *incinerate*   8. *tonsorial*
4. *legion*   9. *tempestuous*
5. *subliminal*   10. *voluptuous*

D. **Matching.** Match the term on the left with its closest definition on the right.

1. *archduke*   a. inherited from a father
2. *regicide*   b. beyond the sea
3. *confraternity*   c. becoming fiery
4. *patrimony*   d. chief leader
5. *immortal*   e. brotherliness
6. *ultramarine*   f. shed light on
7. *equilateral*   g. equal-sided
8. *noctambulate*   h. not dying
9. *elucidate*   i. night walk
10. *ignescent*   j. killing of a king

Mēns quiēta, vīrēs, prūdēns simplicitās, amīcī -
haec vītam beātiōrem faciunt.
A quite mind, strength, prudent simplicity, friends -
these things make life happier.[1]

Chapter Fifteen
Third Declension Nouns (Cont.)
Fourth and Fifth Declension Nouns

This lesson completes our treatment of Latin third declension nouns, begun last chapter. Review the introductory material about them there, especially with regard to gender and the formation of word bases and plurals because the nouns immediately below follow the same rules. Fourth and fifth declension nouns are very few in number and, for purposes of a more ready identification of them, are taken up separately later in this lesson.

Vocabulary (*Third Declension*)

Latin Forms	Gender	Meaning	Derivative
apis	f.	bee	*apiary*
avis	f.	bird	*aviary*
bōs, bōvis	m., f.	ox, cow	*bovine*
calx, calcis	f.	stone	*calcium*
canis	m., f.	dog	*canine*
caput, capitis	n .	head	*capital*
caro, carnis	f.	flesh	*carnal*
cōdex, cōdicis	m .	ancient book	*codex*
cor, cordis	n .	heart	*cordial*
corpus, corporis	n .	body	*corpus*

---

[1] Martial, *Epigrams* 10.47.

cutis	f.	skin	*cuticle*
flōs, flōris	m.	flower	*floral*
gens, gentis	f.	clan, tribe	*gens*
grex, gregis	m.	herd, flock	*congregate*
index, indicis	m., f.	fore-finger	*index*
jūs, jūris	n.	right, law	*jurist*
lac, lactis	n.	milk	*lactic*
laus, laudis	f.	praise	*laudable*
lūmen, lūminis	n.	light	*lumen*
mōs, mōris	m.	custom, habit	*moral*
onus, oneris	n.	burden, load	*onus*
ōs, ōris	n.	mouth	*oral*
os, ossis	n.	bone	*ossify*
pectus, pectoris	n.	breast	*pectoral*
pēs, pedis	m.	foot	*pedal*
piscis	m.	fish	*piscatory*
rādix, rādicis	f.	root	*radix*
rēte, rētis	n.	net	*retiform*
sanguis, sanguinis	m.	blood	*sanguine*
testis, testis	m., f.	witness	*testimony*
vestis	m.	garment	*vest*

Nouns of the *fourth* declension in Latin comprise a relatively small group of words. Those which possess a nominative, singular ending "-*us*" are masculine or feminine in gender; those with an ending in "-*u*" are neuter. Their plural forms, which would likewise apply for English words assumed without other ending modification, are "-*ūs*" and "-*ua*," respectively, added to the word base. As with most instances in the past, the word base consists of every letter in the Latin word prior to any of these endings; however, it should be noted that several English word borrowings from nouns of this declension retain the "*u*" of the ending as well. Study the following examples:

Nominative Sing.	Gender	Word Base	Plural
manus (-us)	*f.*	*man(u)-*	*manūs (-ūs)*
cornū (-ū)	*n.*	*corn(u)-*	*cornua (-ua)*

Vocabulary (*Fourth Declension*)[2]

Latin	Gender	Meaning	Derivative
cornū	n .	horn	*unicorn*
domus	f .	house	*domicile*
genū	n .	knee	*genuflect*
gradus	m .	step, degree	*graduate*
manus	f .	hand	*manual*

The *fifth* declension in Latin is the last and smallest group of nouns to be encountered. Generally feminine in gender, they possess the ending "-*ēs*" in both the nominative singular and plural. The base for words, of course, consists of all the letters prior to this ending. One exception to this rule is the word "*rēs*" which retains the "*e*" as part of its root. The following graph shows the important features to be learned:

Nom. Sing.	Gender	Word Base	Plural
faciēs	*f.*	*faci-*	*faciēs*
rēs	*f.*	*re-*	*rēs*

---

2 Although the Vocabulary List includes only one *masculine* noun, this particular gender actually tends to predominate in this declension.   A few examples, not included in the general vocabulary due to a paucity of English word borrowings, are the following:

Latin	Gender	Meaning	Derivative
arcus	m.	bow	*arc*
fructus	m.	fruit	*fructify*
lacus	m.	lake	*lake*
prospectus	m.	outlook	*prospect*

Vocabulary (*Fifth Declension*)

Latin	Gender	Meaning	Derivative
diēs	f.	day	*diary*
faciēs	f.	face, surface	*facial*
fidēs	f.	trust, faith	*fidelity*
rēs	f.	thing, matter	*real*

Derivative Study

Level A

calcify	*carnage*
gentry	*radical*
mores	*incorporeal*
centipede	*luminous*
codify	*discord*
attest	*divest*
capricorn	*infidelity*
reality	*manufacture*
degrade	*testify*
manicure	*decapitate*
carnation	*florist*
avian	*pedal*
apian	*eradicate*
Pisces	*morality*
corporal	*calculus*
florid	*segregate*
indicator	*lactation*
illuminate	*biped*
testament	*vestment*
domestic	*confident*
republic	*gradual*
gentile	*demoralize*
pedicure	*incorporate*
floribunda	*pedestrian*
cutaneous	*jury*
sanguineous	*corneous*
retina	*superficial*

<u>Level B</u>

apivorous	*occipital*
carnivorous	*cordiality*
lactogenic	*radicle*
pedograph	*gregarious*
genteel	*velocipede*
expectorant	*multiflorous*
subcutaneous	*corpulent*
luminiferous	*divestiture*
intestate	*cornucopia*
centigrade	*manuscript*
rebus	*perfidious*
bicornuate	*emancipate*
retrograde	*diurnal*
bovicide	*reticulum*
reticle	*pedometer*
inflorescence	*longicorn*
sanguiferous	*incarnation*
codicil	*jurisdiction*
pisciculture	*efflorescence*
apiculture	*intracutaneous*
onerous	*orifice*
pedialgia	*lactiferous*
corniculate	*meridian*
infidel	*testator*
reincarnation	*juridical*
laudatory	*immoral*
floriferous	*canicular*
egregious	*quadruped*
calcination	*piscivorous*
ossuary	*florilegium*
genupectoral	*orofacial*
recapitulate	*cordiform*
reticulate	*affidavit*
sanguinaria	*realia*
ossification	*percutinization*
capitulum	*boviform*
corpuscle	*osculate*
luminary	*calciferous*
defloration	*piscine*

impede   *osseus*
uniflorous   *jural*
sanguinivorous

Special Topics

A. The Latin Plural, V

The following English words are formed directly from Latin third, fourth and fifth declension nouns and consequently can take their plural *according to the Latin rules*. Check the rules regarding the formation of plurals for these nouns and see if you can determine the correct form for each. You may wish to consult your English dictionary for those about which you are uncertain.

calyx	*gens*	*occiput*	*pyxis*
codex	*gradus*	*os*	*scabies*
corpus	*index*	*pes*	*superficies*
cornu	*lumen*	*piscis**	*testis*
cutis	*manus*	*pontifex*	*vas*
facies	*mos**	*pubis*	*velamen*

* - actually used only in the plural in English.

B. Latin Phrases

Each of the following Latin phrases contains a word from the Vocabulary List of this lesson. Check your dictionary for both the literal and current meanings for each.

bis in diē (b.i.d.)	*jūs gentium*
bonā fidē	*jūs sanguinis*
Canis Mājor	*jūs solī*
Canis Minor	*Lēgum Doctor (L.D.)*
cavē canem	*magnā cum laude*
corpus callōsum	*magnum opus*
corpus dēlictī	*per capita*
corpus luteum	*per diem*
cum laude	*prō rē nātā (p.r.n.)*
dē jūre	*quater in diē (q.i.d.)*

flōruit	*rāra avis*
hābeās corpus	*rēs ipsa loquitur*
in medias rēs	*semper fidēlis*
in rē	*sine diē*
Jūris Doctor (J.D.)	*summā cum laude*

Exercise

A. **Latin Plurals.** From the list of words given in part "A" of the Special Topics section of this lesson, write both the root meaning and present definition of any *fifteen* examples. You may have to consult both your own English dictionary and the Latin dictionary following lesson twenty.

B. **Latin Phrases.** Using your English dictionary, translate as many of the Latin phrases as you can in part "B" of the Special Topics section of this lesson and relate the present-day context in which each is used.

C. **Matching.** Match the term on the left with its closest definition on the right.

1. *incorporeal*	a. base or foot of a structure
2. *lactiferous*	b. having no will
3. *manicure*	c. lacking a body
4. *expectorant*	d. coming from the chest
5. *exonerate*	e. under the skin
6. *subcutaneous*	f. care of the hands
7. *floriferous*	g. unburden
8. *pedestal*	h. flower-bearing
9. *consanguineous*	i. related by blood
10. *intestate*	j. milk-bearing

D. **Identifying Additional Roots.** Using your English dictionary, identify the Latin third, fourth or fifth declension root in each of the following words.

1. *iridescent*	5. *nativity*
2. *uxorious*	6. *rejuvenate*
3. *casualty*	7. *clavicle*
4. *litigate*	8. *febrile*

E. Animal Roots. Identify the animal named in the words below by the Latin root contained in each before the suffix "*-ine*."

1. *asinine*	6. *taurine*	11. *equine*
2. *vulpine*	7. *vaccine*	12. *ovine*
3. *porcine*	8. *ursine*	13. *bovine*
4. *canine*	9. *hircine*	14. *aquiline*
5. *leonine*	10. *viperine*	15. *serpentine*

DULCE ET DECORUM EST PRO PATRIA MORI. (Sweet and becoming it is to die for one's country.) This patriotic Latin verse which originated with the Roman lyric poet Horace (65-8 B.C.) has been appropriately placed on the entrance gate to Arlington National Cemetery, near Washington, D.C.

Homērus audītōrem in mediās rēs rapit.
Homer hurries his listener into the midst of things.[1]

Chapter Sixteen
Adjectives

Having completed our study of Latin nouns by declension, in this lesson we shall focus our attention on adjectives. Before doing so, however, let us review some characteristics or properties common to all nouns. First, it must be remembered that each Latin noun usually possesses but a single gender (masculine, feminine, or neuter). Upon its appearance in any grammatical setting, the additional determinants of number (singular or plural) and case (nominative, genitive, *etc.*) come into play. In other words, a multitude of word endings exists for Latin nouns of which only one is correct in any single context. This depends not only upon the word's specific declension but also upon whether it functions in the singular or plural and finally whether it is serving as a subject, possessive, object or in some other capacity.

In Latin an adjective serves the same grammatical function as this part of speech does in English, *i.e.*, it modifies a noun in such a way usually as to specify its quality or quantity. Of primary importance in our consideration of it in Latin is the fact that it must agree with the noun it modifies not only in gender but in number and case as well. On the other hand, there is no requirement that it be in the same declension as the noun. While a noun usually possesses but a single gender, an adjective must be able to assume all three genders in its role as a noun modifier. Hence it often possesses three times as many possible word endings. For most adjectives the endings of the first and second declensions provide the necessary variety required for agreement in all three genders, and those which fall into this category are known simply as first and second declension adjectives. Consider carefully each of the following adjective-noun combinations in the graph on the next page. Note that while some nouns among the examples are from the third, fourth and fifth declensions, the adjectives accompanying them remain in either the first or second declension and change only to maintain agreement in gender and number.

---

[1] Horace, *Epistulae* 2.3.148-149.

First/Second Declension Adjective:

magnus (m.), magna (f.), magnum (n.) - large, great

In the Vocabulary List of this lesson these adjectives are identified with the masculine form (given first and spelled out completely) possessing an ending in "*-us*" or "*-er*" followed by the familiar endings of the feminine and neuter, "*-a*" and "*-um*" respectively.

Singular		Meaning	Plural
vīta magna	*(f.)*	a great life[2]	*vītae magnae*
liber magnus	*(m.)*	a large book	*librī magnī*
vīnum magnum	*(n.)*	a great wine	*vīna magna*
pēs magnus	*(m.)*	a large foot	*pedēs magnī*
arbor magna	*(f.)*	a large tree	*arborēs magnae*
corpus magnum	*(n.)*	a large body	*corpora magna*
domus magna	*(f.)*	a large house	*domus magnae*
gradus magnus	*(m.)*	a large step	*gradus magnī*
fidēs magna	*(f.)*	a great faith	*fidēs magnae*

A second group of Latin adjectives, fewer in number but important in any case, exists with all the endings for gender, number and case taken from the third declension. These can be identified in the Vocabulary List of this lesson with the masculine form ending in "*-is*" or "*-er*" followed by the endings "*-is*" and "*-e*" for the feminine and neuter respectively. The single exception in this list is the word *pār* ("equal") which belongs to this declension but possesses this same form in the nominative singular for all three genders. Study these examples of adjective-noun agreement involving a typical third declension adjective.

Third Declension Adjective:

omnis (m.), omnis (f.), omne (n.) - every (sg.), all (pl.)

Singular		Meaning	Plural
vīta omnis	*(f.)*	every life	*vītae omnēs*
liber omnis	*(m.)*	every book	*librī omnēs*

---

2 Latin possesses no separate word equivalent for either the English indefinite article "a" or "an" or for the definite article "the." Therefore, in a translation from Latin we can feel free to use either article or none at all.

vīnum omne	*(n.)*	every wine	*vīna omnia*
pēs omnis	*(m.)*	every foot	*pedēs omnēs*
arbor omnis	*(f.)*	every tree	*arborēs omnēs*
corpus omne	*(n.)*	every body	*corpora omnia*
domus omnis	*(f.)*	every house	*domūs omnēs*
gradus omnis	*(m.)*	every step	*gradūs omnēs*
fidēs omnis	*(f.)*	every faith	*fidēs omnēs*

For words derived from a Latin adjective, most English dictionaries will cite only the masculine, singular form in the nominative case. This is true whether the English word has been created from a simple adjective or is part of a combination of two or more roots. Consider these examples:

English Word	Masc. Adjective Root
certain	*certus* (sure)
sole	*sōlus* (alone)
grave	*gravis* (heavy, serious)
multilingual	*multus* (many); *lingua* (tongue)
equilateral	*aequus* (equal); *latus later-* (side)

The manner in which English dictionaries present the etymology of *abstract* nouns, such as *sanctity, brevity, veracity,* and *antiquity,* is also worthy of note here. Usually borrowed directly from Latin where they also operated in the same capacity, these nouns often possess a simple Latin adjective as their ultimate root. In these situations English dictionaries regularly show first the Latin abstract noun then the simple adjective, as in the following examples:

English Abstract	Latin Abstract	Adjective Root
infirmity	*infirmitas*	*in*, not; *firmus*, strong
altitude	*altitūdo*	*altus*, high, deep
dexterity	*dexteritas*	*dexter*, right
levity	*levitas*	*levis*, light

Vocabulary

Latin Forms	Meaning	Derivative
aequus, -a, -um	equal	*equity*
altus, -a, -um	high	*altitude*
antiquus, -a, -um	old	*antiquity*

bonus, -a, -um	good	*bonus*
brevis, -is, -e	short	*brevity*
castus, -a, -um	pure	*caste*
celer, celeris, -e	swift	*celerity*
certus, -a, -um	sure	*certain*
dexter, dextra, -um	right	*dexterity*
dignus, -a, -um	worthy	*dignity*
dulcis, -is, -e	sweet	*dulcet*
firmus, -a, -um	strong	*firm*
fortis, -is, -e	strong	*fortify*
grātus, -a, -um	pleasing	*gratify*
gravis, -is, -e	heavy	*gravity*
lātus, -a, -um	wide	*latitude*
levis, -is, -e	light	*levity*
magnus, -a, -um	large, great	*magnitude*
malus, -a, -um	bad	*malice*
medius, -a, -um	middle	*mediate*
miser, misera, -um	wretched	*misery*
mollis, -is, -e	soft	*mollify*
multus, -a, -um	much, many	*multitude*
novus, -a, -um	new	*novel*
nūllus, -a, -um	no, none	*nullify*
omnis, -is, -e	every, all	*omnibus*
pār, pār, pār	equal	*parity*
plēnus, -a, -um	full	*plenty*
rectus, -a, -um	straight, right	*rectify*

sacer, sacra, -um	sacred	*sacrifice*
sānctus, -a, -um	holy	*sanctity*
sānus, -a, -um	healthy, sound	*sane*
senex (senis)	old	*senile*
similis, -is, -e	like	*similar*
sinister, sinistra, -um	left	*sinister*
sōlus, -a, -um	alone, single	*sole*
tenuis, -is, -e	thin	*tenuous*
vērus, -a, -um	true	*verify*
vīvus, -a, -um	living	*vivid*

Derivative Study

Level A

sanctify	*veracity*
simile	*insane*
antique	*novice*
equivocal	*bona fide*
magnify	*rectangle*
malpractice	*gratis*
accelerate	*annul*
mediocrity	*multilateral*
dignify	*certify*
par	*dexterous*
abbreviate	*gravitate*
gratuity	*alto*
plenary	*ingratitude*
sanitation	*Mediterranean*
renovate	*certification*
verdict	*infirm*
equator	*indignant*
inequality	*emollient*
miser	*compare*
confirm	*dilate*
sacrament	*rectum*

fortitude	*exalt*
equivalent	*senior*
multivalent	*ambidextrous*
magnificent	*dignitary*
miserable	*mediator*
verily	*sanctuary*
senate	*elevator*
solitude	*equation*

Level B

sinistral	*assimilate*
aver	*vivify*
sanctimonious	*magniloquence*
dextrorse	*soliloquy*
medieval	*rectitude*
equilibrium	*breviary*
decelerate	*incest*
plenitude	*dextral*
ascertain	*mollusk*
omnivorous	*malignant*
antiquarian	*plenilune*
equiponderate	*equinox*
vivisect	*sacrosanct*
commiserate	*replenish*
equilateral	*magnanimous*
novitiate	*multiparous*
confirmation	*viviparous*
malefactor	*gravid*
dulcimer	*gratuitous*
omniscient	*altimeter*
plenipotentiary	*latifundium*
dulciana	*senectitude*
verisimilitude	*solipsism*
sacerdotal	*execrate*
sinistrorse	*facsimile*
attenuate	*desolation*
sanatorium	*extenuate*
annulment	*la dolce vita*
disparity	*multifarious*

certificate	malevolent
omniferous	nullification
innovate	gravitation
omnipotent	levitation
rectilineal	multilingual
brevilineal	altocumulus
alleviate	omnifarious
nullity	multiplicity
senescence	sinistromanual
mollescence	sacrilege
tenuity	desecrate

Special Topics

A. Latin Phrases

The following Latin phrases all possess an adjective from the Vocabulary List of this lesson. Check your English dictionary for a literal translation of those with which you are not familiar.

aequō animō	novus ōrdō sēclōrum
bonā fidē	omnia vincit amor
ceterīs paribus	omnia vincit labor
cui bonō?	omnia vincit vēritas
de novō	parī passū
forāmen magnum	persōna nōn grāta
in mediās rēs	plēnō jūre
justitia omnibus	prō bonō publicō
Magna Charta	similis simili gaudet
magnā cum laude	summum bonum
magnum opus	terra firma
malā fidē	via media
malum in sē	vīvā vōce
multum in parvō	

B. Doublets

Because contact between Latin and English occurred over a broad span of several centuries and along many different routes, we sometimes

managed to borrow two or more words from the same single original
source. Such words are known as *doublets*. Most of the words we have
examined in the Derivative Study of the last several lessons were borrowed
directly from Latin; several others, however, entered English by way of Old
French and consequently assumed a somewhat less recognizable form.
Consider the following:

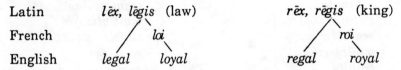

Latin   *lēx, lēgis* (law)   *rēx, rēgis* (king)
French   *loi*   *roi*
English   *legal*   *loyal*   *regal*   *royal*

Several other doublets also trace one part directly from latin and a
second through Old French, such as:

<u>Latin</u>   <u>English</u>

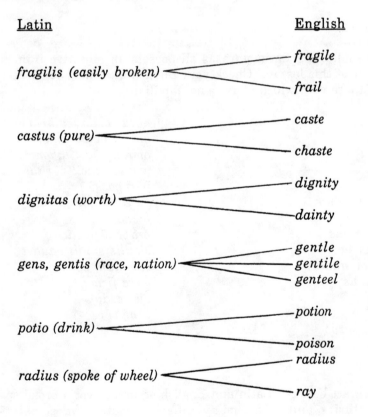

fragilis (easily broken) — *fragile*
                            — *frail*

castus (pure) — *caste*
                — *chaste*

dignitas (worth) — *dignity*
                   — *dainty*

gens, gentis (race, nation) — *gentle*
                              — *gentile*
                              — *genteel*

potio (drink) — *potion*
               — *poison*

radius (spoke of wheel) — *radius*
                          — *ray*

sécūrus (free from care) — secure / sure

Occasionally doublets are the product of a language other than Latin. Among them we can cite:

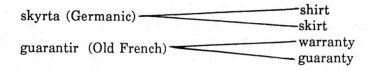

skyrta (Germanic) — shirt / skirt

guarantir (Old French) — warranty / guaranty

Exercise

A. Latin Phrases. Using your English dictionary, translate as many Latin phrases as you can in part "A" of the Special Topics section of this lesson and relate the present-day context in which each is used.

B. Matching. Match the term on the left with its closest definition on the right.

1. *rectitude*   a. strength of mind
2. *similitude*   b. having a broad choice
3. *certitude*   c. condition of being sure
4. *gratitude*   d. right-handedness
5. *fortitude*   e. thinness
6. *plenitude*   f. holiness
7. *latitude*   g. fullness
8. *sanctity*   h. thankfulness
9. *dexterity*   i. likeness
10. *tenuity*   j. righteousness

C. Identifying Additional Roots. Using your English dictionary, identify the Latin adjective root in each of the following words.

1. *audacious*   5. *solidarity*
2. *facilitate*   6. *obdurate*
3. *jocund*   7. *fecund*
4. *paucity*   8. *quantity*

128

E pluribus unum
One from many[1]

Chapter Seventeen
Adjectives (Cont.):
Comparisons, Colors and Numbers

The number of adjectives studied last chapter was indeed quite extensive. Many more could have been presented. To keep the Vocabulary List from becoming too burdensome, however, certain important categories of adjectives were set aside for consideration until this lesson. Our primary consideration at this time will be to examine the way in which Latin adjectives are placed into the comparative and superlative degrees. Most of those we met in the last chapter appeared in their simplest form, that is, in the positive degree. In English we customarily form the comparative degree by adding the suffix "-er" to the positive. The superlative we make by adding the suffix "-est" to the positive. Sometimes in English we place the words "*more*" and "*most*" before the simple form to create the higher levels. Consider these examples:

Positive	Comparative	Superlative
high	higher	highest
strong	stronger	strongest
beautiful	more beautiful	most beautiful

In Latin the comparative degree is formed by adding the suffix "-*ior*" (for masc. and fem.) or "-*ius*" (for the neut.) to the word base of the positive. To make the superlative form, one usually adds the suffix "-*issimus, -a, -um*" (masc., fem., neut., respectively) to the word base. Study the following examples in which only the masculine however is shown.

Positive	Comparative	Superlative
altus (high)	*altior* (higher)	*altissimus* (highest)
dulcis (sweet)	*dulcior* (sweeter)	*dulcissimus* (sweetest)
lātus (wide)	*lātior* (wider)	*lātissimus* (widest)

---

[1] From the Great Seal of the United States of America

These rules hold true for many of the adjectives studied last chapter. On the other hand, just as English has several exceptions (*e.g., good, better, best*), so does Latin. While these would be explained in detail in most elementary Latin textbooks, they are not fully covered in this text. Enough is presented below, however, to provide the reader with a better understanding of many Latin names of plants and muscles of the body, which use these irregular forms often. From the above one should also be able to detect the superlative element in such words as *fortissimo* and *generalissimo*, both outgrowths of Latin by way of Italian. The first is found in music, the second in a military context.

Latin adjectives with irregular comparative and superlative forms have provided many derivatives in English. Listed below are the most important examples in their masculine form only. In some instances, you will note, they are closely tied to prepositions or adverbs, which will be treated in the next chapter.[2]

Positive/Prep.	Comparative	Superlative
bonus "good"	**melior** "better"	**optimus** "best"
malus "bad"	**pejor** "worse"	**pessimus** "worst"
multus "much"	**plūs, plūris** "more"	
magnus "great"	**major** "greater"	**maximus** "greatest"
parvus "small"	**minor, minus** "smaller"	**minimus** "smallest"
juvenis "young"	**jūnior** "younger"	
senex "old"	**senior** "older"	
in(trā) "in(side)"	**interior** "inner"	**intimus** "inmost"
ex(trā) "out(side)"	**exterior** "outer"	**extrēmus** "outermost"
ultrā "beyond"	**ulterior** "farther"	**ultimus** "farthest"
ante "before"	**anterior** "more in front"	
post "after"	**posterior** "more behind"	
suprā "above"	**superior** "higher"	**suprēmus** "highest"
infrā "below"	**inferior** "lower"	

---

2 Latin forms are omitted in places where no English words have been coined.

Derivative Study

ameliorate	*junior*
optimist	*senior*
optimum	*interior*
pejorative	*intimate*
pessimist	*exterior*
pessimistic	*extreme*
plus	*ulterior*
plural	*ultimate*
plurality	*ultimatum*
major	*penult*
majority	*anterior*
maximum	*posterior*
minor	*superior*
minus	*superiority*
minority	*supreme*
minimum	*inferior*
minimal	*inferiority*

All muscles of the body possess a Latin name. Often this name describes the action accomplished by its use, such as *flexor digitōrum* ("bender of the fingers") or *extensor digitōrum* ("extender of the fingers"). Frequently muscles appear in pairs and are differentiated only by an accompanying Latin adjective in the comparative or superlative degree. Since the Latin word for muscle is *musculus* and is masculine in gender, the accompanying adjectives are always in the masculine form. Note how frequently opposites are employed among the few examples which follow.

auriculāris anterior	*(around the ear)*
auriculāris posterior	
auriculāris superior	
constrictor pharyngis superior	*(around the throat)*
constrictor pharyngis medius	
constrictor pharyngis inferior	
pectorālis major	*(around the chest)*
pectorālis minor	

rhomboideus major	*(around the scapula)*
rhomboideus minor	
teres major	
teres minor	
serrātus anterior	*(around the ribs)*
serrātus posterior superior	
serrātus posterior inferior	
glūteus maximus	*(around the buttocks)*
glūteus medius	
glūteus minimus	
lātissimus dorsī	*(on the back)*
longissimus dorsī	

In the assignment of names to plants and flowers the superlative is frequently found. Among the more colorful and interesting adjectives a professional might find would be the following:

acidissimus	*(acidus "acid")*
brilliantissimus	
candidissimus	*(candidus "white")*
delicatissimus	
ēlegantissimus	
foetidissimus	*(foetidus "foul smelling")*
grātissimus	
rāmōsissimus	*(rāmōsus "branchy")*
tenuissimus	

Our next consideration in this lesson is with Latin names for colors. Although the Romans possessed a great abundance of words with which to distinguish colors, only a small number of them are responsible for providing three or more vocabulary words in English. These few are presented in the Vocabulary List which follows.

Vocabulary (Colors)

Latin Forms	Meaning	Derivative
albus, -a, -um	white	*album*
ater, atra, atrum	black	*atrabilious*

flăvus, -a, -um	yellow	*flavin*
ruber, rubra, rubrum	red	*ruby*
viridis, -is, -e	green	*virid*

Derivative Study

alb	*riboflavin*
albescent	*rubella*
albiflorous	*rubefacient*
albino	*rubeola*
albite	*rubescent*
albumen	*rubidium*
alburnum	*rubiginous*
atrocious	*rubric*
atrosanguineous	*bilirubin*
flavine	*biliverdan*
flavism	*verdant*
flavone	*virescence*
flavobacterium	*virid(ian)*
flavoprotein	*viridity*

The vocabulary of Latin numbers is our next consideration. From this category of adjectives our English language has borrowed extensively. The Vocabulary List which follows includes both cardinal numbers (used in simple counting, as 1, 2, 3) and ordinal numbers (used often in ranking, as first, second, third). Only the lowest and most common numbers are included for study here. Note that the cardinal numbers higher than three are indeclinable, *i.e.*, they possess only one form for all genders and cases.

Vocabulary (Numbers)

Cardinal Numbers		Ordinal Numbers	
ūnus, -a, -um	one	**prīmus, -a, -um**	first
duo, -ae, -o	two	**secundus, -a, -um**	second
trēs, tria	three	**tertius, -a, -um**	third
quattuor	four	**quārtus, -a, -um**	fourth
quīnque	five	**quīntus, -a, -um**	fifth

sex	six	**sextus, -a, -um**	sixth
septem	seven	**septimus, -a, -um**	seventh
octō	eight	**octāvus, -a, -um**	eighth
novem	nine	**nōnus, -a, -um**	ninth
decem	ten	**decimus, -a, -um**	tenth
centum	hundred	<u>Adverbial Numbers:</u>	
mīlle	thousand	**semel**	once
sēmi	half	**bīs**	twice
sesqui	one and a half	**ter**	three times
		quater	four times

Derivative Study (Numbers)

<u>*Level A*</u>

duality	*unison*
bilingual	*triple*
sextet	*quarter*
uniform	*September*
centennial	*October*
decimal	*November*
mile	*December*
dual	*unify*
quintet	*trinity*
bigamy	*duplex*
unicorn	*percent*
octet	*octave*
millenium	*unisex*
septet	*bifocal*
trident	*sextuplet*
biannual	*unanimous*
milliliter	*bicentennial*
trivial	*decimate*
bisexual	*duet*

Level B

unilateral	univalent
bilateral	bivalent
trilateral	trivalent
quadrilateral	quadrivalent
uniparous	trijugate
sesquicentennial	millipede
decemvir	triumvirate
novena	centimeter
bicameral	quintessence
biramous	bicornuate
unifoliate	quadruped
binary	unicameral
quinquefoliate	decanal
octogenarian	dean
centigrade	unijugate
bicuspid	triceps
quadrennium	quadriceps
septuagenarian	biceps
biped	centipede
binomial	tertiary
trinomial	Septuagint

Special Topics

A. Roman Numerals

Although Arabic numbers today represent the standard by which nearly all aspects of mathematics are figured, some attention to Roman numerals ought to be given here. Indeed this form of calculation is encountered yet with some frequency. In many books, for example, the introduction is enumerated with Roman numerals, generally in the lower case. Elsewhere, in uppercase form, we can readily find them as chapter numbers for books, as volume numbers in journals and in the establishment dates of institutions or buildings. Since Roman numerals are traditionally studied at some point in elementary education, only a quick review will be given here. The following table shows the numerical value for the most common Roman letter symbols.

$$I = 1 \qquad V = 5$$
$$X = 10 \qquad L = 50$$
$$C = 100 \qquad D = 500$$
$$M = 1000 \qquad \underline{V} = 5000$$

Various combinations of these letters produce the numbers in between. In regard to this, however, two special rules apply. First, symbols representing larger values are regularly placed before those representing smaller amounts and the total is simply determined by addition. The second rule comes into play as an exception to this. In situations where the same symbol might otherwise be required four times in succession, the Romans preferred to employ a different technique. In such cases a smaller numeral is placed before a larger one and accordingly is subtracted from it. In numbers below 1,000 the following subtraction possibilities existed:

"I" before "V" = 4
"I" before "X" = 9
"X" before "L" = 40
"X" before "C" = 90
"C" before "D" = 400
"C" before "M" = 900

Study the following examples:

CCLIX = 259   DCCLIII = 753

MCMXCIV = 1,994   CDLXXXIV = 484

xxviii = 28   ccxxii = 222

B. The Metric System

Greek and Latin play a very important part in the vocabulary of the metric system. In their role as prefixes Greek numbers always represent *whole numbers* above "1." The corresponding prefixes in Latin, on the other hand, in all cases represent *decimals* (or fractions). The numbers employed most frequently are the following:

Greek	Latin
deka- = 10	deci- = .1
hecto- = 100	centi- = .01
kilo- = 1000	milli- = .001

Examine these systems which measure length, capacity, and weight.

Unit of Measure	Abbreviation	Number
kilometer	km	1,000
hectometer	hm	100
dekameter (decameter)	dkm	10
meter	m	1
decimeter	dm	.1
centimeter	cm	.01
millimeter	mm	.001
kiloliter	kl	1,000
hectoliter	hl	100
dekaliter (decaliter)	dkl	10
liter	l	1
deciliter	dl	.1
centiliter	cl	.01
milliliter	ml	.001
kilogram	kg	1,000
hectogram	hg	100
dekagram (decagram)	dkg	10
gram	g	1
decigram	dg	.1
centigram	cg	.01
milligram	mg	.001

C. Latin Phrases with Comparisons, Numbers & Colors

The following Latin phrases contain either an adjective in the comparative or superlative degree, a color or a number. They are arranged in categories according to the context in which each is generally employed.

Mottoes
E plūribus ūnum - "Out of many one" (U.S.A.)
Salūs populī suprēma lēx estō - "Let the safety of the people be the highest
                              law" (Missouri)

Philosophy
ā fortiōri - "from the stronger (argument)"
ā minōri - "from the lesser (argument)"

ā posteriōri - "from the latter;" inductive reasoning (Aristotle)
ā priōri - "from the former;" deductive reasoning (Plato)
summum bonum - "the highest good"
ūnā vōce - "with one voice"
ūnō animō - "with one mind"

Law
Dē minimīs nōn cūrat lēx. - "The law does not care about very small matters."
prīmā facie - "on the first face (appearance)"

Pharmacy
bīs in diē (b.i.d.) - "twice daily"
ter in diē (t.i.d.) - "three times daily"
quater in diē (q.i.d.) - "four times daily"

Trees, Plants, Animals
Acer rubrum - "red maple"
Digitālis purpurea - "foxglove"
Quercus rubra - "red oak"
Juglans nigra - "black walnut"
Elephās maxima - "Indian elephant"
Vulpes fulva - "red (tawny) fox"

Exercise

A. Each of the following English words contains a Latin root word that is the
name of a color. Using your dictionary, write the Latin word for each and
its English meaning.

1. *oriole*	5. *rufous*	9. *verdant*
2. *candidate*	6. *cerulean*	10. *lurid*
3. *nigrescent*	7. *jaundice*	11. *luteous*
4. *obfuscate*	8. *livid*	12. *fulvous*

B. Write the following Arabic numbers as Roman numerals and the
Roman numerals as Arabic numbers.

1. 2,943	4. 34	7. 278
2. 1,993	5. 422	8. 862
3. 3,726	6. 4,444	9. 8,238

10. MDCLXVI	12. DLIX	14. cvii
11. MMCCXXII	13. MXCI	15. xlix

Ad astra per aspera
To the stars through difficulties[1]

Chapter Eighteen
Prefixes and Adverbs

In this lesson we shall examine Latin prepositions and adverbs. These two parts of speech share some interesting features. In the first place, they regularly possess only a single form in Latin (although most adverbs can be put into a comparative and superlative level). Nouns, pronouns, adjectives and verbs, on the other hand, all possess an extensive system of endings which can be added to each word's base. The singleness of form in Latin for prepositions and adverbs can be found in many Latin phrases employed in English. In the examples which follow note their separate and unique character.

Prepositions		Adverbs
ad infinītum	*ad hoc*	*semper fidēlis (parātus)*
ex librīs	*ex officiō*	*notā bene*
dē jūre	*dē factō*	*vidē suprā*
post mortem	*post partum*	*nunc prō tunc*

In addition to their possession of a separate and unchangeable form in Latin, these same two parts of speech likewise happen to assume the more integral role of word prefix in English. Directly attached to various Latin word roots, prepositions and adverbs assist in the formation of thousands of English words. Among the many possibilities are the following examples:

Prepositions	Adverbs
defoliate	*peninsula*
expectorant	*supraliminal*
incorporeal	*ultramarine*

With regard to their function as prefix, two linguistic phenomena recur with some frequency. They are *assimilation* and *vowel weakening*. The first of these is the result of the juxtaposition of two consonants (sometimes

---

[1] Motto of the state of Kansas.

of two vowels) in such a way that the second causes the first to change to conform more pleasantly with it in sound. In most cases, but not always, the changed consonant simply becomes a duplicate of the consonant which it precedes. Study the following examples (hyphens have been added only to highlight the orthographic changes).

"in-" (in, on)	"con-" fr. cum (with)
in-undate	*con-cord*
il-luminate	*col-lateral*
im-press	*com-press*
ir-rigate	*cor-respond*

A knowledge of the interworking of prefixes and word roots in these circumstances will often lead to improved spelling habits for most individuals, especially in areas where one might wonder whether or not a consonant is "doubled." For instance, if you are already familiar with a word such as "illuminate" and know that its parts mean "light" and "in," you ought to be able to conclude that there are two *l*'s near the beginning (and not just one) due to the change in the prefix from "*in* -" to "*il* -" by reason of assimilation.

The second phenomenon to occur frequently in word formation of this sort is *vowel weakening*. In this situation the union of the prefix to the main root causes the initial vowel in the second root to weaken or shorten. Examine the most common vowel changes below.

Change	Reg. Latin	Change with Prefix	Derivative
a > e	annus	biennium	*biennial*
a > i	caput, capitis	occiput, occipitis	*occipital*
ae > ī	quaerere	inquīrere	*inquire*
au > ū	claudere	inclūdere	*include*

Of course, not all Latin roots undergo vowel shortening simply because they are preceded by a prefix. Using the examples above, one could readily cite such common words as *biannual* and *decapitate,* both of which keep the original vowels in spite of the prefixes.

In the Vocabulary List which follows the simple Latin preposition is given first. This is the customary way it will appear in the etymological portion of your English dictionary and in Latin phrases sometimes employed in English. Various prefix alternatives often arising from assimilation are then given for each in parentheses. Only the meanings which are most commonly found in English derivatives are presented.

Vocabulary (Prepositions)

Prefix	Meanings	Derivatives
ab (ā-, abs-)	away, from	*abduct, abstain*
ad (a-, ac-, af-, ag-, al-, an-, ap-, ar-, as-, at-)	to, toward	*adhere, affirm aver*
ambi	both, around	*ambidextrous*
ante	before	*antedate*
circum	around, about	*circumnavigate*
cum (co-, col-, com-, con-, cor-)	with, together	*concord, compete*
contrā	against	*contradict*
dē	down, off, from, about	*deduct, descend*
dis- (di-, dif-)	apart, not	*dissolve, divert*
ex (ē-, ef-)	out of, from	*extend, eject*
in (il-, im-, ir-)	in, on	*inform, impose*
in- (il-, im-, ir-)	not	*infidel, illegal*
inter	between	*intercede*
ob (oc-, of-, op)	in the way, toward	*obstacle, offer*
per	through, to the bad, by	*perspire*
post	after	*postscript*
prae (pre-)	before, in front	*prefix*
prō	forward, for	*promote*
re- (red-)	back, again	*recede, redeem*
sē- (sēd-)	apart, without	*secede, sedition*
sub (suc-, suf-, sug-, sup-, sus-)	under	*subscribe, sustain*
super	above, over	*supervision*
trāns (trā-, trān-)	across, through	*transcribe, traverse*

It was pointed out at the beginning of this chapter that Latin adverbs were like prepositions in that in Latin they exist as separate words and possess only a single form (that is, they are indeclinable). Moreover, in English they regularly serve as prefixes. An interesting characteristic about a few of the adverbs in the Vocabulary List which follows is that in English they exist in a different part of speech. Consider the following examples:

1. *Let's hear your **alibi**.*
2. *The team elected an **interim** president.*
3. *After the trial they discovered the defendant's **alias**.*

Vocabulary (Adverbs)

Latin Form	Meaning	Derivative
aliās	at another time	*alias*
alibī	at another place	*alibi*
bene (adv. of bonus)	well	*benefit*
extrā	beyond, outside	*extra*
infrā	below	*infrared*
interim	meanwhile	*interim*
intrā (intrō-)	within	*intramural*
male	badly	*malevolent*
nunc	now	
paene (pen-)	almost	*peninsula*
retro	backward	*retrograde*
satis	enough	*satisfy*
semper	always	*sempervivum*
suprā	above	*supraliminal*
tunc	then	
ultrā	beyond	*ultramarine*

In the list which follows a few examples will contain roots from verbs which are yet to be studied. In most instances where this occurs, however, the word is already well known and is presented here only to highlight the prepositional or adverbial element.

Derivative Study

Level A

abbreviate	adequate
annul	affiliate
circumlunar	exculpate
subpoena	subterranean
expectorant	immortal
devious	conjugal
congregate	decapitate
irradiate	interlunar
incarnation	secure
subjugate	transmarine
recapitulate	associate
condominium	dissociate
exonerate	inadequate
inculpable	degradation
decelerate	dislocate
accelerate	allocate
alleviate	aggravate
accord	disburse
transform	translucent
suburb	segregate
illuminate	exterminate
collaborate	rebel
infidel	insatiable
introspection	retrospect
ultramarine	peninsula
benefactor	comfort
collateral	ultraviolet
satiate	malnutrition
exalt	intramural
extraneous	submarine

<u>*Level B*</u>

infrastructure	*benign*
intravenous	*commiserate*
irrevocable	*supraorbital*
disburse	*antediluvian*
aggregate	*postdiluvian*
rejuvenate	*obfuscate*
subaqueous	*sublunar*
superannuate	*transvestite*
supercilious	*supernumerary*
subcutaneous	*retroversion*
substratum	*annihilate*
adrenalin	*adumbrate*
perfidious	*occipital*
impervious	*combine*
cooperate	*intercostal*
sublingual	*antepenult*
reincarnation	*impecunious*
exceed (cedere = to go)	*precede*
proceed	*recede*
succeed	*accede*
intercede	*concede*
secede	*antecedent*

Special Topics

A. <u>Latin Phrases</u>

Each of the following Latin phrases contains a word from the Vocabulary List of this lesson. See how many you know.

ā posteriōri	*cum grānō salis*
ā priōri	*cum laude*
ab ōvō	*dē factō*
ad hoc	*dē jūre*
ad infinītum	*deus ex māchinā*
ad nauseam	*ē plūribus ūnum*
ante bellum	*ex cathēdrā*

ex librīs	*per annum*
ex officiō	*per capita*
in camerā	*per diem*
in locō parentis	*post mortem*
in mediās rēs	*post partum*
in situ	*post scrīptum*
in vinō vēritas	*prō fōrmā*
in vītrō	*quid prō quō*
inter vīvōs	*sine diē*
nunc prō tunc	*sine quā nōn*

Exercise

A. **Latin Phrases.** Using your English dictionary, translate as many Latin phrases as you can in part "A" of the Special Topics section of this lesson and relate the present-day context in which each is used.

B. **Matching.** Match the term on the left with its closest definition on the right. The Latin verb *ducere* (to lead), which you will encounter in the next chapter, is just one of many verbs that readily joins with the prefixes of this lesson.

1. reduce	a. lead forth
2. induce	b. lead back
3. adduce	c. lead astray
4. educe	d. evoke or lead out
5. introduce	e. lead on
6. traduce	f. degrade, defame
7. seduce	g. lead forth as proof or example
8. conduce	h. infer from a principle
9. produce	i. bring on for the first time
10. deduce	j. contribute to an end

C. **Greek/Latin Comparisons.** Match words in each of the three columns below according to their similar meanings.

English	Greek	Latin
1. under	A. en-	a. super-
2. away from	B. syn-	b. contra-
3. around	C. hypo-	c. per-
4. in	D. dia-	d. ultra-
5. above, over	E. anti-	e. re-
6. with	F. ana-	f. circum-
7. against	G. apo-	g. ab-
8. through	H. meta-	h. con-
9. back, again	I. hyper-	i. sub-
10. beyond	J. peri-	j. in-

This sidewalk mosaic from Pompeii gives trespassers ample warning of what to expect ahead with the intimidating Latin message "Cave canem." Can you guess its meaning?

Errāre humānum est.
To err is human.

Chapter Nineteen
Verbs: Infinitives and Perfect Passive Participles

In earlier chapters of this text you saw that Latin nouns are separated into different groups known as declensions due to the fact that each group possesses a unique set of "word endings." These endings not only help in identifying the number of a noun (whether it is singular or plural) but also show the grammatical function or role the noun plays in a sentence. They indicate, among other things, whether a noun is the subject, the direct object, or a possessive.

In many respects the Latin verb works much like the noun. Through its own system of "word endings" the various properties of this part of speech can be identified. These unique verb forms give us important information about *voice, mood, tense, person* and *number*.

voice	(whether it is) active or passive;
mood	indicative, imperative or subjunctive;
tense	present, future, imperfect, perfect, *etc.*
person	first, second or third person;
number	singular or plural.

In English these verbal characteristics are revealed by the use of helping words, such as "will," "been," "is," "was," and "have." Moreover, instead of being joined to part of the verb stem, these auxiliary forms are placed separately near it. Examine carefully the difference of approach toward this same phenomenon employed by the two languages in the following examples.

Latin	English	Grammatical Form
portāre	*to carry*	active present infinitive
portābimus	*we shall carry*	act., ind., fut., 1st, plur.
portābat	*he was carrying*	act., ind., imperf., 3rd, sg.
portantur	*they are carried*	pass., ind., pres., 3rd, pl.
portēs	*you may carry*	act., subj., pres., 2nd, sg.
portābor	*I shall be carried*	pass., ind., fut., 1st, sg.

The number of endings for Latin verbs is quite large indeed and students in traditional Latin courses spend a good deal of time learning them in order to read Latin literature correctly. For our purposes in derivative study, however, it is necessary to learn only two specific forms of most verbs. The first is the *present active infinitive* and the second is the *perfect passive participle*. From the verb "carry" in the examples above, the first form in Latin happens to be *portāre* and is translated "to carry." The second is *portātus* and can be translated as either "having been carried" or simply "carried." Most English dictionaries regularly cite one or both of these forms when giving the etymology of an English word with a Latin verb root. For this reason the Vocabulary List of this lesson and the next will present these two forms. Just as Latin possesses five separate declensions for nouns, it employs four separate *conjugations* for most verbs.

The Present Active Infinitive. Sample infinitives of verbs from the four Latin conjugations are presented in the following table. Note the infinitive ending for each conjugation. Upon its removal, the remaining portion provides us with the word base or stem. It is this part which is generally included in English word borrowings.

Conjugation	Infinitive	Root/ Ending		Derivative
1st	*portāre* (to carry)	port-	-*āre*	*import*
1st	*putāre* (to think)	put-	-*āre*	*compute*
2nd	*docēre* (to teach)	doc-	-*ēre*	*docent*
2nd	*vidēre* (to see)	vid-	-*ēre*	*provide*
3rd	*dūcere* (to lead)	dūc -	-*ere*	*induce*
3rd	*petere* (to seek)	pet-	-*ere*	*compete*
4th	*audīre* (to hear)	aud-	-*īre*	*audible*
4th	*venīre* (to come)	ven-	-*īre*	*intervene*

It occasionally happens in Latin that a verb is somewhat defective in that it possesses only about half the number of forms of a regular verb. The endings which it for the most part employs are those of the passive voice. A peculiar aspect of such verbs, which are said to be *deponent*, is that the passive voice forms are translated into English as if they were active. Deponent verbs can be readily recognized in English dictionaries and the Vocabulary Lists of this text by the substitution of the present passive infinitive for the corresponding active form. The passive infinitive ending for the four conjugations can be observed from the following examples.

Conj.	Passive Infin.	Root/Ending		Derivative
1st	*mīrārī*(to wonder at)	mīr-	-*ārī*	*admire*
2nd	*verērī*(to fear)	ver-	-*ērī*	*revere*
3rd	*gradī*(to step)	grad-	-*ī*	*degrade*
4th	*partīrī*(to share)	part-	-*īrī*	*impart*

The Perfect Passive Participle.   The Latin perfect passive participle has likewise been responsible for providing us with numerous derivatives in English. Due to its participial nature, it assumes both the character and form of an adjective and resembles the first-second declension type with the endings "-*us , -a, -um*" for the masculine, feminine and neuter genders, respectively. Commonly the masculine form in "-*us*" is the only one cited in dictionaries. As in the case of adjectives, the stem or base of the participle includes each letter prior to the familiar adjective ending. At this point it is important to note any and all differences in form which may exist between the stem of the participle and that of the present active infinitive. Study the following examples.

Conj.	Infin.	Root	Participle	Root
1st	*portāre*	*port-*	*portātus*	*portat-*
2nd	*vidēre*	*vid-*	*vīsus*	*vis-*
3rd	*scrībere*	*scrib-*	*scriptus*	*script-*
4th	*audīre*	*aud-*	*audītus*	*audit-*

Finally, the difference in voice between the present active infinitive and the perfect passive participle can *sometimes* be detected in the meanings of English derivatives taken from each. Consider examples from the Latin verbs just mentioned:

Deriv. from Infin.		Deriv. from Participle	
deport	*(carry out)*	deportation	*(carried out)*
provide	*(see before)*	provision	*(seen before)*
inscribe	*(write on)*	inscription	*(written on)*
audible	*(able to hear)*	audition	*(hearing)*

In the last chapter you saw numerous examples of vowel shortening or weakening when prefixes were added to roots. Since this phenomenon is very common in the case of Latin verbs, the weakened form, where it exists, is regularly given in parentheses in the Vocabulary List below.

Vocabulary

Infinitive	Participle	Meaning	Derivative
agere (-igere)	**āctus**	to do, act	*transact*
amāre	**amātus**	to love	*amatory*
ambulāre	**ambulātus**	to walk	*ambulate*
audīre	**audītus**	to hear	*audience*
cadere (-cidere)	**cāsus**	to fall	*cadence*
caedere (-cīdere)	**caesus (-cīsus)**	to cut, kill	*incision*
capere (-cipere)	**captus (-ceptus)**	to take, seize	*capture*
cēdere	**cessus**	to go, yield	*concede*
claudere (-clūdere)	**clausus (-clūsus)**	to shut	*exclude*
clīnāre	**clīnātus**	to lean	*incline*
crēdere	**crēditus**	to believe	*credit*
currere	**cursus**	to run	*recur*
damnāre (-demnāre)	**damnātus**	to declare guilty	*condemn*
dāre (-dere)	**dātus (-ditus)**	to give	*tradition*
dīcere	**dictus**	to say, tell	*dictate*
docēre	**doctus**	to teach	*doctor*
dūcere	**ductus**	to lead	*induce*
facere (-ficere)	**factus (-fectus)**	to do, make	*factory*
fārī	**fātus**	to speak	*fate*
ferre	**lātus**	to bear, carry	*transfer*
findere	**fissus**	to split	*fission*
flectere	**flexus**	to bend	*reflex*
fluere	**flūxus**	to flow	*fluent*
frangere (-fringere)	**fractus**	to break	*fracture*

fugere	**fugitūrus**	to flee	*fugitive*
fundere	**fūsus**	to pour	*infuse*
gerere	**gestus**	to bear, bring	*gestation*
gignere	**genitus**	to bring forth	*genital*
gradī (-gredī)	**gressus**	to step, move	*progress*
habēre (-hibēre)	**habitus (-hibitus)**	to have, hold	*habitate*
haerēre (HER-)	**haesus (HES-)**	to stick	*adhere*
incendere	**incensus**	to burn	*incense*
īre (usu. -IENT)	**itum**	to go	*exit*
jacere	**jactus (-jectus)**	to throw	*eject*
jūrāre	**jūrātus**	to swear	*abjure*
lābī	**lapsus**	to slip	*lapse*
legere (-ligere)	**lectus**	to read, choose	*lector*
loquī	**locūtus**	to speak	*eloquent*
lūdere	**lūsus**	to play	*prelude*
mergere	**mersus**	to plunge	*merge*

Derivative Study

Level A

antecedent	*circumflex*
concur	*incident*
interlude	*coherent*
belligerent	*contradict*
congress	*confuse*
regress	*predict*
profuse	*secede*
seclude	*transgress*
introduce	*cohabit*
incredible	*ambition*
ingredient	*illusion*
fissure	*infringe*

infant

intercede

coincidental

exceed

decide

reflect

object

submersion

inaudible

amorous

decadent

confer

collapse

occur

inherent

infantry

infringe

deflect

conception

circumference

reject

perjury

subject

immerge

react

ambulance

recipient

superfluous

include

decline

conducive

affable

Level B

abduction

ambient

circumcision

efferent

afferent

collate

precede

prelate

illegible

refuge

confluence

somnambulate

congenital

prefactory

objection

fissiparous

translate

aqueduct

cohesive

submersion

recession

incisor

accident

circumambulate

interjection

deference

deciduous

interdict

occlusion

fissile

emerge

frangible

refund

concurrent

viaduct

recluse

prolapse

sedition

seduction

benediction

affluence

precursor

incendiary

egress

influence	*influx*
genuflect	*legend*
funambulist	*inflection*
benefactor	*perfection*
collusion	*ventriloquist*
labile	*soliloquy*
credulous	*refract*
referendum	*refrangible*

Special Topics

<u>Latin phrases</u>

The following phrases all possess a verb from the Vocabulary List of this lesson. See how many you can translate before consulting a dictionary.

fierī faciās	*rēs ipsa loquitur*
habeās corpus	*scire faciās*
obiter dictum	*subpoena dūcēs tēcum*
quod erat faciendum	*tempus fugit*
furor loquendī	*lapsus linguae*
ipsō factō	*dē factō*

Exercise

A. **Latin Phrases.** Using your English dictionary, translate as many of the Latin phrases as you can in the Special Topics section of this lesson and relate the present-day context in which each is used.

B. **Identifying additional verbs.** Using your English dictionary, identify and translate the Latin verb in the following words or phrases.

1. *imprimatur*	6. *illicit*
2. *mandamus*	7. *fiat*
3. *affidavit*	8. *ad libitum*
4. *caveat*	9. *nolo contendere*
5. *recipe*	10. *veto*

Dum spīrō, spērō.
As long as I breathe, I hope.[1]

Chapter Twenty
Verbs: Present Active Participles and Gerundives

Last lesson it was pointed out that two specific forms of Latin verbs were regularly employed in English dictionaries in indicating etymologies from words of this part of speech. They were the present active infinitive and the perfect passive participle. In this chapter you will discover two additional Latin verb forms which also play a significant role in English vocabulary. They are the *present active participle* and the *gerundive.* Let us consider them separately.

<u>Present Active Participle</u>   This form of the verb in both English and Latin functions as a verbal adjective. In English it regularly carries the suffix ending "*-ing.*" Consider its use and form in these sentences:

The *barking* dog caused the burglars to flee.
The old man, *resting* on the park bench, cannot see.

In Latin the specific form which reflects this verbal adjective always ends in "*-ns, -ntis*" with the vowel or vowels preceding indicative of the specific conjugation to which each verb belongs, as noted below.

<u>Conj.</u>	<u>Latin Example</u>	<u>Derivative</u>	<u>Ending</u>
1st	*secāns, secantis (cutting)*	*secant*	**-ant**
2nd	*vidēns, videntis (seeing)*	*evident*	**-ent**
3rd	*tangēns, tangentis (touching)*	*tangent*	**-ent**
4th	*oriēns, orientis (rising)*	*orient*	**-ient**

Important for our study of derivatives is the fact that all first conjugation verbs, *i.e.,* those with the present active infinitive ending in "*-āre,*" will form their Latin present active participle with the ending "*-āns, -antis.*" Consequently, when an English derivative is formed from this verbal adjective, it will always possess the ending "*-ant.*" The same pattern holds true for derivatives from second, third and fourth conjugation verbs, as

---

[1] Motto of the state of South Carolina.

noted above, where the endings "-*ent*" or "-*ient*" are employed. When, on occasion, an English derivative from the latter category possesses the ending "-*ant*" instead of "-*ent*," we can suspect that some other linguistic factor is responsible. In this situation it often happens that the word entered the English language not directly from Latin but only after having first passed through French, where all present active participles end in "-*ant*."

Because speakers of English today frequently do not give clear pronunciation to final unaccented syllables of words, orthographical errors are particularly apt to be made in cases of words formed from a Latin present active participle. You may often wonder, for instance, whether a specific word ends in "-*ant*" or "-*ent*." Certainly having a knowledge of the correct Latin conjugation from which a word is originally derived will be the greatest source of help in reducing mistakes of this sort.

<u>Gerundive</u>   The final Latin verb form we shall examine is the gerundive. Its effect on the meaning of words is to show necessity. Usually in English we can say that someone or something "*must be...*" or "*is to be...*" The Latin form of this verbal adjective for first conjugation verbs is:

-andus, -anda, -andum

The gerundive forms of second, third and fourth conjugation verbs are like those of the first except that they are introduced by the characteristic vowel of "-*e*-" (or "-*ie*-") instead of "-*a*-." Gerundives are similar to regular adjectives of the first and second declension, which you studied some time ago. As such, they possess the same possibe adjective endings in *-us, -a,* and *-um* for agreement with masculine, feminine, and neuter nouns. (The typical forms for *magnus*, you will recall, are also made plural with the endings "-*i*," "-*ae*," and "-*a*.") Although any of these endings may be reflected in English derivatives, the neuter (sing.) tends to be preferred. Check the following examples:

<u>Derivative</u>		<u>Meaning</u>
Amanda	*(f., sg.)*	to be loved
agendum	*(n., sg.)*	to be done
referendum	*(n., sg.)*	to be referred
addendum	*(n., sg.)*	to be added
corrigendum	*(n., sg.)*	to be corrected
propaganda	*(n., pl.)*	to be spread
pudendum	*(n., sg.)*	to be ashamed

memorandum (n., sg.)   to be remembered

In some English words the gerundive may lose the adjective suffix of its form and keep only the "-*and*" or "-*end*," as in the following examples:

<u>Derivative</u>	<u>Meaning</u>
legend	to be read
reverend	to be respected
multiplicand	to be multiplied
dividend	to be divided
addend	to be added
minuend	to be lessened
subtrahend	to be subtracted

Vocabulary

<u>Latin Forms</u> <u>Pres., Act., Inf.</u>	<u>Perf., Pass., Part.</u>	<u>Meaning</u>	<u>Derivative</u>
miscēre	**mixtus**	to blend, mingle	*mix*
mittere	**missus**	to send	*admit*
monēre	**monitus**	to warn	*admonition*
movēre	**mōtus**	to move	*promote*
nāscī	**nātus**	to be born	*natal*
parere	**partum**	to give birth	*parent*
pendere	**pensus**	to hang, weigh	*pendent*
petere	**petītus**	to seek	*petition*
plicāre	**plicātus (-plicitus)**	to fold	*implicate*
pōnere	**positus**	to put, place	*deposit*
portāre	**portātus**	to carry	*import*
premere	**pressus**	to press	*impress*
putāre	**putātus**	to think	*compute*
quaerere **(-quīrere)**	**quaesītus** **(-quīsītus)**	to seek	*inquire*

rapere	raptus (-reptus)	to snatch	*rapacious*
rumpere	ruptus	to break	*rupture*
scandere (-scendere)	scansum (-scensum)	to climb	*ascend*
scrībere	scriptus	to write	*scribe*
secāre	sectum	to cut	*dissect*
sedēre	sessus	to sit	*session*
sequi	secūtus	to follow	*sequence*
solvere	solūtus	to loosen, destroy	*solvent*
spīrāre	spīrātus	to breath	*inspire*
stāre	status	to stand	*status*
sūmere	sūmptus	to take (up)	*assume*
tangere (-tingere)	tāctus	to touch	*tangent*
tendere	tentus (tensus)	to stretch	*tense*
tenēre (-tinēre)	tentus	to hold	*tenure*
trahere	tractus	to drag, draw	*tractor*
trūdere	trūsus	to thrust, push	*protrude*
valēre	valitūrus	to be strong, well	*equivalent*
venīre	ventum	to come	*convene*
vertere	versus	to turn	*invert*
vīdēre	vīsus	to see	*vision*
vincere	victus	to conquer	*convince*
volvere	volūtus	to roll	*evolve*
vorāre	vorātus	to eat	*devour*

Derivative Study

Level A

remit	inquire
depress	compete
convene	presume
involve	sequel
describe	dissolve
descend	provide
interrupt	depend
inspire	inscription
scripture	demote
monitor	intermix
transport	appendix
evict	carnivorous
retention	intrude
victory	divert
retract	invalid
extend	section
complicate	sedan
viviparous	stable
cognate	report
obstacle	perspire
postscript	subscribe
subtract	admit
absolve	circumstance
intersect	universe
contact	supervise
attract	portable
opponent	corrupt
anniversary	scan
emit	contingent
solution	spirit
invisible	revolve
prescription	sediment
extract	transmit
miscellaneous	avert
tactile	compress
suspense	subscription
dispute	manuscript
intermittent	expensive

Level B

subsequent
transcribe
independent
suppository
condescend
repute
omnivorous
apposition
ascribe
compendium
univalent
explicate
consecutive
obtrude
persecute
sedentary
subversion
piscivorous
rapine
insoluble
providence
secant
preposition
sequential
miscegenation
inadvertent
erupt
convolution
distend
assumption
scansorial
oviparous
introvert

transverse
supersede
suspend
transpire
nascent
surreptitious
proscription
ambivalence
circumvent
expiration
sumptuous
contravene
promiscuous
pervert
obverse
superscript
parturition
indisputable
prerequisite
aspirant
rape
scriptorium
petulance
raptorial
premonition
extrusive
interpose
abstinence
multivalent
miscible
oppression
proposition
explicit

Special Chapter Topics

A. Latin Phrases

The following phrases all possess a verb from the Vocabulary List of this lesson. See how many you can translate before consulting a dictionary.

dum spī rō, spē rō	*omnia vincit amor*
furor scrībendī	*post scriptum (p.s.)*
labor omnia vincit	*prō rē nātā (p.r.n.)*
lēx scripta	*quod vidē (q.v.)*
līs pendēns	*rēbus sīc stantibus*
locum tenēns	*stāre dēcīsīs*
locus stāndī	*stāre in jūdiciō*
nōn sequitur	*status quō (ante)*

B. Verbal Suffixes

The suffixes listed below are used in English to make Latin words of various parts of speech into verbs. Generally, the effect they have on the word base is to "cause" or "make something to be."

Suffix	Examples
-ize	*verbalize, localize, finalize, patronize*
-ate	*terminate, nominate, locate, stimulate*
-ify	*magnify, pacify, verify, rectify, ramify*

The Romans often employed another verbal suffix to denote "becoming" or "beginning," and the group of words that carried this suffix became known as "inchoatives" (from the Latin verb *inchoāre* meaning "to begin"). Slightly modified, this suffix can also be found in noun and adjective forms in English. It has the following characteristics:

Inchoative Suffix	Examples
-esce (v.)	*convalesce, coalesce, effloresce*
-escence (n.)	*convalescence, coalescence*
-escent (adj.)	*ignescent, incandescent, fluorescent*

Exercise

A. **Latin Phrases.** Using your English dictionary, translate as many Latin phrases as you can in part "A" of the Special Topics section of this lesson and relate the present-day context in which each is used.

B. **Present Participle Suffix.** Determine which word in each set below is spelled correctly. Each contains a present participle suffix. Check your answers in any standard English dictionary.

1. *exponant - exponent*
2. *aspirant - aspirent*
3. *regant - regent*
4. *recipiant - recipient*
5. *decedant - decedent*
6. *currant - current*
7. *docant - docent*
8. *fluant - fluent*
9. *ingrediant - ingredient*
10. *inherant - inherent*
11. *conveniant - convenient*
12. *repugnant - repugnent*

13. *ambiant - ambient*
14. *adjacant - adjacent*
15. *eloquant - eloquent*
16. *emergant - emergent*
17. *remittant - remittent*
18. *nascant - nascent*
19. *parant - parent*
20. *pendant - pendent*
21. *solvant - solvent*
22. *tenant - tenent*
23. *sedantary - sedentary*
24. *disputant - disputent*

General Vocabulary: Latin[1]

A

ā, ab "(away) from," "by" (18)

abacus "square slab on column," "counting board" (12)

ac "and"

acer, aceris "maple tree"

ācer, ācris, ācre "sharp"

acidus "acid"

ad "to," "toward" (18)

addendum "thing to be added" (13)

addere, additum "to add"

aequus "equal" (16)

agendum "thing to be done" (13)

ager, agrī "field" (12)

agere, āctus (-igere) "to do," "to drive" (19)

agricola "farmer"

āla "wing" (11)

albus "white" (17)

alga "sea-weed" (11)

aliās "at another time" (18)

alibī "at another place" (19)

alimōnia "sustenance"

almus "nourishing"

altus "high" (16)

alumna "foster-daughter" (11)

alumnus "foster-son" (12)

alveolus "small cavity" (12)

amāre, amātus "to love" (19)

ambi "both," "around" (18)

ambitiō, ambitiōnis "canvassing"

ambulāre, ambulātus "to walk" (19)

amīcitia "friendship"

amīcus "friend"

amor "love"

ancilla "maid-servant" (11)

angustus "narrow"

anima "soul," "breath" (11)

animus "mind"

annus "year" (12)

ante "before" (18)

antenna "sail-yard" (11)

anterior "more in front" (17)

antīquus "old" (16)

apex, apicis "high point" (14)

---

[1] In this listing, nouns are presented only in the nominative, singular form unless a change of root occurs, in which case the genitive, singular is also given. Adjectives are likewise shown in the nominative case, but generally only in the masculine, singular form. Most prepositions appear only in their standard form, not as they sometimes occur as prefixes in words. For verbs only the present active infinitive and perfect passive participles are given. Additional information can sometimes be found in the lesson, indicated in parentheses, where the word is initially presented for study.

apis "bee" (15)
appendix, appendicis "hanging
   on to" (14)
aqua "water" (11)
aquila "eagle" (11)
arbor "tree" (14)
arēna "sand" (11)
argentum "silver" (13)
argumentum "proof," "subject"
ars, artis "craft," "skill" (14)
asinus "donkey" "ass"
asper, aspera,asperum "rough"
astrum "star"
ater, atra, atrum "black" (17)
ātrium "central room or hall in
   a Roman house" (13)
audax, audācis "daring," "bold"
auditor, audītōris "listener"
audīre, audītus "to hear" (19)
aureus "golden"
auriculāris "pert. to the ear"
auris "ear"
aurum "gold" (13)
austrālis "southern" (11)
auxilium "help," "aid"
avis "bird" (15)

B
bacca "berry" (11)
baccalaureus "bachelor"
bacillus "small staff" (12)
bactērium "staff" (13)
baculum "staff"
beātus "happy"
bellum "war" (13)
bene "well" (18)
bibere "to drink"
biennium "two-year period" (13)
bīs "twice" (17)

bonus "good" (16)
boreālis "northern" (11)
bōs, bōvis "ox" (15)
brevis "short" (16)
bronchus "bronchial tube" (12)

C
cactus "prickly plant" (12)
cadere, cāsus (-cidere) "to fall"
   (19)
caecum "blind" (13)
caedere, caesus (-cīdere,
   -cīsus) "to cut," "to kill"
caeruleus "dark blue"
calamitas "disaster"
calcāneum "heel" (13)
calculus "little stone" (12)
callōsus "hardened," "callous"
calx, calcis "stone" (15)
camera "room" (11)
cancer, cancrī "crab"
candidus "white"
canis "dog" (15)
caper, caprī "goat"
capere, captus (-cipere,
   -ceptus) "to take, to seize" (19)
capillus "hair"
capitulum "little head" (13)
caput, capitis "head" (15)
cāritas, cāritātis "love"
caro, carnis "flesh" (15)
cārus "dear"
castus "pure" (16)
cāsus "opportunity," "chance"
   (13)
causa "reason," "motive" (11)
cavēre, cautus "to beware"
cēdere, cessus "to go," "to yield"
   (19)

celer "swift" (13)
cella "store room" (11)
centum "hundred" (14)
cerēbellum "little brain" (13)
cerēbrum "brain" (13)
cernere, crētus "to separate"
certus "sure" (16)
cervix, cervīcis "neck" (14)
cēteri, cēterae, cētera "other"
charta "charter," "paper"
cibōrium "drinking cup" (13)
cicāda "cricket" (11)
cicātrix, cicātrīcis "scar" (14)
cilium "eye-lid" (13)
cinerārium "place for ashes"
  (13)
cinis, cineris "ashes"
circum "around," "about" (18)
circus "ring" (12)
cirrus "curl" (12)
cisterna "subterranean
  reservoir" (11)
citāre, citātus "to cite" (12)
civis "citizen" (14)
classicus "significant" (12)
claudere, clausus, (-clūdere,
  -clūsus) "to shut" (19)
clāvis "key"
clīnāre, clīnātus "to lean" (19)
coccus "berry" (12)
cōdex, cōdicis "ancient book" (15)
colōnia "farm," "estate"
colossus "large statue" (12)
coma "hair of the head" (11)
compos, compotis "in
  possession of"
consortium "fellowship" (13)
constringere, constrictus
  "to draw together"
continuum "uninterrupted" (13)

contrā "against" (18)
cōpia "abundance" (11)
cor, cordis "heart" (15)
corium "hide," "skin" (13)
cornū "horn" (15)
corolla "little crown" (11)
corōna "crown" (11)
corpus, corporis "body" (15)
cortex, corticis "bark" (14)
crēdere, crēditus "to believe"
  (19)
crīmen, crīminis "accusation,"
  "fault" (14)
crocus "saffron" (12)
crux, crucis "cross" (14)
cubiculum "bedroom"
cubīle "bed"
culīna "kitchen" (11)
culpa "fault," "blame" (11)
cum "with" (18)
cumulus "heap," "mass" (12)
cuneus "wedge" (12)
cūra "care" (11)
cūrāre, cūrātus "to care for"
currere, cursus "to run" (19)
curriculum "little course" (13)
cutis "skin" (15)

D

damnāre, damnātus (-demnere)
  to declare guilty" (19)
damnum "loss," "injury"
dare, datus (-dere, -ditus) "to
  give" (19)
datum "something given" (13)
dē "down," "off," "about" (18)
decimus "tenth" (17)
dēlicātus "soft," "delightful"
dēlictum "crime"
dens, dentis "tooth"

desiderātum "something desired" (13)
deus "god" (12)
dexter "right" (16)
dīcere, dictus "to say," "to tell" (19)
diēs "day" (15)
digitus "finger" (12)
dignus "worthy" (16)
dis- "apart" (18)
discus "flattened disk" (12)
docēre, doctus "to teach" (19)
doctor "teacher"
dominus "lord," "master"
domus "house" (15)
dōnum "gift," "present"
dormīre, dormītus "to sleep"
dorsum "back" (13)
dūcere, ductus "to lead" (19)
dulcis "sweet" (16)
dum "while," "as long as"
duo "two" (17)
duodēnum "length of twelve" (12 fingers' breadth) (13)
dūrus "hard"
dux, ducis "leader" (15)

E

elephās, elephantis "elephant"
equus "horse" (12)
errāre, errātus "to stray"
errātum "fault," "error" (13)
est "(he, she, or it) is"
ex (ē) "out of," "from" (18)
exemplum "sample," "copy" (13)
exterior "outer" (17)
extrā "outside," "beyond" (18)
extrēmus "outermost" (17)

F

facere, factus (-ficere, fectus) "to do," "to make" (19)
faciēs "face," "surface" (15)
facilis "easy"
fāma "reputation" (11)
familia "family"
fārī, fātus "to speak" (19)
fatuus "foolish"
fēbris "fever"
fēcundus "fruitful"
fēlix, fēlicis "happy"
fēmina "woman" (11)
ferre, lātus "to bear," "to carry" (19)
ferrum "iron" (13)
fiat "let there be made"
fidēlis "faithful," "true"
fidēs "trust," "faith" (15)
fierī, factus "to become," "to be made" (19)
fīlia "daughter" (11)
fīlius "son" (12)
fīlum "thread" (13)
findere, fissus "to split" (19)
fīnis "end" (14)
firmus "strong"
fiscus "purse," "treasury" (12)
flāvus "yellow" (17)
flectere, flexus "to bend" (19)
flōrēre "to flower," "to flourish"
flōs, flōris "flower" (15)
fluere, fluxus "to flow" (19)
focus "hearth" (12)
foetidus "foul-smelling"
folium "leaf" (13)
forāmen, forāminis "opening" (14)
forma "shape," "figure" (11)

formula "pattern," "scheme"
(11)
fortis "strong," "brave" (16)
fortūna "fate" (11)
forum "market-place,"
"meeting-place" (13)
fragilis "easily broken"
francus "Frankish," "French"
(11)
frangere, fractus (-fringere)
"to break" (19)
frāter, frātris "brother" (14)
frīgus, frīgoris "coldness"
fugere, fugitūrus "to flee" (19)
fulvus "tawny"
fūmus "smoke" (12)
fundere, fūsus "to pour" (19)
fungus "mushroom" (12)
furor, furoris "madness"
fuscus "dark brown"

G
galbinus "(greenish) yellow"
gaudēre "to rejoice"
gelāre, gelātus "to freeze"
gemma "bud," "gem"
genius "guardian spirit" (12)
gens, gentis "clan," "tribe" (15)
genū "knee" (15)
genus, generis "race," "class"
"birth" (14)
gerere, gestus "to bear," "to
bring" (19)
gignere, genitus "to bring forth"
(19)
gladius "sword" (12)
glōria "renown" (11)
glūteus "buttock"
gradī, gressus (-gredī) "to step"
"to move" (19)

gradus "step," "degree" (15)
grānum "seed" (13)
grātia "favor"
grātus "pleasing" (16)
gravis "heavy," "serious" (16)
grex, gregis "flock," "herd" (15)
gubernāre "to govern"
gutta "to drop"

H
habēre, habitus (-hibēre,
-hibitus) "to have" "to hold" (19)
haerere, haesus "to stick" (19)
hālāre, hālātus "to breathe"
helix, helicis "spiral" (14)
herba "plant," "grass" (11)
hic, haec, hoc "this"
hircus "goat"
homō, hominis "human being,"
"man" (14)
hōra "hour"
hortus "garden"
humerus "shoulder" (12)
hūmānus "human"

I
ignis "fire" (14)
ilium "flank"
imperium "power," "rule" (13)
in "in," "into," "on" (18)
in- "in," "on," "not" (18)
incendere, incensus "to burn"
(19)
incognitus "unknown" (11)
incūnābulum "beginning,"
"cradle" (13)
index, indicis "forefinger" (15)
inferior "lower" (17)
infīnitus "infinite"
infrā "below" (18)

insignis "remarkable"
īnsula "island" (11)
inter "between," "among" (18)
interim "meanwhile" (18)
interior "inner" (17)
intimus "inmost" (17)
intrā "within" (18)
ipse, ipsa, ipsum "himself, ..."
īre, itum (-ient) "to go" (19)
īris, iridis "rainbow"

J

jacere, jactus (-jectus) "to
   throw" (19)
jocundus "cheerful"
jūdex, jūdicis "judge" (14)
jūglans, jūglandis "walnut"
jugum "yoke"
jūrāre, jūrātus "to swear" (19)
jūs, jūris "right," "law" (15)
jūnior "younger" (17)
justitia "justice"
juvenis "young" (17)

L

lābī, lapsus "to slip" (19)
labium "lip" (13)
labor "work"
lapsus "slip" (11)
lac, lactis "milk" (15)
lacrima "tear"
lacūna "hole," "gap" (11)
lāmella "small, thin plate" (11)
lāmina "thin plate," "covering"
   (11)
larva "specter," "mask" (11)
latex, laticis "fluid" (14)
lātus "wide"
latus, lateris "side," "flank"

laus, laudis "praise" (15)
legare, legatus "to send"
legere, lectus (-ligere) "to read,"
   "to choose" (19)
legiō, legiōnis "legion"
leō, leōnis "lion"
levis "light" (16)
lēx, lēgis "law" (14)
liber, librī "book" (12)
licēre, licitum "to be permitted"
lignum "wood" (13)
līmen, līminis "threshold,"
   "door"
linere, litus "to smear"
lingua "tongue," "language"
   (11)
līs, lītis "legal suit"
lit(t)era "letter" (11)
literātim "letter for letter" (11)
līvidus "blue"
locus "place" (12)
loquī, locūtus "to speak" (19)
lōrīca "breastplate" (11)
lucrum "gain," "profit" (13)
luctārī "to struggle"
lūdere, lūsus "to play" (19)
lūmen, lūminis "light" (15)
lūna "moon" (11)
lūridus "pale yellow"
lūteus "yellowish"
lūx, lūcis "light" (14)

M

māchina "machine" (12)
macula "stain," "blotch" (11)
magister, magistri "teacher"
   (12)
magnus "large," "great" (16)
mājestas, mājestātis "dignity"

major "greater" (17)
male "badly" (18)
malleus "hammer" (12)
malus "bad" (16)
manus "hand" (15)
mare, maris "sea" (14)
māter, mātris "mother" (14)
mātrix, mātricis "womb" (14)
maximus "greatest" (17)
medicus "physician" (12)
medius "middle" (16)
melior "better"
memorandum "that to be mentioned" (13)
memorāre, memorātus "to mention"
mēns, mentis "mind" (14)
mercēs, mercēdis "pay"
mergere, mersus "to plunge" (19)
meus, mea, meum "my"
mīles, mīlitis "soldier"
mille "thousand" (17)
mina "ancient coin" (11)
minimus "smallest" (17)
minor "smaller" (17)
miscēre, mixtus "to blend," "to mingle" (20)
miser "wretched" (16)
mittere, missus "to send" (20)
mōbilis "mobile," "movable"
modulus "small measure" (12)
modus "measure," "method" (12)
mollis "soft" (16)
mōmentum "period of time" (13)
monēre, monitus "to warn" (20)
mora "delay"
moratōrium "period of delay" (13)

morbus "disease" (12)
mors, mortis "death" (14)
mos, moris "custom," "habit" (15)
movēre, mōtus "to move" (20)
multus "much," "many" (16)
mundus "world," "universe"
mūrex, mūricis "shell-fish"

N

naevus "mole" (12)
nascī, nātus "to be born" (20)
nātivitas, nātivitātis "birth"
nauta "sailor" (11)
nāvis "ship"
nē "that...not"
nebula "mist," "cloud" (11)
nec ... nec "neither ... nor"
nervus "cord," "sinew" (12)
nexus "binding" (12)
niger, nigra, nigrum "black"
nimbus "storm," "cloud" (12)
nōmen, nōminis "name" (14)
nōn "not"
nōnus "ninth" (17)
noster, nostra, nostrum "our"
novem "nine" (17)
novus "new" (16)
nox, noctis "night" (14)
noxa "harm"
nucleus "kernel of nut" (12)
nūllus "no," "none" (16)
nunc "now" (18)
numerus "number" (12)
nūntium "message" (13)

O

ob "in the way," "toward," "on account of" (18)
obiter "in passing"

obscūrus "dark" (11)
occidere, occasus "to fall,"
   "to set"
ocellus "little eye" (12)
octāvus "eighth" (17)
octō "eight" (17)
oculus "eye" (12)
odium "hatred" (13)
officium "duty," "service" (13)
oleum "oil"
ōmentum "entrails" (13)
omnis "every," "all" (16)
onus, oneris "burden," "load"
   (15)
operārī, operātus "to work"
optimus "best" (17)
opus, operis "work," "labor" (14)
ōrdō, ōrdinis "order," "series"
   (14)
orīrī, ortus "to rise"
ōs, ōris "mouth" (15)
os, ossis "bone" (15)
ōtium "leisure" (13)
ovis "sheep"
ōvum "egg" (13)

P
paene "almost" (18)
paenitēre "to be sorry"
pandere, pansus "to stretch"
pār "equal" (16)
parēns, parentis "parent" (12)
parere, partum "to give birth"
   (20)
parvus "small" (17)
pater, patris "father" (14)
patī, passus "to suffer," "to
   endure" (20)
patina "shallow dish" (11)

pātria "fatherland" (11)
paucī, paucae, pauca "few"
pāx, pācis "peace" (14)
peccāre, peccātum "to sin"
pectorālis "pert. to the chest"
pectus, pectoris "breast(-bone)"
   (15)
pecūnia "money" (11)
pejor "worse" (17)
pendere, pensus "to hang," "to
   weigh" (20)
penna "feather," "wing" (11)
per "through," "by" (18)
per- "through," "to the bad" (18)
persōna "character," "mask"
   (11)
pēs, pedis "foot" (15)
pessimus "worst" (17)
petere, petītus "to seek" (20)
pharynx, pharyngis "throat"
piscis "fish" (15)
pius "tender," "pious"
plaudere, plausus "to clap
   hands"
plēnus "full" (16)
plicāre, plicātus (-plicitus) "to
   fold" (20)
plumbum "lead" (13)
plūs, plūris "more" (17)
poena "punishment" (11)
poēta "poet"
poēticus "poetic"
pōnere, positus "to put," "to
   place" (20)
pontifex, pontificis "priest" (15)
populus "people" (12)
porcus "pig"
portāre, portātus "to carry" (20)
possum, posse "can," "be able"

post "after" (18)
posterior "further behind" (17)
pōtio, pōtiōnis "drink"
prae "before," "in front" (18)
prehendere, prehensus "to
  seize"
premere, pressus "to press" (20)
pretium "value," "worth" (13)
primus "first" (17)
prō "forward," "for" (18)
pūbes, pūbis "body hair" (15)
publicus "public"
pudendum "that to be ashamed
  of" (13)
pudēre, puditum "to be
  ashamed"
pugna "fight" (11)
pulpitum "platform"
pungere, punctus "to prick"
purgāre, purgātus "to purify"
purpureus "purple"
putāre, putātus "to think" (20)
pyxidium "little box" (13)
pyxis, pyxidis "box" (15)

Q

quaerere, quaesītus (-quīrere
  -quīsītus) "to seek" (20)
quālis "what kind"
quantus "how much," "how
  many" (13)
quartus "fourth" (17)
quater "four times" (17)
quattuor "four" (17)
quercus "oak"
quī, quae, quod "who," "which"
quiētus "quiet"
quīnque "five" (17)
quīntus "fifth" (17)
quis, quid "who," "what"

quō "where"

R

racēmus "bunch of grapes,"
  "cluster" (12)
radius "ray," "staff" (12)
rādix, rādicis "root" (15)
rāmōsus "branchy"
rāmus "branch" (12)
rapere, raptus (-reptus) "to
  snatch" (20)
rārus "rare"
rāsus "smoothed," "blank" (11)
re- "back," "again" (18)
rectus "straight," "right" (16)
rēgius "royal" (11)
remedium "remedy"
rēs, reī "thing," "matter" (15)
rēte, rētis "net" (15)
retrō "backward" (18)
reus "accused," "guilty"
rēx, rēgis "king" (14)
rhomboideus "similar to a
  rhombus"
rhombus "parallelogram"(12)
rhonchus "snoring" (12)
rigor "stiffness"
rīpa "river bank"
rōdere "to gnaw"
rostrum "ship's beak,"
  "speaker's platform" (13)
ruber, rubra "red" (17)
rufus "red," "ruddy"
rūga "wrinkle" (11)
rūmen, rūminis "gullet,"
  "throat" (14)
rumpere, ruptus "to break (20)

S

sacer, sacra "sacred" (16)

saec(u)lum "age," "world" (13)
saeptum "fence," "wall" (13)
sāl, salis "salt" (14)
salūs, salūtis "health," "welfare"
sanctus "holy" (16)
sanguis, sanguinis "blood" (15)
sānus "healthy," "sound" (16)
sapiēns, sapientis "wise"
satis (sat) "enough" (18)
scalprum "knife," "chisel"
scandere, scansum (-scendere,
  -scensum) "to climb" (20)
scapula "shoulder blade" (11)
scīre, scītum "to know"
scrībere, scriptus "to write" (20)
sē "himself," "herself," "itself"
sē- "apart," "without" (18)
secāre, sectum "to cut" (20)
secundus "second" (17)
sedēre, sessus "to sit" (20)
semel "once" (17)
sēmen, sēminis "seed" (14)
sēmi "half" (17)
semper "always" (18)
senior "older" (17)
senex (senis) "old" (16)
septem "seven" (17)
septimus "seventh" (17)
sequī, secūtus "to follow" (20)
serpere "to creep"
serrātus "toothed like a saw"
serum "fluid" (13)
sesqui "one and one half" (17)
sex "six" (17)
sextus "sixth" (17)
sīdus, sīderis "star"
sigillum "seal," "stamp" (12)
similis "like" (16)

simplicitas, simplicitātis
  "simplicity"
sinister, sinistra "left" (16)
situs "place"
socius "companion," "ally" (12)
sōl, sōlis "sun" (14)
solidus "dense," (12)
solum "ground," "soil" (13)
sōlus "alone," "single" (16)
solvere, solūtus "to loosen," "to
  destroy" (20)
somnus "sleep" (12)
soror, sorōris "sister" (14)
sopor "deep sleep"
spatium "distance" (13)
spectāre, spectātus "to look at"
spectrum "image" (13)
speculum "mirror" (13)
spērāre, spērātus "to hope for"
spīrāre, spīrātus " to breathe"
  (20)
stāre, status "to stand" (20)
statuere, statūtus "to put,"
stēlla "star" (11)
stimulus "whip," "goad" (12)
strātum "covering" (13)
strātus "spread out" (12)
sub "under" (18)
sūmere, sūmptus "to take" (20)
super "above," "over" (18)
superior "higher" (17)
suprā "above" (18)
suprēmus "highest" (17)
suus, sua, suum "one's own"

T
tabula "table," "list" (11)
tāliō, tāliōnis "retaliation"

tangere, tāctus (-tingere) "to touch" (20)

taurus "bull" (12)

tēcum (cum tē) "with you"

tempestās, tempestātis "storm"

tempus, temporis "time" (14)

tendere, tentus (tensus) "to stretch" (20)

tenēre, tentus (-tinēre) "to hold" (20)

tenuis "thin" (16)

ter "three times" (17)

terere, trītum "to rub (off)"

teres "rounded"

tergum "back" (13)

terminus "boundary," "end" (12)

terra "earth," "land" (11)

tertius "third" (17)

testis "witness" (15)

thallus "green sprout" (12)

theca "case," "cover" (11)

thyrsus "stalk of a plant" (12)

tibia "shin-bone," "flute" (11)

toga "outer gown"

tolerāre, tolerātus "endure"

tōnsor, tōnsōris "barber"

torquēre, tortus "to twist"

trahere, tractus "to drag," "to draw" (20)

tranquilitas, tranquilitatis "calmness"

trāns "through," "across" (18)

trapezium "little table" (13)

trēs, tria "three" (17)

trūdere, trūsus "to push," "to thrust" (20)

tunc "then" (18)

turba "crowd," "uproar"

U

ulterior "farther" (17)

ultimus "farthest" (17)

ultrā "beyond" (18)

umbra "shade" (11)

unda "wave" (11)

urbs, urbis "city" (14)

ursus "bear"

uterus "womb"

uxor "wife"

V

vacca "cow"

vacuum "empty (thing)" (13)

vādere, vāsum "to go"

valēre, valitum "to be strong," "to be well" (20)

vēlāmen, vēlāminis "covering" (15)

venīre, ventum "to come" (20)

venter, ventris "belly"

vēnum (acc.) "sale"

venus, veneris "love," "beauty"

ver, veris "spring" (season)

verbātim "word for word" (11)

verbum "word" (13)

vēritas, vēritātis "truth"

vertebra "joint" (11)

vertere, versus "to turn" (20)

vertex, verticis "whirlpool," "summit" (14)

vērus "true" (16)

vestis "garment" (15)

vetāre "to forbid"

via "way," "road" (11)

vidēre, vīsus "to see" (20)

vindex, vindicis "claimant"

vincere, victus "to conquer" (20)

vīnum "wine" (13)

vīpera "snake"

vir, virī "man" (12)

virgo, virginis "maiden"

viridis "green" (17)

virīlis "manly" (12)

vīs (pl. vīrēs) "force," "power"

vīta "life" (11)

vitium "flaw," "defect" (13)

vīvus "living" (16)

voluptās, voluptātis "pleasure"

volvere, volūtus "to roll" (20)

vorāre, vorātus "to eat" (20)

vortex, vorticis cf. vertex

vōx, vōcis "voice" (14)

vulpes "fox"

Part III

Derivatives in Selected Fields
(Including Latin Phrases,
Expressions and Abbreviations)[1]

Chapter Twenty-One
Literature and the Arts

In Chapter One on the Greek alphabet it was pointed out that the ancient Greeks were not the first people to express their ideas in written form. Nevertheless, although other people wrote before them, it was not until around 750 B.C., with the advent of Homer's *Iliad* and *Odyssey,* that we can really say that secular literature, as we know it, truly began to develop. From this point in time the Greeks steadily moved forward in sophistication not only with an increasing number of writing styles (*genres*) but also with an ever-increasing complexity of expression within the various styles. In the centuries that followed, the Romans and all other western people imitated the awesome achievements of the Greeks in both these areas. Consequently, the names of nearly all literary genres are of Greek (or Latin) origin. Such is also the case with most rhetorical and poetic devices. Even the simple labels we employ when talking about the fundamentals of grammar are Greek or Latin.

Some of the more interesting Greek and Latin terms or names are given in their original forms in the vocabulary list that follows. Others you may

---

[1] The purpose of the first two parts of this text was to meet the linguistic and general vocabulary needs of students majoring in a great variety of subjects. In part three the focus shifts to the more detailed vocabulary of selected fields. Since it is not expected for students majoring in one field to become steeped in the vocabulary of another, it is recommended that from this point on they be assigned to complete only those remaining chapters which satisfy or meet their individual academic interests.

173

have to find in your English dictionary. Although their contemporary meanings have sometimes changed greatly over a period of centuries, it will still be helpful to examine the original terms before studying the specialized lists.

Vocabulary

Greek	**Meaning**
ἀν ἀκολουθός	not, following
ἀναπαιστός	struck back (reverse of dactyl)
ἀπὸ σιωπή	away from, silence
βουκόλος	cowherd
διδάσκειν	to teach
δρᾶν	to do; to act
ἔλλειψις	omission
ἐπιστολή	letter
Θέσπις	Thespis (first Gk. actor)
Λακωνισμός	imitating Lacedemonians
ὀρχήστρα	place for dancing
πανηγυρικός	public, festive assembly
πλεονασμός	more than enough
ῥαψωδία	recitation of epic poem
τραγωδία	goat song
Φιλιππικός	having to do with Philip

Latin	**Meaning**
forensis fr. forum	pert. to the public speaking place
histrio, -ōnis	actor
pastōrālis fr. pastor	pert. to a shepherd
praefātio	a saying beforehand

Examine the following lists of words arranged by category and, when necessary, consult your English dictionary to note not only the etymology of each word but also the distinctions in definition which separate the terms from one another within the same list. When you are confident that you know them well, complete the exercise for each group at the end of this chapter.

I. Genres and Related Terms

amatory (erotic)	*encyclopedia*
biography	*epic*
bucolic	*epigram*
comedy	*epistolary*
didactic	*epitome*
drama	*epode*
elegy	*fable*
encomium	*fiction*
history	*poetry*
lyric	*prose*
novel	*romance*
ode	*satire*
oration	*tragedy*
panegyric	

II. Grammar and Related Terms

active	*mood*
adjective	*noun*
adverb	*number*
antecedent	*object*
appositive	*paragraph*
article	*parsing*
capitalization	*passive*
case	*participle*
clause	*perfect*
comparative	*person*
composition	*plural*
conjugation	*possessive*
conjunction	*predicate*
coordinate	*preposition*
declarative	*pronoun*
declension	*sentence*
exclamatory	*singular*
gender	*subject*
imperative	*subjunctive*
imperfect	*subordinate*
indicative	*syntax*

infinitive   *tense*
interjection   *transitive*
interrogative   *verb*
intransitive   *voice*

III. Terms in Metrics

anapestic   *iambic*
dactylic   *spondee*
elegiac   *trochaic*
hendecasyllabic   *tetrameter*
dimeter   *pentameter*
trimeter   *hexameter*

IV. Rhetorical and Poetic Terms

alliteration   *litotes*
anacoluthon   *metaphor*
anaphora   *metonymy*
anastrophe   *onomatopoiesis*
antithesis   *oxymoron*
aposiopesis   *personification*
apostrophe   *pleonasm*
asyndeton   *polysyndeton*
ellipsis   *preterition*
euphemism   *prolepsis*
euphony   *simile*
hendiadys   *synecdoche*
hyperbole   *synesis*
hysteron proteron   *transferred epithet*
irony   *zeugma*
laconism

V. Additional Terms Related to
Literature, Drama and Public Speaking

antistrophe   *monologue*
declamation   *orchestra*
dialogue   *paleography*
elocution   *parody*

epigraphy	*pastoral*
epilogue	*philippic*
episode	*philology*
epithet	*preface*
eulogy	*prolegomenon*
forensic	*prologue*
hapax legomenon	*rhapsody*
histrionic	*strophe*
invective	*thespian*
lacuna	*transcript*
lexicography	*translation*
linguistics	*trilogy*

VI. Latin Phrases

Over the centuries many Latin phrases dealing with various aspects of literature and the arts have become an integral part of our language. Especially prominent in this category are phrases related to early printing. Also included are some terms in the arts which are more of a directional or instructional nature for drama and music or are formulae for authorship in the field of art. The following are the most significant.

Latin Phrase	Meaning	Notes
addenda (et corrigenda)	things to be added (and corrected)	*additions and corrections*
apparātus criticus	critical material	*variant text readings*
ars poētica	art of poetry	*Horace's treatise on writing poetry*
ēditio princeps	first printed edition	*after A.D. 1450*
et aliī	and others	*other authors*
ex librīs	from the library	*on bookplates with the owner's name affixed*
fiat	let it be done	
foliō versō	the back side of a page	
furor loquendī	frenzy for speaking	

furor poēticus	poetic frenzy	
furor scrībendī	frenzy for writing	
imprimātur	let it be printed	*license or sanction to publish a book*
in mediās rēs	into the midst of things	*beginning a work with a later event*
in memoriam	to the memory (of)	*with the name added; dedications / epitaphs*
inter alia	among other things	
lapsus calamī	slip of the pen	
lapsus linguae	slip of the tongue	
lapsus memoriae	slip of the memory	
lībra (lb.)	pound (weight)	*scales; a balance*
locus classicus	classic reference	*passage that clarifies a word's meaning*
Magna Charta	great charter	*constitutional guarantees of 1215 in Eng.*
magnum opus	great work	*one's best literary or artistic work*
multum in parvō	much in a little	
obiter dictum	something said in passing	*non-binding or incidental remark*
per capita	by heads	
per centum (percent)	by the hundred	
prō formā	for the sake of form	*for the record*
prō ratā (parte)	in proportion to liability	
suō locō	in its own place	
tabula rasa	clean slate (tablet)	*unprejudiced mind*

terra firma	solid ground	
ultimātum	last or final offer	
verbātim (ac litterātim)	word for word (and letter for letter)	
vice versā	with the order reversed	

Terms or Phrases in Art, Drama or Music

ad libitum (ad lib)	at pleasure	*sung or played according to one's feeling*
bis	twice	
ter	three times	
fēcit	he (she) made it	*with maker's name*
pinxit	he (she) painted it	*with painter's name*
sculpsit	he (she) sculpted it	*with sculptor's name*
facsimile	reproduction ("make similar")	
terracotta	baked earth	
deus ex machinā	god from the machine	*one who appears late in a play and resolves problems*
dramātis persōnae	characters of a play	
exit	he (she) goes out	
exeunt omnēs	all depart	
secundum artem	according to art	
solus	alone	
tacē, tacet	be silent; it is silent	

Exercise

Matching. Show that you know the terms in the various categories above by matching them with the definitions or etymologies below.

I. *Genres and related terms.*

    1. writing in a format of letters or correspondence
    2. polished, terse poem or saying
    3. writing about the "life" of a person
    4. long lyric verses originally sung after ("upon") short ones
    5. a "pastoral" poem
    6. a song of mourning
    7. writing created or "made" for a theme, meter, and mood
    8. poem often sung with "stringed" accompaniment
    9. an imagined or feigned tale
10. humorous type of drama
11. a compilation of many subjects
12. writing intended to "teach"
13. "cutting upon" a comprehensive work, taking its best parts
14. "love" poetry
15. long narrative poem about a hero
16. a "medley" of writings scorning human vices and follies
17. "straightforward" writing
18. a work intended to depict life by "doing" or "acting"
19. an enthusiastic expression of praise for someone
20. a legend or story with speaking animals
21. a "small, new" writing about unreal people and events
22. a writing about imaginary people remote in time and place
23. an eulogy before "all the assembly"
24. a poem usually sung in exalted style
25. an account about past human events, intended to be true
26. formal dignified speech, usually written
27. serious drama for which originally a "goat" was the prize

II. *Grammar and Related Terms* (not all employed)

    1. the "command" mood
    2. the subject shown as "suffering," *i.e.*, receiving the action
    3. a word which "goes before"
    4. the subject shown as "doing" the action
    5. a clause that "ranks together" equally with another
    6. a clause that "ranks under" another
    7. words, phrases, and clauses properly "arranged together"

8. that which is "proclaimed about the subject
9. an identifying noun "put near" another noun
10. a qualifying word usually placed "near the verb"
11. the mood that often shows contingency or possibility
12. verb designation indicating "time"
13. verb designation indicating a "completed" past act
14. showing the "parts of speech" of words in a sentence
15. the sentence type that "asks a question"
16. the verb mood that "points out" a fact
17. verb type that possesses, or "goes across" to, a direct object
18. part of speech that "joins together" two or more words
19. "put before" an object, it should never end a sentence
20. sentence type that shouts out loudly

III. *Terms in Metrics* (not all employed)

1. a verse with eleven syllables
2. a metrical foot with a long (accented) syllable followed by two short (unaccented) ones
3. a metrical foot with two short (unaccented) syllables followed by a long (accented) one
4. a metrical foot with two long (accented) syllables
5. a metrical foot with a long (accented) syllable followed by a short unaccented one
6. a metrical foot with a short (unaccented) syllable followed by a long accented one

IV. *Rhetorical and Poetic Terms* (not all employed)

1. repetition (or "bringing back") of the same word or phrase at the beginning of clauses
2. leaving of an idea only partially expressed by a sudden "silence"
3. exaggeration ("excessive throwing") to highlight a point
4. repetition of the same "letter" at the beginning of words or syllables
5. the parallel arrangement of ideas syntactically "placed opposite" each other to show contrast
6. conciseness or terseness in speech

7. the "leaving out" of a word that syntactically belongs but in any case is easily understood from the context
8. the sudden "turning away" in a passage to address an absent person or thing
9. the substitution of a word that "speaks well" for one that may be offensive
10. a syntactical shift where one construction does "not follow" properly an initial construction
11. the omission of conjunctions in (or the "non-binding together" of) words or phrases in a series
12. the expression of "one" idea "through two" nouns joined by a conjunction
13. "dissembling" or incongruent speech, often meaning the opposite of that spoken
14. the inversion (or "turning back") of the usual order of words
15. understatement in which an idea is affirmed by the use of the negative of the opposite
16. the use of one word for another in which the meaning by analogy "carries beyond" the literal meaning
17. the substitution of one word for another or the "change of name" with which it is associated
18. the "making of a word" (or use of one) whose sound suggests the meaning
19. the combination of words whose meanings are contradictory or incongruous
20. words so arranged as to "sound well"
21. the giving of human or "personal" qualities to inanimate things
22. the use of "more" words than necessary to convey an idea
23. the use of "many" conjunctions that "bind together" words in a series
24. the intentional mentioning of past events while claiming to "pass over" them
25. the use of part for the whole or the reverse

V. *Additional Terms Related to Literature, Drama and Public Speaking* (not all employed)

1. the study of ancient inscriptions
2. having to do with theatrical performances

3. a missing part or gap in a text
4. insulting, abusive language
5. the countermovement/song of the chorus in Greek drama
6. the exercise of reciting rhetorically
7. the editing of a dictionary
8. the conversation between two or more actors in a play
9. the study of human speech and language
10. a word occurring or "spoken once" in early literature
11. the concluding part of a play or book
12. a speech of praise
13. the art of effective public speaking
14. a descriptive word or phrase of a person or thing
15. the discourse or debate on public issues, as was commonly held in ancient Rome
16. the study of ancient manuscripts or writing
17. the introduction to a Greek play
18. the presentation of a single theme in "three" separate parts
19. literature about shepherds and rural life
20. the recitation of selections from epic poetry
21. circular space where the chorus in Greek drama sang and danced
22. the rendering of one language in another
23. the comic imitation of the style of one's work
24. an official (usually certified) copy of a record
25. an introduction to a work

Chapter Twenty-Two
Abbreviations in Formal Writing

Several Latin abbreviations and expressions continue to be employed in the formal writing of English. Some appear merely as terms for citing notes of reference while others occur parenthetically in the body of a text. In nearly all cases they can be found in scholarly articles of professional or scientific journals or those with a recognized international readership. In some cases young students still have occasion to use them when writing formal term papers. The most common ones to appear in all these settings are listed below. Although no special vocabulary is provided in this chapter, you should make an effort to memorize the abbreviations as well as the complete phrases and their meanings.

Latin Phrase	Abbreviation	Meaning
ad locum	ad loc.	at or to the place
circā	ca.	approximately, around
confer	cf.	compare
et alii (et alia)	et al.	and other persons (things)
et cētera	etc.	and other things; and so forth
et sequēn s	et seq.	and the following (sg.)
et sequentes	et seqq.	and the following (pl.)
exemplī gratiā	e.g.	for example
flōruit	fl.	he (she) flourished
ibīdem	ibid.	in the same place
id est	i.e.	that is
īdem	id.	the same
infrā (vidē infrā)		(see) below
locō citātō	loc. cit.	in the place cited
notā bene	n.b.	mark well

Latin Phrase	Abbreviation	Meaning
opere citātō	op. cit.	in the work cited
passim		everywhere (as in a chapter)
post scriptum	p.s.	written after
quod (quae) vidē	q.v.	which see (which things see)
scīlicet	sc.	namely
sīc		thus
suprā (vidē suprā)		(see) above
ut dictum	ut dict.	as directed
vidēlicet	viz.	that is to say; namely

When you have learned the meanings of these phrases and their uses, complete the exercise that follows.

Exercise

In the completely fictitious essay that follows replace the Latin terms or abbreviations in italics with their respective English equivalent.

Whither Now the Olympians?
by
I. M. Smart, R. U. Wise, *et Al.* *

In his recent article, "Old Arguments for Evolution," Mr. N. O. Detective[1] masterfully argues that the newly discovered *Vīta Lucretiī* (*Life of Lucretius*) by the biographer Cornelius Nepos (*c.** 99 - *c.** 25 B.C.) a contemporary of the great Roman poet-philosopher Lucretius (*fl.** 60 B.C.), contains a good deal of evidence that modern theories of evolution were actually pirated from this hitherto lost work from antiquity. To prove his

---

[1] N. O. Detective, "Old Arguments for Evolution," *Journal of Inquiring Minds,* 7.1 (Nov., 1984), p. 382.

point, Detective[2] quotes several lines thought to have been originally contained in Book Seven of the *De Rerum Natura* (*On the Nature of Things*) in which the origin of man is said to have developed from the chimpanzee, the gorilla, the peacock, *etc.** Several classical scholars, *i.e.,** Slow, Clever and Thorough[3], have taken issue with these findings. Angered by the admission of the chimp into the chain of development, they have claimed the entire *vita* to be a forgery. "The peacock, yes; the gorilla, maybe; but don't inspect (*sic**) us to buy that chimp bit,"[4] they protest. However, even if Lucretius' expressions about man's development are found to be authentic, they clearly were not original. The *Encyclopedia of Brilliant Ideas* identifies several predecessors of the Roman poet who offered additional thoughts on man's ties to the animal kingdom. In its treatment of human origins, it states:

> According to various writers in antiquity, man is thought to have evolved from several lower animal species. Democritus (*q.v.**) thought he was a monkey; Aristophanes (*q.v.**), a bird; and Socrates (*q.v.**), a gadfly.

Detective[5] believes the *vita* was discovered and translated a couple centuries ago by scholars who claimed the ideas as their own (*cf.** Darwin's *Origin of Species*) and who destroyed what they thought was the sole surviving copy of this text. If this is so, *i.e.,** if these arguments from antiquity were so purloined, we ask, by Zeus, what is one to believe about all those recent stories linking us so closely to that heavenly family of Olympians.

Translate and explain the context of the following Latin words and abbreviations used in the essay.

1. *et Al.*	7. *q.v.*
2. *c.*	8. *cf.*
3. *fl.*	9. *i.e.*
4. *etc.*	10. *ibid.*
5. *e.g.*	11. *passim*
6. *sic*	12. *op. cit.*

---

2 *Ibid.,** pp. 384-385.

3 J. Slow, R. Clever and N. Thorough, *Missing Links*, pp. 32, 36-37; ch. 4 "Not that Chimp Again" (*passim**).

4 *Ibid.,** p. 64.

5 Detective, *op. cit.,** p. 388.

Chapter Twenty-Three
Medicine and the Human Body

In *A.D.* 1542 a renowned anatomist by the name of Andreas Vesalius assembled the latest evidence of more than two thousand years of study on the subject of anatomy and published it in his famous treatise *Dē Humānī Corporis Fabricā.* In an *Epitomē* appended to his book he included a brief section delineating the proper names for the external parts of the body as they were known in *Greek.* Plate drawings of a nude male and female similar to those that appear on the next two pages accompanied his text with the appropriate vocabulary labels placed nearby.[1]

Vesalius followed a long list of physicians or scholars who published works on medical subjects, a list that goes back as far as the fifth century B.C. to Hippocrates who among other things wrote the famous *Hippocratic Oath.* Other writers on medical subjects in antiquity whose works survive to this day include a Latin encyclopedist named Celsus who lived in the early Roman Empire during the reign of Tiberius (*A.D.* 14-37). His work covered a wide range of medical topics and exerted a strong influence in the field during the Renaissance. Another famous writer was Galen (*c. A.D.* 129-199). Famous especially for anatomy and physiology, this physician also wrote about pharmacology and dietetics. All these writings were employed extensively in medical schools at the time that Vesalius wrote his masterpiece. From this long history it is not difficult to see why the disciplines of medicine and anthropology today still employ many Greek and Latin labels for body parts.

I. <u>Major Body Parts</u>

Study the Greek and Latin names on the next two pages with a view toward recognizing each proper body part in derivatives in the exercise section of this lesson.

---

[1] Since Vesalius wrote in *Latin*, it was not necessary for him to include a list of special labels in that language. However, modifications have been made to the plate drawings in this text to include a similar list of Latin terms.

Greek Word	*English Root*	*Meaning*
κεφαλή	**cephal-**	head
θρίξ, τριχός	**trich-**	hair
πρόσωπον	**prosop-**	face
μέτωπον	**metop-**	forehead
βλέφαρον	**blephar-**	eyelid
ὀφθαλμός	**ophthalm-**	eye
ῥίς, ῥινός	**rhin-**	nose
οὖς, ὠτός	**ot-**	ear
στόμα, στόματος	**stom(at)-**	mouth
γλῶσσα, γλῶττα	**gloss-; glott-**	tongue
ὀδούς, ὀδόντος	**odont-**	tooth
χεῖλος	**ch(e)il-**	lip
γένειον	**geni-**	chin
γνάθος	**gnath-**	jaw
τράχηλος	**trachel-**	neck
ὠμός	**om-**	shoulder
κλείς, κλειδός	**cl(e)id-**	clavicle
βραχίον	**brachi-**	arm
καρπός	**carp-**	wrist
χείρ	**ch(e)ir-**	hand
δάκτυλος	**dactyl-**	finger
ὄνυξ, ὄνυχος	**onych-**	nail
θώραξ, θώρακος	**thorax; thorac-**	thorax
στῆθος	**steth-**	chest
μαστός	**mast-**	breast
ὀμφαλός	**omphal-**	navel
νῶτον	**not-**	back
γλουτός	**glut-**	buttock
φαλλός	**phall-**	penis
πρωκτός	**proct-**	anus
γόνυ	**gon(y)-**	knee
κνήμη	**cnem-**	leg, shin
ταρσός	**tars-**	ankle
ὀστέον	**oste-**	bone
σάρξ, σαρκός	**sarc-**	flesh
φλέψ, φλεβός	**phleb-**	vein
νεῦρος	**neur-**	nerve
πλευρά	**pleur-**	side, rib
μῦς, μυός	**my-**	muscle
νεφρός	**nephr-**	kidney
ἧπαρ, ἥπατος	**hepat-**	liver
κύστις	**cyst-**	bladder, cyst
πνεύμων	**pneum(on)-**	lung
καρδία	**cardi-**	heart
ἐγκέφαλος	**encephal-**	brain

Τὸ Σῶμα Ἀνθρώπου

Latin Word	English Root	Meaning
caput, capitis	capit-	head
faciēs	faci-	face
frōns, frontis	front-	forehead
cilium	cili-	eyelid
oculus	ocul-	eye
nāsus	nas-	nose
auris	aur-	ear
bucca	bucc-	cheek
maxilla	maxill-	jaw
ōs, ōris	or-	mouth
lingua	lingu-	tongue
dēns, dentis	dent-	tooth
labium	labi-	lip
cervix, cervīcis	cervic-	neck
scapula	scapul-	shoulder blade
clāvicula	clavicul-	collar bone
humerus	humer-	upper arm
ulna	uln-	bone of forearm
radius	radi-	bone of forearm
manus	manu-	hand
digitus	digit-	finger
unguis	ungui-	nail
pectus, pectoris	pector-	chest
mamma	mamm-	breast
abdōmen, -minis	abdomin-	belly
venter, ventris	ventr-	belly
umbilīcus	umbilic-	navel
dorsum	dors-	back
lumbus	lumb-	loin
pudenda	pundend-	(female) genitals
crūs, crūris	crur-	leg
femur, femoris	femor-	thigh bone
genu	genu-	knee
patella	patell-	kneecap ("small pan")
tībia	tibi-	shin bone
fibula	fibul-	lower leg bone ("pin")
pēs, pedis	ped-	foot
os, ossis	oss-	bone
caro, carnis	carn-	flesh
cutis	cut-	skin
vēna	ven-	vein
nervus	nerv-	nerve, sinew
costa	cost-	rib
musculus	muscul-	muscle
rēn, rēnis	ren-	kidney
vesīca	vesic-	bladder
pulmō, pulmōnis	pulmon-	lung
cor, cordis	cord-	heart
cerēbrum	cerebr-	brain

Corpus Humānum

II. Latin Phrases

Often in professional journals the first citation of a specific medical condition or disease is officially identified with its Latin name. Sometimes it is merely placed in parentheses following its English name. In most instances the technical name appears as a two-word phrase. In the medical fields of anatomy and physiology, the muscles, nerves, arteries and veins all possess official Latin names consisting of two words by which they are universally known. The most common type of phrase is that of a noun followed by an adjective in agreement in gender and number, like the binomial nomenclature for most plants and animals. Note that the Latin words for "muscle" (*musculus*) and "nerve" (*nervus*) are masculine in gender, while those for "artery" (*artēria*) and "vein" (*vēna*) are feminine. Study the few examples below.[2]

Latin Phrase	English Meaning	Notes
acne vulgāris	common acne	*skin disease*
anorexia nervōsa	nervous loss of appetite	
arthrītis dēformāns	deforming arthritis	
corpus luteum	yellow body	*an ovarian follicle*
dēmentia praecox	precocious insanity	*schizophrenia*
dermatītis gangrenōsa	gangrenous skin inflammation	
diabētes mellītus	(honey-)sweet diabetes	
herpes simplex	simple creeping (disease)	
impetīgo contāgiōsa	contagious impetigo	*skin disease*
lupus vulgāris	common lupus	*skin disease*
maculae albidae	white spots	

---

2   Most of these phrases and numerous English terms derived from Greek and Latin words in the following sections can be found in any medical dictionary, such as *Taber's Cyclopedic Medical Dictionary*.

muscae volitantes	flitting flies	*spots in vision*
myasthenia gravis	serious muscle weakness	
partus caesareus	Cesarean birth	
pavor nocturnus	nocturnal anxiety	
substantia alba	white matter	
(musculus) flexor digitōrum	bender of the fingers	
(musculus) levātor labīi superiōris	raiser of the upper lip	
(musculus) glūteus maximus	largest buttock muscle	
(nervus) opticus	optic nerve	
(nervus) zygomaticus	zygomatic nerve	*near cheek bone*
(artēria) coronāria dextra	right coronary artery	
(artēria) genus media	middle artery of the knee	
(vēna) linguālis	tongue vein	
(vēnae) rēnālēs	kidney veins	

A less common type of Latin phrase is that of two nouns in which the second is in the genitive case and can usually be translated with the word "*of*." Consider these examples:

Latin Phrase	English Meaning
angīna pectoris	(suffocative) pain of the chest
asphyxia neonātōrum	suffocation of new-borns
encephalītis neonātōrum	brain inflammation of new-borns
pediculōsis capitis	louse infestation of the head
tinea barbae	(ring-)worm of the beard

III. Additional Medical Terms

Vocabulary The terms listed below, presented in Greek alphabetical order, do not appear in earlier chapters.

Greek	Translit./Root	Latin	Meaning
ἀδήν	aden-	glans, glandis	gland
ἀγγεῖον	angi-	vas	vessel
ἄρθρον	arthr-	artus	joint
δάκρυ	dacry-	lacrima	tear
ἔντερον	enter-	intestīnum	intestine
ἱστίον	hist-		tissue ("web")
κρανίον	crani-	crānium	skull
κύτος	cyt-	cella	cell ("vessel")
λίπος	lip-	adeps, adipis	fat
μῆνιγξ, μήνιγγος	mining-	membrana	membrane
μυελός	myel-	medulla	marrow
οὖρον	ur-	urīna	urine
πυλωρός	pylor-		gatekeeper
πύον	py-	pūs, puris	pus
σφόνδυλος	spondyl-	vertebra	vertebra
ὑστέρα	hyster-	uterus	womb
χόνδρος	chondr-	cartilāgō	cartilage

A mosaic in the Museo della Terme in Rome with the famous Greek saying "Know thyself." Note the formation of the Greek letters: ΓΝΩΘΙ ΣΑΥΤΟΝ.

Exercise

A. In the following medical terms identify the Greek root body part that was presented in section one of this chapter.

1. *stethoscope*	26. *metopion*
2. *amyotonia*	27. *mastopexy*
3. *nephrolith*	28. *cnemial*
4. *omphalorrhea*	29. *gnathoschisis*
5. *metacarpal*	30. *stomatitis*
6. *cheiloplasty*	31. *proctology*
7. *notochord*	32. *stethometer*
8. *otorrhagia*	33. *blepharism*
9. *cleidotomy*	34. *omitis*
10. *hepatitis*	35. *thoracoscopy*
11. *rhinoscleroma*	36. *hypoglossal*
12. *pachyonychia*	37. *pneumonomycosis*
13. *encephalasthenia*	38. *sarcoid*
14. *podalgia*	39. *osteodystrophia*
15. *cardiomegaly*	40. *osphyitis*
16. *cystolithiasis*	41. *phallodynia*
17. *odontalgia*	42. *chiromegaly*
18. *brachiocephalic*	43. *syndactylism*
19. *gluteal*	44. *carpoptosis*
20. *trachelodynia*	45. *genioplasty*
21. *tarsometatarsal*	46. *prosopoplegia*
22. *pleuroperitoneal*	47. *trichotrophy*
23. *phleboplasty*	48. *myomalacia*
24. *gonyoncus*	49. *prognathism*
25. *ophthalmoscope*	50. *gastroenteritis*

B. In the following medical terms identify the Latin root body part that was presented in section one of this chapter.

1. *ventrofixation*	6. *vesicocele*
2. *superciliary*	7. *maxillofacial*
3. *pulmonary*	8. *musculocutaneous*
4. *genupectoral*	9. *digital*
5. *mammography*	10. *abdominovesical*

11. *occipital*
12. *ungual*
13. *cerebrifugal*
14. *crural*
15. *fibulocalcaneal*
16. *carneous*
17. *oculonasal*
18. *pedialgia*
19. *pedodontist*
20. *submammary*
21. *subungual*
22. *cordiform*
23. *humeroradial*
24. *monobrachius*
25. *supralumbar*
26. *labiodental*
27. *cervicobuccal*
28. *dorsiflexion*
29. *scapuloclavicular*
30. *adrenal*

31. *patellofemoral*
32. *oronasal*
33. *radioulnar*
34. *umbilical*
35. *tibiofemoral*
36. *frontomaxillary*
37. *lumbocostal*
38. *nervomuscular*
39. *ventomy*
40. *tibiofemoral*
41. *pudendagra*
42. *manual*
43. *subcutaneous*
44. *subcrureus*
45. *subpatellar*
46. *subumbilical*
47. *abnerval*
48. *ciliectomy*
49. *uniocular*
50. *suprarenal*

C. In the following medical terms identify the Greek or Latin root that was presented in section three of this chapter.

1. *angiostenosis*
2. *syndesmotomy*
3. *poliomyelitis*
4. *uremia*
5. *lipoid*
6. *spondylodynia*
7. *histogenous*
8. *dacruorrhea*
9. *hysteroophorectomy*
10. *cytopathology*

11. *vas deferēn s*
12. *adenomalacia*
13. *adipose*
14. *meningitis*
15. *medullocell*
16. *pyorrhea*
17. *enterospasm*
18. *arthroplasty*
19. *lacrimation*
20. *chondrotomy*

Chapter Twenty-Four
Law

It should be clear to see from the terms in the last chapter that Greek played a dominant role in the creation of medical vocabulary. In the present chapter we shall discover a similar dominance of Latin in the field of law. Certainly examples of codification of laws can be found long before the rise of the Romans. It was the Roman people, however, who developed a sophisticated system of civil law that pervaded political and social developments throughout much of the history of western Europe. In the sixth century *A.D.* the Roman emperor Justinian ordered the codification of Roman civil law and had it published as the *Corpus Juris Civilis.* Together with the canon law of the Roman Christian church that developed in the twelfth century, the educated and literate people possessed systems by which to regulate themselves in society. Side by side with these systems for several centuries in England, however, was the common law of the Anglo-Saxons, widely known but originally unwritten and not taught in universities until the mid-eighteenth century. Amid this setting law developed in England and its many colonies, including the United States.

Many derivatives in law arrived from other cultural settings, especially French. The words and phrases below, however, are from Latin. While most can be found in standard English dictionaries, their legal implications are more readily observed in a law dictionary such as *Black's Law Dictionary*, which now can be obtained in abridged form. The terms below are grouped into certain broad categories of law, but in many cases they are not restricted to one area alone.

I. Criminal and Penal

abduction	*deterrent*
aggravated	*extortion*
alibi	*homicide*
allocution	*incarceration*
asylum	*infraction*
capital	*mitigating*
conspiracy	*penal*
culpable	*penitentiary*
detention	*probation*

recidivism   *stigma*
reformatory   *violation*
retaliation

II. Domestic Relations

abortion   *divorce*
adoption   *emancipation*
adultery   *filiation*
alimony   *illegitimate*
annulment   *impediment*
bigamy   *incest*
carnal   *majority*
coercion   *minority*
cohabitation   *pander*
condonation   *pederasty*
conjugal   *pornographic*
consanguinity   *prostitution*
consummation   *seduction*
custody

III. Contracts and Debts

accommodation   *illusory*
bona   *liable*
collateral   *novation*
consideration   *patent*
contingent   *rescission*
contract   *subrogation*
covenant   *usury*
creditor   *vitiation*

IV. **Property and Wills**

accretion
administrator
adverse
affinity
agrarian
alluvian
benevolent
codicil
condominium
confiscation
consanguinity
decedent
domicile
ejection
eluviation

executrix
heir
intestate
legacy
maritime
nautical
perpetuity
preemption
probate
residuary
reversion
riparian
servitude
tenement

V. **Other Areas of Law**

abdication
abjure
abolition
abrogation
abscond
absolution
abstract
accession
accident
accredit
adjudication
advocate
affidavit
ancillary
appendant
ascendancy
attestation
calumny
casus

collusion
concurrent
defalcation
defamation
desecration
dilatory
divestment
estuary
evasive
extenuating
fiduciary
fiscal
fortuitous
gratuitous
illicit
intangible
illusory
incorporeal
jurisprudence

latent	*peripheral*
libel	*plenary*
litigation	*plebiscite*
mandamus	*protocol*
mittimus	*quasi*
pecuniary	*quorum*
peremptory	*revocable*
posthumous	*supervening*

Latin Phrases[1]

Latin Phrase	English Meaning
ab initiō	(a contract void) from the beginning
ab intestātō	from one who made no will
ab invītō	by an unwilling person; unwillingly
actio in rem	action for a thing (to recover what is in another's possession)
ad arbitrium	at will (according to judgment)
ad damnum	to the loss (damage)
ad litem	(guardianship) for a lawsuit
ad rem	to the point; pertinent; a propos
ad testificandum	(a subpoena) for the purpose of testifying
ad valōrem	according to value
aliās	another name
alibī	elsewhere; in another place
aliud est celāre, aliud tacēre	"It is one thing to hide (a fault), another to be silent about it" (in a contract of sale).

---

[1] The Latin phrases for law are not divided into categories in this text, yet many of them clearly belong to only a single aspect of law. Others have a wider context.

amīcus curiae	friend of the court
animus testandī	the intention of making a will
apologia prō vītā suā	defense of one's life
aquā et igni interdictus	forbidden to be furnished with water and fire; outlawed
argumentum ad hominem	argument directed against the person
argumentum ad rem	argument directed against the issue
audī alteram partem	hear the other side (Juvenal, *Sat.*)
bonā fide (emptor)	(a buyer) in good faith
causa proxima (remōta)	proximate (or remote) cause
cavē canem	beware of the dog
caveat emptor	let the buyer beware
caveat venditor	let the seller beware
caveat viātor	let the treveller beware
certiorārī	to be informed of
cēterīs paribus	other things being equal
compos mentis	sound of mind; capable of making a will
consensus ad idem	consensus for the same thing; meeting of minds
corpus dēlictī	substance of a crime; proof that a crime was committed
corpus juris	body of law
damnum absque injuriā	loss or harm without injury
dē factō	according to fact
dē jure	according to right (law)
dē minimīs nōn cūrat lex	the law takes no account of trifles; re. a nuisance claim

dē praesenti	about the present (legal status)
dolī capax	capable of crime (usually 7 years or older)
dolī incapax	incapable of crime
donātio inter vīvōs	gift among the living
dūcēs tēcum	(subpoena) you shall bring with you (certain documents)
eiusdem generis	of the same kind
ex curiā	out of court
ex parte	regarding (in the interest of) only one part
ex post factō	based on what is done afterwards
exitus acta probat	the end justifies the means
ferae nātūrae (animal)	(an animal) of a wild nature; not a domestic animal (*domitae nātūrae*)
fiat justitia	let justice be done
fiat justitia, ruat caelum	let justice be done though heaven falls
fierī faciās	(we order that) you cause (an award) to be made (fr. sale of the defendant's goods)
habeās corpus	(we order that) you have the body (of a person detained brought to court)
ignorantia jūris nēmi-nem excūsat	ignorance of the law excuses no one
impretiābilis	priceless; invaluable
in camerā	in chambers (in a private room)
in esse, in posse, in fierī	in being (state of existence); in being able (realm of possibility); in becoming (actual state of development) - used separately
in flagrante dēlictō	while the crime was blazing (caught red-handed)
in invītum (-am)	against an unwilling person

in locō parentis	in place of a parent
in persōnam	against the person (not a thing)
in re	in the matter (case) of
in rem	against the thing (not a person)
in situ	in its (natural or original) place
in uterō	in the womb; an unborn child
infrā aetātem	under age
inter vīvōs	(gift to be shared) among those alive
intestābilis	a witness not capable or competent to testify
ipsō jūre	by the law itself
jūs accrescendī	right of survivorship
jūs civīle	civil law
jūs divīnum	divine law
jūs gentium	law (right) of nations
jūs nātūrāle	natural law
jūs osculī	right of a kiss (In the past within certain degrees of kinship where the right to kiss existed, the right to marry was prohibited.)
jūs sanguinis	right of blood (citizenship as determined by that of the parents)
jūs solī	right of soil (citizenship as determined from place of birth)
jūs ūtendī	right to use (certain property or goods)
lēx (nōn) scripta	(un-)written law
lēx taliōnis	law of retaliation
licet	it is permitted
līs pendēns	a suit pending

locum tenēn s	one holding a place (or office) temporarily for another
locus contractus	the place of a contract
locus criminis	the place of a crime
locus dēlictī	the place of a crime
locus poenitentiae	place for repentence (opportunity for a person to withdraw from some engagement so long as a particular step has not been taken)
locus sigillī	place of the seal (on a document)
locus stāndī	place of standing; a right to appear in court
malā fidē (venditor)	(a seller) in bad faith
malum prohibitum	thing that is legally rather than morally wrong
mē jūdice	while I am judge; in my judgment
mēns rea	guilty mind (criminal intent)
modus operandī	manner of working
modus vivendī	manner of living
mortis causā	(action) for the sake of (approaching) death
nē exeat	let him not leave (the court's jurisdiction)
nolle prōsequi	(plaintiff's declaration) to be unwilling to prosecute
nolō contendere	I do not wish to contest (the charge)
nōn compos mentis	not sound of mind
nōn licet	it is not permitted (lawful)
nūdum pactum	a bare agreement (contract lacking consideration)
nunc prō tunc	now for then

obiter dictum	incidental remark (in passing); non-binding, judicial opinion
onus probandī	burden of proof
ope et consiliō	(an accessory) with aid and counsel
parī passū	(creditors) on an even footing (for recovering)
particeps criminis	accomplice; a sharer in a crime
per capita	(distributing a legacy equally) by heads
per stirpēs	(distributing a legacy) by branches
persōna (nōn) grāta	a (not) acceptable person (diplomatically among nations)
pignus	pledge
plēnō jūre	with full right
prīmā faciē	on first face (or look)
prō bonō publicō	for the public good (services provided free)
prō dēfectū haerēdis	for want of an heir
prō et con	for and against
prō formā	as a matter of form
prō ratā (ratiōne)	according to one's share
prōpriā manū	by one's own hand
quantum valēbant	as much as they (damaged or lost goods) were worth
quī facit per alium facit per sē	he who does something though another does it through himself
quid prō quō	something for something (consideration)
quō jūre?	by what right?
rē infectā	the business being unfinished; without accomplishing one's purpose

rēbus sīc stantĭbus	with things standing thus; in these circumstances
rēs ipsa loquitur	the matter speaks for itself
rēs jūdicāta	a case decided
rēs publica	the commonwealth; republic
scīre faciās	(we demand that) you cause to know (why a certain court action should not be taken)
sē dēfendendō	in self-defense
senātus consultum	a decree of the senate
sine diē	without a day (being set for reconvening)
sine morā	without delay
sine prōle	(probate of a will of one) without offspring
solvere poenas	to pay the penalty
stāre dēcīsīs	to stand by decisions
stāre in jūdiciō	to stand before a tribunal
stātus quō (ante)	a condition something had before
suā sponte	of his (her) own free will; voluntarily
sub conditiōne	on condition
sub jūdice	(case) before the judge (and not yet decided)
sub suō periculō	at one's own risk
sub rosā	secretly (under the rose)
suī jūris	(guardianship) of one's own right; having the power to act for oneself
suō jūre	in his (or her) own right
summum jūs	the highest law (right)
tabulae nuptiāles	a marriage document
tē jūdice	you being judge

testis	witness
totiēs quotiēs	as often as the occasion arises
uxor (... et ux.)	a wife (... and wife)
vinculum matrimoniī	the bond of marriage

Exercise

Matching. Show that you know the terms in the various categories above by matching them with the definitions or etymologies in the following exercises.

I. Criminal and Penal Terms (not all employed)

1. act of a "falling back" (into past criminal behavior)
2. serving to inhibit or "frighten" one from a criminal act
3. kidnapping or "leading away" of someone
4. conditions that make an offense "milder"
5. period of "testing" the fitness of one to return to society
6. placing of someone "into prison"
7. the "holding away" of imprisoning of someone
8. place for "reshaping" someone
9. blameworthy
10. "mark" of shame or discredit

II. Domestic Relations (not all terms employed)

1. relationship "by blood"
2. release from parental care (literally "from the hand")
3. process or act of determining a child's relationship to a parent
4. guardianship
5. intercourse involving a man and a boy
6. allowance "for food" and other necessary goods
7. an obstacle (to a marriage)
8. force used to dominate or nullify another's free choice
9. implied pardoning of a spouse by continuing a marital relationship
10. the declaring of a marriage void

III. Contracts and Debts (not all terms employed)

1. goods
2. legal bond that "draws" the parties "together"
3. a binding agreement
4. the act of "taking back" or voiding a contract
5. substitution of one (creditor) for another
6. (excessive) charge or interest for "using" money
7. security that indirectly supports a loan
8. act of invalidating an agreement due to a "flaw"

IV. Property and Wills (not all terms employed)

1. something that depends or "touches" upon act or event
2. not having made a will
3. goods (remaining) after the fixed allotments have been distributed
4. property touching a river bank
5. a person who has died
6. relationship by marriage
7. act or process of "turning back" to a previous condition
8. one (f.) who puts a will into effect

V. Other Areas of Law (not all terms employed)

1. something that "lies hidden," especially a defect
2. something that can be "called back"
3. "we command" performance of an act
4. "we send" someone to prison
5. a "full" session or meeting
6. embezzlement or "sickling away" of goods for one's own use
7. after one's death and burial
8. lacking a body, immaterial
9. untouchable, immaterial
10. to "hide away" usually with goods
11. deliberate, malicious misrepresentation of another's character
12. (another term for #11)
13. (a third term for #11)

14. "delaying" tactics
15. secret cooperation ("playing together") for fraudulent purposes
16. "lessening" the seriousness of an act
17. the record or draft of a document
18. "he has sworn"
19. act of violating the sanctity of something
20. happening by chance or accidentally

Chapter Twenty-Five
Philosophy and Theology

Beginning with the pre-Socratics in the sixth and fifth centuries B.C., most early philosophical literature among the ancient Greeks investigated the origins of the universe and similar matters relative to nature. Socrates turned the focus of debate to man and human behavior. The writings of his pupil Plato and Plato's pupil Aristotle treat a multitude of subjects which have dominated western thought for more than two millennia. During Hellenistic times Diogenes Laertius wrote the first history of philosophy, titled *Lives of Eminent Philosophers*. Generally regarded as less original than the Greeks in the development of philosophical ideas, the Romans nevertheless still produced such philosophical writers as Lucretius, Cicero, Seneca the Younger and Marcus Aurelius. In the area of theology Hesiod's *Theogony (Race of the Gods)* composed about 700 B.C., stands as the earliest Greek work devoted strictly to their gods, the Olympians. Elsewhere these gods appear in countless myths beginning with Homer and continuing well into Roman times. From our rich Judeo-Christian heritage critical studies about the Bible, both old and new testaments, appeared in Greek and Latin from early Christian times. Over the centuries these contributed much to the eventual development of a sophisticated vocabulary in English in this subject.

Examine the following lists of words from Greek and Latin roots, arranged by category for philosophy and theology. When necessary, consult your dictionary to note not only the etymology of each word but also the distinctions in definition which separate the terms from one another within the same list. When you are confident that you know them well, complete the exercises at the end of this chapter.

I. Beliefs (*-isms*)

agnosticism	*naturalism*
anthropomorphism	*nominalism*
atheism	*pacifism*
atomism	*pantheism*
deism	*pluralism*
determinism	*polytheism*
empiricism	*pragmatism*

existentialism	*rationalism*
extremism	*relativism*
fanaticism	*scepticism*
gnosticism	*sophism*
hedonism	*spiritualism*
humanism	*stoicism*
idealism	*transcendentalism*
materialism	*unitarianism*
monasticism	*universalism*
monotheism	*utilitarianism*
mysticism	*vitalism*

II. Specialized Studies (*-logies; -ics*)

axiology	*hermeneutics*
cosmology	*metaphysics*
ecclesiology	*ontology*
epistemology	*soteriology*
eschatology	*synoptics*
ethics	*teleology*

III. Logic/Philosophy

abduction	*hypothetical*
absolute	*illogical*
aesthetics	*induction*
apodeictic	*intuition*
category	*judgment*
causation	*justice*
cognitive	*morality*
conscience	*objective*
contingent	*paradox*
deduction	*phenomenon*
dialectic	*presumption*
essence	*subjective*
etiological	*tautologous*
genesis	*voluntary*

IV. Religion/Spiritualism

animism
apocryphal
baptism
canonical
catechumen
catholic
censorship
communion
conversion
creation
decalogue
demonical
eulogy
evangelism
evolution
excommunicate
hierarchy
idolatry
immortality

incarnation
inspiration
liturgy
martyr
miracle
monastery
obscene
occult
orthodox
parable
paraclete
paradise
prophecy
redemption
sacrament
sacrilege
schism
spirituality
synagogue

V. Latin Phrases

Many terms and phrases pertaining to philosophy and disputation have been taken directly into English. Some describe strict thought processes or steps of argumentation. Others are philosophical only in a loose sense as when we say, for example, *in vino veritas* (In wine there is truth).

Latin Phrase	Meaning	Notes
ā fortiōrī	from the stronger (reason)	*with even greater reason*
ā minōrī	from the lesser (reason)	*all the less reason*
ā posteriōrī	from the latter (reason)	*fr. observed facts; empirical knowl.; inductive (Aristotle)*
ā priōrī	from the former (reason)	*fr. self-evident propositions; cause to effect; deductive (Plato)*

ad hoc	for this (purpose or thing)	*temporary*
aequō animō	with even mind	*equanimity*
alter ego	another I	*dear friend*
alter īdem	a second self; another I	
amīcus humānī generis	friend of the human race	
amor patriae	love of country	
aurea mediocritas	golden mediocrity	*the golden mean*
cāsus bellī	opportunity for war	
cōgitō ergō sum	I think, therefore I am	*Descartes*
cum grānō salis	with a grain of salt	
dē factō	from the (actual) fact	*according to fact*
dē gustibus nōn est disputandum	concerning taste it ought not to be disputed	
dē jūre	from right (law)	*according to law*
dēsiderātum	something desired/needed	
dictum	something said; an opinion	
ēns	being	
errātum	an error	
errāre humānum est	to err is human	
est modus in rēbus	there is (always) a proper measure in things	*golden mean should be observed*
ex animō	from the heart	*sincerely*
ex cathēdrā	from the (official) chair	*official*
exceptiō probat rēgulam (dē rēbus nōn exceptīs)	The exception proves the rule (as to things not excepted).	
exceptīs excipiendīs	with the things excepted that should be excepted	*if one makes the necessary exceptions*

ex officiō	from one's office	*resulting fr. one's duty*
expressiō unīus est exclūsiō alterīus	Express mention of one implies the exclusion of the other.	
gnōthi sauton	know thyself	*a Greek expression*
hominis est errāre	It is man's nature to err.	*fr. Terence*
Homō sapiēn s	intelligent (wise) human	*mankind*
in līmine	on the threshold	*at the beginning*
in parte	in part	*partly*
in tōtō	in entirety	*completely*
in vīnō vēritas	In wine there is truth.	
inter aliōs	among other persons	
inter nōs	between (or among) us	
inter sē	among themselves	
ipsissima verba	the very words themselves	
ipsō factō	by the very fact	
īra furor brevis est	Anger is a brief madness.	*fr. Seneca*
malum in sē	bad in itself	*intrinsic evil*
mēden agan	nothing in excess	*Greek expression*
medio tutissimus ibis	By the middle course you will go most safely.	
mūtātīs mūtandīs	with things changed that should be changed	*after making the necessary changes*
nē quid nimis	nothing in excess	
nōn constat	it (an account) does not agree (or balance)	
nōn libet	it is not pleasing (to me)	

nōn licet	it is not permitted	
nōn (nil) obstante	not withstanding	*with nothing standing in the way*
nōn sequitur	it does not follow	*an argument*
omnia vincit vēritas (amor)	truth (love) conquers all	
per accidēn s	by accident	*by chance*
per sē	by itself	*essentially*
placet	it pleases	*official sanction*
post hoc ergō propter hoc	after this therefore on account of it	*a fallacy of argument*
quod erat dēmon- strandum (q.e.d.)	which was to be proved	*in logic or math*
quod erat faciendum	which was to be done	
quod semper, quod ubīque, quod ab omnibus	what (has been held) al- ways, everywhere & by everybody	
rāra avis	a rare bird	*unusual person or thing*
reductio ad absurdum	reduction to absurdity	
secundum nātūra m	according to nature	
similia similibus cūrantur	Like things are cured by like.	
similis similī gaudet	Like takes pleasure in like.	
sine quā nōn	without which (it is) not (possible)	*an essential*
stātus quō (ante)	standing where it was before	*pre-existing condition*
suī generis	of his (her) own kind	*unique*
summum bonum	highest good	
suum cuique	to each his own	

tabula rāsa	blank slate	*mind before influenced by experiences*
terminus ad quem	point to which	*in time or place*
terminus ā quō	point from which	*in time or place*
terra incognita	unknown land	*early maps (geography)*
ūnā vōce	in one voice	*unanimously*
ūnō animō	with one mind	*unanimously*
ut mos est	as is the custom	
verbum sat sa- pienti (est)	a word to the wise is sufficient	
via media	the middle path	
volēns nolēns	willing or not (willing)	*willy-nilly*

Exercise

Matching. Show that you know the terms in the various categories above by matching them with the definitions or etymologies in the following exercises.

I. Beliefs (not all terms used)

1. giving "humans characteristics" to the divine
2. teaching that everything is composed of very small particles
3. belief that all knowledge originates in experience
4. theory that the ultimate reality is composed of two or more entities
5. belief that everything is composed of physical matter
6. belief in only one God
7. belief that God is manifested in everything
8. the practice of practical consequences guiding one's actions
9. the belief that "pleasure" or happiness should guide one's actions
10. belief that emphasizes knowledge from the spiritual or super-natural over experience
11. (another possibility for #10)
12. (a third possibility for #10)

II. *Specialized Studies* (not all terms used)

1. Study dealing with the "last" things (end of the world)
2. Study dealing with the "salvation" of mankind
3. Study dealing with the "interpretation" of religious writings
4. Study dealing with the origin and structure of the universe
5. Study dealing with the "end" or purpose of phenomena
6. Study dealing with the principles of human conduct
7. Study dealing with the nature of human "knowledge"
8. Study dealing with the nature of "being" or "existence"

III. *Logic or Philosophy* (not all terms used)

1. reasoning from the particular to the general, from individual to universal
2. reasoning from the general to the particular, from universal to individual
3. "showing" of necessary truth or absolute certainty
4. "shown" or observed by the senses
5. true by virtue of logical "sameness"
6. "contrary to opinion" and yet possibly true
7. pertaining to knowledge with awareness and judgment
8. the real, ultimate nature of something
9. having to do with the "causes" of things (other than "causation")
10. intellectual investigation by reasoning and discussing in dialogue manner
11. something "taken for" granted due to probability
12. insight to knowledge without rational thought

IV. *Religion or Spiritualism* (not all terms used)

1. one receiving instruction in the doctrine of a faith
2. the "ten" commandments
3. (books) "hidden away" due to doubted authenticity
4. the act of "buying back" and thereby releasing from debt
5. a "split" among religious groups
6. a "comforter"
7. place of worship where people are "brought together"
8. act of a divinity taking on human "flesh"
9. sign or symbol of religious belief
10. "witness" of one's belief often shown by death
11. "worship of an image" or phantom as a god
12. disgusting to the senses and inciting to depravity

Chapter Twenty-Six
Botany & Botanical Nomenclature

The science of systematically arranging plants and animals according to their relationships in nature is known as *taxonomy*. At least as far back as the fourth century B.C. scientists carried on this process of categorizing. Through this technique, which led to many advances in philosophy too, attempts were made to define with logical precision not only visible objects of creation but also the abstract ideas of man. The renowned philosopher-scientist Aristotle (384-322 B.C.) was the first to assign binomial definitions for each plant species. This he did in Greek. For him the genus represented the general class to which a particular living thing belonged; the species identified the uniqueness possessed within the specified class. For nearly 2,000 years Aristotle's scientific classifications were universally employed and accepted. It was not until the eighteenth century that a Swedish scientist named Carolus Linnaeus (1707-1778) greatly expanded the Greek philosopher's system and at the same time converted the universal language to Latin. Separated according to structure within each genus, plants and animals were each assigned distinctive Latin names. Since the time of Linnaeus scientist-scholars around the world have continued the process of labeling in Latin. This is in recognition of the fact that all modern languages constantly undergo change with regard to semantics (word meanings). Because Latin is not spoken anywhere in the world today and its vocabulary cannot undergo further semantic change, the adoption of this language, it was hoped, would remove confusion from nation to nation and age to age.

On the pages that follow the official two-part Latin name is given for some of the more common trees, plants, flowers and vegetables. It would be impossible to reproduce in this space of this small text the tens of thousands of species belonging to the various categories. Scientific dictionaries are available to scholars to consult when necessary. It should be noted, however, that agreement in gender is required for each name combination, *i.e.*, each Latin adjective must agree with its noun. Frequently adjectives and nouns in agreement will end with the same letter as, for example, *Lilium longiflorum* (the Easter Lily). In the lists below you will note that the names of many specific trees and plants in Latin are words of the second or fourth declension and as such end in "*-us*." In most instances, however, their gender is not masculine, but feminine. Therefore, although it may appear odd, an adjective ending in "-*a*" may well be required for agreement in gender with an accompanying noun in "-*us*." Thus *prūnus persica* ("peach") assumes a form that looks, upon first glance, to be incorrect but is correct nonetheless because *prūnus* is a feminine, not masculine, noun.

TREES
(Divided as broadleafed or needleleafed)

A. <u>Common Broadleaf Trees</u>

Acer rubrum	red maple
Acer saccharum	sugar maple
Aeschylus hippocastānum	horse chestnut
Betula papȳrifera	paper birch
Carya illinoensis	pecan
Carya ovata	shagbark hickory
Castanea dentāta	American chestnut
Cercis canadensis	Eastern redbud (Judas)
Citrus limonia	lemon
Citrus sineenis	orange
Cornus flōrida	flowering dogwood
Fāgus grandifolia	American beech
Fraxinus americāna	white ash
Gleditsia triacanthos	honey locust
Ilex opāca	American holly
Jūglans nigra	black walnut
Liquidambar styraciflua	sweet gum
Liriodendron tulipfera	tulip tree
Magnolia grandiflōr	southern magnolia

Mālus pumila	apple
Mŏrus rubra	red mulberry
Platanus occidentālis	American sycamore
Pŏpulus deltoides	Eastern cottonwood
Prūnus armeniāca	apricot
Prūnus avium	sweet cherry
Prūnus domestica	plum
Prūnus persica	peach
Prūnus virginiāna	wild cherry
Quercus lobāta	California white oak
Quercus rubra	red (northern) oak
Robinia pseudoacacia	black locust
Salix babylonica	weeping willow
Sassafras albidum	sassafras
Sobrus americāna	American white ash
Tilia americāna	American linden
Ulmus americāna	American elm

B. Common Needleleaf Tree

Abiēs balsamea	balsam fir
Cupressus macrocarpa	Monterey cypress
Jūniperus chinensis columnāris	blue column juniper
Jūniperus virginiāna	red juniper
Picea mariāna	black spruce
Pīnus ponderōsa	ponderosa pine
Pīnus resinōsa	red pine
Pīnus strobus	white pine

Pseudotsuga menziesii taxifolia	Douglas fir
Sequoia sempervirēn s	redwood
Thuja occidentālis	American arborvitae
Tsuga canadensis	eastern hemlock

HOUSE PLANTS

Asparagus plumōsus	asparagus fern
Brassaia actinophylla	scheflera
Cholorophytum comōsum	spider plant
Euphorbia pulcherrima	poinsettia
Ficus elastica	India rubber tree
Gardenia jasminoides veitchii	gardenia
Hedera helix	English ivy
Lilium longiflōrum	Easter lily
Nephrolepsis exaltāta Bostoniensis	Boston Fern
Philodendron radiātum	philodendron
Saintpaulia ionantha	African violet

GRASSES

Axonopus affinis	carpet grass
Cynodon dactylon	Bermuda grass
Festūca arundinacea	tall fescue
Lolium perenne	perennial rye grass
Poa prātensis	Kentucky blue grass

FLOWERS

Althea rosea	hollyhock
Antirrhinum majus	snapdragon
Begonia semperflōrēn s	wax begonia
Dianthus barbātus	sweet William

Digitālis purpurea	foxglove
Gladidus psittacinus	gladiola
Helianthus annuus	common sunflower
Hemerocallis hybrida	day lily
Hymenocallis occidentālis	spider lily
Ipomoea purpurea	morning glory
Narcissus incomparābilis	daffodil
Papāver orientāle	Oriental poppy
Sanvitalia procumbēns	creeping zinnia
Tagetes tenuifolia pūmila	dwarf marigold

VEGETABLES

Apium graveolēns	celery
Brassica oleracea botrytis	cauliflower
Brassica oleracea capitāta	cabbage
Cucumis satīvus	cucumber
Daucis carota	carrot
Lactūca satīva	lettuce
Lycopersicum esculentum	tomato
Pīsum satīvum	pea
Sōlānum tuberōsum	potato
Spinacia oleracea	spinach
Zea Maya	corn

Terms Related to Botany

abaxial	*agronomy*
abscission	*allelopathy*
achene	*angiosperm*
adhesion	*anther*

anthesis	*heterotrophic*
anthocyanin	*heterozygous*
autoecious	*homologous*
autogamy	*homozygous*
autotrophic	*hormone*
bifrenaria	*hypogeal*
biocide	*mesophyll*
brachyanthus	*metabolism*
callus	*micropyle*
calyx	*mitochondria*
carotene	*monoecious*
carpel	*mycology*
caryopsis	*osmosis*
chlorophyll	*parenchyma*
cohesion	*parthenocarpy*
conifer	*perianth*
corolla	*pericarp*
cortex	*pistil*
cytology	*pheromone*
deciduous	*photophilous*
diffusion	*photosynthesis*
dioecious	*phototropism*
diploid	*phytochrome*
diurnal	*pollen*
edaphic	*raceme*
endogenous	*rhizome*
epidermis	*semiarid*
epigeal	*senescence*
epigyny	*sepal*
epiphyte	*stamen*
exogenous	*symbiosis*
flocculate	*synergids*
gametophyte	*tetraploid*
geotropism	*thallophyte*
germination	*transpiration*
guttation	*vernalization*
gynoecium	*xanthophyll*
herbaceous	*xylem*
hermaphrodite	*zygote*

Exercise

A. Many colorful adjectival labels accompany nouns in the labeling of plants. Some can be translated into English from our past study of Latin vocabulary. Others are easily recognized from similar existing English words. Identify the meaning of the following:

1. *grandiflōra*	8. *semperviren s*
2. *parviflōra*	9. *augustifolia*
3. *penduliflōra*	10. *rotundifolia*
4. *orientālis*	11. *brilliantissima*
5. *occidentālis*	12. *ēlegantissima*
6. *deliciōsa*	13. *minutissima*
7. *amābilis*	14. *incomparābilis*

B. Identify the (transliterated) Greek or Latin roots in the left column below that appear in one or more of the many terms for botany (listed earlier in the chapter) with their closest definition or etymology on the right.

1. *carpos*	A. fine flour
2. *phellos*	B. drops
3. *thallos*	C. virgin, lacking fertilization
4. *corolla*	D. fruit
5. *cary*	E. bark, cork
6. *pollen*	F. walnut, nut kernel
7. *parthenos*	G. cup
8. *gutta*	H. small crown, garland
9. *rhizoma*	I. root, stem
10. *calyx*	J. twig, young shoot

C. Identify the *gender* (*m.*, *f.*, or *n.*) of each of the words below based on the accompanying adjectival form appearing with them in the list of binomial examples earlier in the chapter.

1. *acer*	6. *pīnu s*
2. *citrus*	7. *philodendron*
3. *jūglans*	8. *helianthus*
4. *mālus*	9. *hemerocallis*
5. *salix*	10. *cucumis*

Chapter Twenty-Seven
Zoological Nomenclature

In the last chapter the Latin scientific names for many common plants were listed according to the binomial classification system developed by the eighteenth-century, Swedish scientist Carolus Linnaeus in his *Systēma Nātūrae*. The same technique of identification was established for the animal world as well. In both cataloguing systems the scientist created several divisions and subdivisions. The names of these divisions are given below in such a way that each general category heading is listed on the left with the corresponding particular name for "*man*" at each level noted on the right.

Except for obvious differences in anatomy, the labeling of body parts and related vocabulary for most animals remains practically the same as that for humans. Since that list was already presented in chapter twenty-three, it will not be repeated in this chapter. Other words related to the field, however, are included below.

Classification

Kingdom	**Animālia** (Animals)
Phylum	**Chordāta** (Chordates)
Subphylum	**Vertēbrāta** (Vertebrates)
Class	**Mammālia** (Mammals)
Subclass	**Euthēria** (Eutherians)
Order	**Prīmāta** (Primates)
Suborder	**Anthrōpoidea** (Anthropoids)
Family	**Hominidae** (Hominids)
Genus Species	**Homō sapiēns** (Mankind)

All animals, from the smallest insect to the largest of beasts, not only possess a binomial Latin name such as that for humans (*homō sapiēns*) but also fall into one of the divisional categories at each level. For example, some *classes* in addition to *Mammālia* (Mammals) include:

Avēs	birds
Reptilia	reptiles
Amphibia	frogs, *etc.*
Osteoichthyes	bony fish[1]
Chondrichthyes	cartilage fish[1]

Orders in addition to *Prīmāta* (Primates), with an example on the right for each, are as follows:

Marsupiālia	kangaroos
Insectivora	moles
Chiroptera	bats
Rodentia	mice
Carnivora	lions
Proboscidea	elephants
Perissodactyla	horses

Since the scope of this text is concerned with English derivatives from Greek and Latin as well as with complete Latin phrases which occasionally appear in English, two special lists are presented in this chapter. In the first, only the simple Latin name is given for some of the more common animals. From most of these simple English derivatives have been created. *E.g.*, *"canine"* from *canis* (dog). The second list contains the scientific binomial name for many animals, mostly mammals. In this type of listing, you should note, it has become accepted practice to present the genus first with a capital letter followed by the species (epithet) in a small letter. Of course, agreement in gender is also required. Today the International Commission on Zoological Nomenclature periodically reviews animal classifications and occasionally approves new entries in the field.

---

[1] In modern times the names *osteoichthyes* and *chondrichthyes* have been modified to *Piscēs* (fish) and *Selachiī* (shark), respectively.

Simple Latin Names
for Common Animals

apis	*bee*
aquila	*eagle*
asinus	*ass, donkey*
avis	*bird*
bōs, bovis	*ox*
canis	*dog*
cervus	*deer*
crocodīlus	*crocodile*
elephantus	*elephant*
equus	*horse*
fēlis	*cat*
formīca	*ant*
hircus	*goat*
leō, -ōnis	*lion*
mūs, mūris	*mouse*
ovis	*sheep*
piscis	*fish*
porcus	*pig*
serpēns, -entis	*snake*
sīmia	*monkey*
taurus	*bull*
tīgris	*tiger*
ursus, ursa	*bear*
vacca	*cow*
vulpes, -pis	*fox*

Binomial Listing of Animals
Some Examples

Equus caballus	*domestic horse*
Equus asinus	*ass, donkey*
Equus zebra	*zebra*
Rhinoceros ūnicornis	*Indian rhinoceros*
Diceros bīcornis	*black rhinoceros*
Fēlis catus	*domestic cat*
Fēlis rufa	*bobcat*
Panthēra tīgris	*tiger*
Panthēra leō	*lion*
Panthēra pardus	*leopard*
Mūs musculus	*house mouse*
Apodēmus sylvāticus	*field mouse*
Ursus americānus	*black bear*
Ursus arctos	*brown bear*
Thalarctos maritīmus	*polar bear*
Ailuropoda melanoleuca	*giant panda*
Canis familiāris	*dog*
Canis lupus	*grey wolf*
Canis lātrāns	*coyote*
Vulpes fulva	*red fox*
Vulpes leucopōs	*dessert fox*
Procyon lōtor	*North American raccoon*
Mustēla nivālis	*weasel*
Mustēla nigripēs	*ferret*

Elephas maximus	*Indian elephant*
Loxodonta africāna	*African elephant*
Sūs scrōfa	*European pig*
Hippopotamus amphibius	*hippopotamus*
Camēlus dromedārius	*one-humped camel*
Camēlus bactriānus	*two-humped camel*
Cervus elephas	*red deer*
Rangifer tarandrus	*reindeer*
Giraffa camēlopardālis	*giraffe*
Oreamnos americānus	*Rocky Mountain goat*
Ovis ariēs	*domestic sheep*
Capra aegagros	*wild goat*
Delphīnus delphis	*common dolphin*
Phōcaena phōcaena	*porpoise*
Phōca vitulīna	*seal*
Crocūta crocūta	*hyena*
Passer domesticus	*domestic sparrow*
Coturnix coturnix	*quail*
Pelicānus occidentālis	*pelican*
Apterodytes patagonica	*penguin*
Gymnogyps californiānus	*condor*

Derivative Study

agnatha	*cynodont*
bicameral	*deuterostome*
carnivorous	*diarthrognathus*
centriole	*dipleurula*
chela	*embryology*
cloaca	*entomostracan*

euryphagous	*pterygian*
exteroceptor	*pygidium*
flagellum	*pyrenoid*
gastrula	*radula*
glabrous	*rhyncodeum*
invagination	*rostrum*
isolecithal	*scutellum*
labyrinthodont	*scyphistoma*
maxilliped	*spiracle*
nematocyst	*squamata*
ocellus	*stenophagous*
ossicle	*tentacle*
oviparous	*ungulate*
poikilotherm	*vestigial*

Exercise

A. According to their etymology with which animal would the following words be associated?

1. *apiary*	5. *apian*
2. *feline*	6. *vaccinate*
3. *formicary*	7. *murine*
4. *piscary*	8. *simian*

B. Prepare a list of body parts of various animals for which there is no comparable human equivalent. Give the etymology of each word in your list. *E.g., antennae* (sail-yard). A few examples appear in the derivative study list above.

Chapter Twenty-Eight
Astronomy

Of all the recognized subject areas of inquiry, certainly one of the oldest is astronomy. We know, for instance, that the Egyptians and Babylonians were quite active in the study of the stars. The earliest Greek philosophers, i.e., those prior to Socrates, also seem to have been concerned rather narrowly with the origins of the universe and similar aspects of nature. Thales (c. 625-547 B.C.), for example, knew well of the division of the solar year into 365 days and supposedly predicted correctly the solar eclipse of May 28, 585 B.C. Pythagoras, Aristarchus, Hipparchus, and Ptolemy all wrote extensively on the subject. It is no wonder then that much of our terminology in this subject field is derived directly from Greek and Latin.

Derivative Study

aberration	*comet*
absolute	*composition*
absorption	*conic*
acceleration	*constellation*
altimeter	*convection*
altitude	*conversion*
angular	*corona*
apolune	*cosmic*
ascension	*cosmology*
asteroid	*crater*
astrophysics	*declination*
astronomy	*deferent*
atmosphere	*diffraction*
atom	*diffuse*
autumnal	*dispersion*
bolometer	*eclipse*
binary	*ecliptic*
calendar	*emission*
celestial	*energy*
collimate	*ephemeris*
collision	*epicycle*

equilibrium
equinox
exponent
filament
fission
fusion
galactic, galaxy
geocentric
globular
gravitation
granule
heliocentric
hemisphere
hydrogen
inclination
ionosphere
isotope
kinetic
latitude
libration
longitude
Lucifer
luminosity
lunar
magnification
magnitude
meridian
meteor
molecule
nebula
nucleus
occultation
opacity
orbit
parabola
parallax
penumbra
perigee
perihelion

perilune
photometer
photosphere
planetarium
potential
pulsate
quantum
radiation
radical
rectilinear
recurrent
reflection
refraction
regression
resolution
retardation
retrograde
revolution
satellite
seismograph
sidereal
solstice
spectroheliogram
spectrum
sphere
stellar
stratosphere
synthesis
tangent
telescope
terminator
terrestrial
transverse
troposphere
universe
vector
velocity
vernal
zodiac

Names of the Planets

Mercury   **Mercurius** Roman god of commerce and travel, messenger

Venus   **Venus, Veneris** Roman god of love and beauty

Mars   **Mars, Martis** Roman god of war

Jupiter   **Jupiter, Iovis** Roman sky god, chief god

Saturn   **Saturnus** Roman god of agriculture, father of Jupiter

Uranus   **Uranus** Greek sky god, personification of "heaven"

Neptune   **Neptunus** Roman god of the sea, brother of Jupiter

Pluto   **Pluto** Roman god of the underworld, brother of Jupiter

Signs of the Zodiac

Leo	Sagittarius	Aries
Virgo	Capricornus	Taurus
Libra	Aquarius	Gemini
Scorpius	Pisces	Cancer

Constellations and Stars

Aquila   *coma Berenices*
Arcturus   *Columba*
Auriga   *Cygnus*
Aurora Borialis   *corona Australis*
canes Venatici   *corona Borealis*
Capella   *Delphinus*
Cassiopeia   *Draco*

Hercules	*Serpens Caput*
Hydra	*Taurus*
Leo Minor	*Trapezium*
Orion	*Tricuspis*
Pegasus	*Virgo*
Polaris	*Vulpecula*
Serpens Cauda	

Although astronomers in ancient times devoted much attention to the moon, it was not until the early seventeenth century with the use of the telescope that its surface was studied. In 1609 the Italian scientist Galileo charted several surface formations and assigned Latin names to them. Before long moon map-makers standardized these names which are still in use today. Although some "mountains" (*montes*) rise more than 20,000 feet, the "seas" (*maria*) were incorrectly named as such since they are now known to contain no water. See the map on the next page.

Exercise

A. Identify as many Greek and Latin animal names as you can after which constellations and stars are named. A few appear above.

B. Explain the Greek and Roman myths associated with any fifteen constellations.

THE MOON

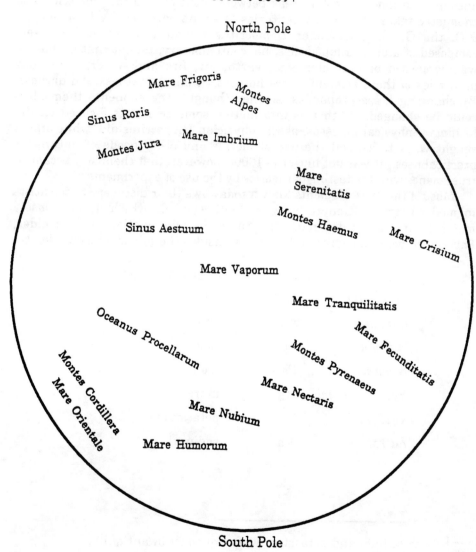

North Pole

Mare Frigoris

Montes Alpes

Sinus Roris

Montes Jura

Mare Imbrium

Mare Serenitatis

Montes Haemus

Mare Crisium

Sinus Aestuum

Mare Vaporum

Mare Tranquilitatis

Mare Fecunditatis

Oceanus Procellarum

Montes Pyrenaeus

Mare Nectaris

Montes Cordillera

Mare Orientale

Mare Nubium

Mare Humorum

South Pole

Chapter Twenty-Nine
Chemical & Pharmaceutical Terms

Just as thousands of words unique to medicine and other sciences have entered the English language from Greek and Latin, so also is the case with chemistry and pharmacy. The history of these related subjects is indeed ancient even though a clear break between alchemy and the true science of chemistry takes place many centuries later. As early as the fifth century B.C. the Greek philosopher Democritus taught that substances were composed of atoms. Empedocles, his contemporary, taught that all nature was composed of four elements: earth, air, fire and water. The four properties of these elements were hotness, coldness, wetness and dryness. By changing these properties, so they thought, the elements themselves could be changed. With this information some scientists focused on the healing of physical illnesses, as the physician Hippocrites did, while others sought ways to expand the use of metals and other goods of nature for practical uses. It was not until the 1600s, however, that chemistry became a true science with the testing of theories by the use of experiments.

Most of the 100+ elements known today owe their discovery to scientists in modern times. Generally, a few with symbols which do not closely match their modern-day name but carry the abbreviation of their older, Latin form were known in antiquity. Consider the following examples.

Latin	Symbol	Element
argentum	Ag	silver
aurum	Au	gold
cuprum	Cu	copper
ferrum	Fe	iron
hydrargyrum	Hg	mercury
kalium	K	potassium[1]
natron	Na	sodium[1]

---

1 Both sodium and potassium were unknown in antiquity.

plumbum	Pb	lead
stannum	Sn	tin
stibium	Sb	antimony

The naming of complexes in chemistry has an interesting history. Originally named after their discoverer, they soon often assumed names associated with their color. Presently, however, rules for nomenclature are approved by the International Union of Pure and Applied Chemistry. As expected, numerical attachments appear in Latin forms. To indicate the number of each kind of substance when more than one kind is present, Greek numbers are employed in transliteration as prefixes. To indicate the oxidation state, on the other hand, Roman numerals are added as suffixes.

The following words are proper to either chemistry or pharmacy.

Derivative Study

affinity
amorphous
amphoteric
analgesic
antipruritic
antipyretic
antisudorific
antithrombin
antitoxin
apothecary
barometer
bicapsular
bivalent
calation
calorimetry
cation
chromatic
chromophore
coagulant
codeine
colation
colligation

constituent
converge
covalence
crystallization
desalination
desiccation
dialysis
diffusion
disinfect
diverge
dosage
effusion
electron
empirical
emulsification
enzyme
equilibrium
equivalence
exothermic
fluctuation
generic
gelatin

germicidal	node
hallucinogen	nucleus
halogen	opiate
hemolysis	pharmacodynamics
heterogenous	pharmacopsychosis
homogenous	precipitation
hypothesis	photon
hydrolysis	proton
injection	radiation
insulin	radical
intratracheal	repulsion
intravenous	semipermeable
isomerism	spectrometer
isotope	sublimation
metathesis	syringe
molecule	thermodynamics
mutation	toxin
narcotic	univalent
neutron	vial

Latin phrases dealing with the administration of drugs in pharmacy can be divided into two groups below. The first relates to directions of TIME when medication should be given or applied, as follows:

Latin Phrase	Abbreviation	Meaning
ad libitum	ad lib.	at will; as it pleases
bīs in diē	b.i.d.	twice a day
ter in diē	t.i.d.	three times a day
quater in diē	q.i.d.	four times a day
quāque diē	q.d.	every day
omnī hōrā	o.h.	every hour
in diēs	in d.	daily
quotidie	quotid.	daily
alternīs diēbus	alt. dieb.	on alternate days
quāque hōrā	q.h.	every hour

hōrā somnī	*h.s.*	at bedtime
omnī hōrā	*omn. hor.*	every hour
ante cibum	*a.c.*	before a meal
post cibum	*p.c.*	after a meal
māne et nocte	*m. et n.*	morning and night
prō rē nātā	*p.r.n.*	as occasion arises
si opus sit	*s.o.s.*	if necessary

The second group relates to directions for the preparation or administration of medication.

da	*d.*	give, administer
dīluē	*dil.*	dilute
miscē	*m.*	mix
notā bene	*n.b.*	mark well
recipē	*Rx*	take
signētur	*sig.*	let it be labelled
solvē	*solv.*	dissolve
sumē	*sum.*	take
cum	*c*	with
sine	*s*	without
circā	*c.*	about, approximately
aqua	*aq.*	water
quantum libet	*q.l.*	as much as desired
quantum satis	*q.s.*	as much as is sufficient
ut dictum	*ut dict.*	as directed

Exercise

1. Analyze and define the terms in the derivative section of this lesson.

2. Write ten chemical complexes and show how the various parts in their technical name employ Greek and Latin roots.

Chapter Thirty
Terms in Psychology and Sociology

To some degree psychology and sociology may be regarded as relatively new subjects of study in higher education, more recent than philosophy, but much older than such technical fields as computer science. The same can be said of the other social sciences: anthropology, political science and economics; for they all can trace their academic origins back only a couple hundred years to the Age of Enlightenment. Although this may be so, any student of classics can still readily point out that the customary objects of investigation in all these fields were invariably discussed and debated with vigor in Greek and Roman times. The one thing most treatises then lacked was an accompanying statistical or scientific survey that most scholarly investigations possess today. Herodotus, Thucydides, Livy, Tacitus and other historians from antiquity, for example, offered many insights not only into the social institutions of their time in their respective Greek and Roman worlds but also into those of tribes beyond their borders. Moreover, beginning with Socrates in the fifth century B.C., philosophers began to focus on man and his behavior (ethics), on logical reasoning and on just how things were known. Finally, the surviving speeches of such orators as Demosthenes and Cicero indicate how hotly debated were political institutions and the interpretations given to society's laws. For these reasons it is not unexpected for us to find that present-day technical vocabulary in these fields owes a significant debt to the Greek and Latin languages.

Derivative Study

A. Terms in Psychology

acquiescence	*amnesia*
acrophobia	*androgynous*
aesthetics	*anima*
afferent	*animus*
aggression	*anorexia nervosa*
agnostic	*anosmia*
agoraphobia	*aphagia*
ambivalence	*autokinetic*

aversion
bipolar
bulimia nervosa
catatonic
catharsis
charismatic
claustrophobia
coercion
cognition
cohesion
complement
compulsive
concordant
congruity
consumption
contingency
delirium tremens
dementia
divergent
delusion
dichotic
dyslexia
echoic
eclectic
efferent
egocentrism
eidetic
Electra
emanation
empiricism
extravert
facilitation
gregariousness
hallucinogen

homeostasis
hyperphagia
hypnosis
hypochondriasis
id
idiosyncrasy
implicit
in vivo
ingratiation
inhibition
introvert
kinesics
latent
libido
masochism
mimicry
mnemonic
narcissism
obtrusion
Oedipus
phallicism
placebo
predatory
psychodelic
psychogenic
psychokinesis
repression
repulsion
schizoid
segregation
subliminal
tabula rasa
telepathy
thanatos

B. Terms in Sociology

acculturation
affiliation
aggregate
agnates

agrarian
anomie
assimilation
attraction

autonomy
bigamy
capitalism
chromosome
cognates
colonialism
communism
conjugal
contingency
convergence
cooptation
delusion
democracy
demography
demonic
deprivation
deviance
dramaturgy
dyad
ecology
ectomorph
ecumenical
empathy
enculturation
endogamy
endomorph
ethics
ethnocentrism
evolutionary
exogamy
fecundity
hedonism
hermaphrodite
heterosocial
homicide
homogamy
hormone

hypothesis
illegitimate
incarceration
incest
inferiority
integration
intergenerational
intimacy
latent
megalopolis
mesomorph
misogamy
monogamy
mores
nomadic
oligarchy
paradigm
polyandry
polygamy
polygyny
promiscuity
propaganda
radicalism
reciprocity
rehabilitation
retaliation
retribution
segregation
socioeconomic
somtatotype
stigma
suicide
totalitarian
transvestite
triangulation
urbanization
xenophobia

Exercise

1. **Phobias**. The fear of objects often reflects a condition or state of the mind that deserves psychological attention. Review the "phobias" in exercise "C" of Chapter Six. These were based mostly on roots encountered in earlier chapters. Below, match the object feared in the right column with its proper term on the left. You may encounter some difficulty finding each phobia in your dictionary, but usually the Greek or Latin root can be found in related word borrowings.

1. *hylophobia*		A. wind	
2. *entomophobia*		B. forests	
3. *pharmacophobia*		C. sea	
4. *brontophobia*		D. poison	
5. *triskaidekaphobia*		E. glass	
6. *trichopathophobia*		F. medicine	
7. *harmatophobia*		G. blushing	
8. *toxicophobia*		H. dampness	
9. *anemophobia*		I. number "13"	
10. *thalassophobia*		J. insects	
11. *erythrophobia*		K. hair	
12. *hyelophobia*		L. sin	

2. **Killings (-cides)**. Acts of violence against individuals or objects in nature have often been described with the Latin suffix "-cide" (from the verb *caedere* meaning "to kill"). Identify what is being killed by matching the terms on the left with their proper etymology or definition on the right.

1. *fratricide*	A. oneself
2. *patricide*	B. grass
3. *ecocide*	C. brother
4. *herbicide*	D. king
5. *tyrannicide*	E. environment
6. *fungicide*	F. seed
7. *regicide*	G. father
8. *suicide*	H. life
9. *biocide*	I. absolute ruler
10. *spermicide*	J. bacteria

Chapter Thirty-One
Mottoes in Government & Education,
Degree Titles, Terms in Education

Most Latin (and Greek) mottoes that can be found today contain a cleverly-worded phrase from biblical or classical literature. The Roman poet Vergil, for example, was the inspiration for the phrases *annuit coeptis* and *novus ordo seclorum* on the Great Seal of the United States. The first is taken from his *Aeneid* 9.625, the second from his *Bucolics* 4.5. Mottoes of states and universities are also dependent on this great master. In almost all cases, the phrases contain an uplifting message or espouse a virtue, such as courage, hope, justice, truth, wisdom or knowledge. Reference to light (standing no doubt for wisdom) seems to be a particularly favorite theme of educational institutions as students are hopefully raised from the darkness of ignorance. Others possess a religious overtone.

A. Mottoes in the U.S. Government

From the Great Seal

(These can be found on the back of the one dollar bill.)

Annuit coeptīs	He (God) has nodded assent to our undertakings.
Novus ōrdō sēclōrum	A new order of ages
E plūribus ūnum	One out of many

Governmental Departments and Academies

Acta nōn verba	Acts, not words. (U.S. Merchant Marine Academy)
Ex scientiā tridens	The trident from knowledge. (U.S. Naval Academy)
Quī prō dominā justitiā sequitur	Who pursues for Lady Justice. (Dept. of Justice)

Scientiae cēdit mare	The sea yields to knowledge. (U.S. Coast Guard Academy)
Semper Fidēlis	Always faithful. (U.S. Marine Corps)
Spēs anchora vītae	Hope the anchor of life. (Dept. of Health, Educ. & Welfare)

B. State Mottoes

Ad astra per aspera	To the stars through difficulties. (KA)
Audēmus jūra nostra dēfendere	We dare defend our rights. (AL)
Cēdant arma togae	Let arms yield to the toga. (WY*)
Crēscit eundō	It grows as it goes. (NM)
Dīrigō	I direct. (ME)
Dītat Deus	God enriches. (AZ)
Dum Spīrọ, Spērō	As long as I breathe, I hope. (SC)
Ense petit placidam sub lībertāte quiētem	By the sword he seeks a peaceful quiet with liberty. (MA)
Esse quam vidērī	To be rather than to seem. (NC)
Estōperpetua	Be forever! (ID)
Eurēka	I have discovered it! (CA)
Excelsior	Higher. (NY)
Imperium in imperiō	An empire in an empire. (OH*)
Justitia omnibus	Justice to all. (D.C.)
Labor omnia vincit	Work conquers all. (OK)
Montāni semper līberī	Mountaineers are always free. (WV)
Nil sine nūmine	Nothing without Providence. (CO)
Quī trānstulit sustinet	He who transplanted sustains. (CN)

Regnat populus	The people rule. (AR)
Salūs populī suprēma lēx estō	Let the safety of the people be the supreme law. (MO)
Scūtō bonae voluntātis tuae corōnāsti nōs	With the shield of your good will you crowned us. (MD)
Si quaeris pēninsulam amoenam, circumspice	If you are seeking a pleasant peninsula, look around. (MI)
Sīc semper tyrannīs	Thus always to tyrants. (VA)
Virtūte et armīs	By virtue and arms. (MS)

* Former motto or motto as a territory.

C. Mottoes of Colleges and Universities

Latin/Greek Motto	Translation
Ad majōrem Deī glōriam	To the greater glory of God. (Loyola Univ., IL)
Artēs, scientia, vēritās	Arts, science, truth. (U. of Michigan)
Certā bonum certāmen	Fight the good fight. (Iona Coll., NY)
Cīvium in mōribus rei pūblicae salūs	The safety of the republic is in the morals of its citizens. (U. of Florida)
Crēscat scientia vīta excōlātur	Let knowledge grow, let life be perfected. (Univ. of Chicago, IL)
Dābō tibi corōnam vītae	I shall give you the crown of life. (Bard Coll., NY)
Deī sub nūmine viget	Under the providence of God it flourishes. (Princeton Univ., NJ)
Eruditio et religio	Learning and religion. (Duke U., NC)
Ex ūnō fonte	From one source. (Coll. of Wooster, OH)

In Deō spērāmus	In God we trust. (Brown Univ., RI)
In fide vestra virtūtem, in virtūte autem scientiam	Courage in your faith, but knowledge in your courage. (Agnes Scott Coll., GA)
In lūmine tuō vidēbimus lūmen	In your light we shall see the light. (Ohio Wesleyan Univ., OH)
Ineāmus ad discendum, exeāmus ad merendum	Let us enter to learn, let us leave to acquire. (Jersey City St. Coll, NJ)
Incipit vīta nova	A new life is beginning. (Scripps Coll, CA)
ΛΑΜΨΑΤΩ ΤΟ ΦΩΣ	Let the light shine. (Adrian Coll., MI)
Lēgēs sine mōribus vānae	Laws without morals are vane. (Univ. of Pennsylvania)
Lūx et vēritās	Light and truth. (Yale, CN; Indiana U)
Lūx fiat	Let there be light. (Albion Coll., MI; Alfred Coll., NY)
Lūx vestra lūceat	Let your light shine. (Notre Dame Coll., NH)
Macte virtūte sīc itur ad astra	Well done! Thus one approaches the stars. (Manhattan Sch. of Music,NY)
Mēns et manus	Mind and hand. (Massachusetts Institute of Technology)
Nūmen lūmen	Providence, light. (U. of Wisconsin)
Nūmen flūmenque	Providence and river. (Marquette U,WI)
Palmam quī meruit ferat	Let him who has deserved the palm carry it. (U of Southern California; Roanoke Coll., VA)
Perstāre et Praestāre	To persist and excel. (New York U.)
ΠΙΣΤΕΙ ΤΗΝ ΑΡΕΤΗΝ, ΕΝ ΔΕ ΤΗΙ ΑΡΕΤΗΙ ΤΗΝ ΓΝΩΣΙΝ	Courage in your faith, but knowledge in your courage. (Allegheny Coll. PA)

Post tenebrās lūx	After darkness light. (American Internat. Coll, MA)
Prō Deō et Patriā	For God and Country. (American Univ., Washington, D.C.)
Prōdesse quam conspicī	To benefit rather than to observe. (Miami Univ., OH)
Quaecumque sunt vēra	Whatever are true. (Northwestern U., IL)
Religio, doctrīna, cīvīlitas, prae omnibus virtūs	Religion, learning, civility, but courage before all. (Ohio Univ.)
Religiōni et bonīs artibus	To religion and the liberal arts. (Boston Coll., MA; St. Louis Univ., MO)
Rosam quae meruit ferat	Let her who has deserved the rose carry it. (Sweet Briar Coll., VA)
Sapientia et doctrīna	Wisdom and learning. (Fordham U., NY)
Sīcut lilium inter spīnās	As a lily among thorns. (Marian Coll. of Fond du Lac, WI)
Terrās irradient	They shall light up the lands. (Amherst Coll., MA)
Vēritās	Truth. (Radlcliffe Coll., MA)
Vēritās Christō et ecclēsiae	Truth to Christ and the church. (Harvard Univ., MA)
Vēritās et justitia	Truth and justice. (Albright Coll, PA)
Vēritātem dīlexi	I have loved the truth. (Bryn Mawr, PA)
Vincit quī sē vincit	He conquers who conquers himself. (Mount Vernon Coll., Wash., D.C.)
Vīta sine litterīs mors est	Life without literature is death. (Adelphi Univ., NY)
Vōx clāmantis in dēsertō	Voice of one shouting in the desert. (Dartmouth Coll., NH)

D. Academic Degree Titles

Artium Baccalaureus	A.B.	Bachelor of Arts
Baccalaureus Artium	B.A.	
Artium Magister	A.M.	Master of Arts
Magister Artium	M.A.	
Scientiae Baccalaureus	Sc. B.	Bachelor of Science
Scientiae Magister	Sc.M.	Master of Science
Scientiae Doctor	Sc.D.	Doctor of Science
Divinitātis Doctor	D.D.	Doctor of Divinity
Jŭris Doctor	J.D.	Doctor of Law
Jurum Doctor	J.D.	Doctor of Laws
Juris Canonici Doctor	J.C.D.	Doctor of Canon Law
Jŭris Utriusque Doctor ***	J.U.D.	Doctor of Both (Civil & Canon) Laws
Lĕgum Baccalaureus*	LL.B.	Bachelor of Laws
Lĕgum Magister	LL.M.	Master of Laws
Lĕgum Doctor*	L.D.	Doctor of Laws
Litterārum Doctor**	Litt.D.	Doctor of Letters (or Literature)
Medicīnae Doctor	M.D.	Doctor of Medicine
Philosophiae Doctor	Ph.D.	Doctor of Philosophy
Scientiae Jŭridicae Doctor	S.J.D.	Doctor of Juristic Science
Sacrae Theologiae Doctor	S.T.D.	Doctor of Sacred Theology

* No longer in common use
** Honorary degree (*honoris causa*)
*** European/Latin American

E. Educational Terms

ad hoc	for this (purpose, and therefore often for a limited time)
alma māter	foster mother
alumna (pl., -*ae* -) fem.	foster child
alumnus (pl., -*ī*) masc.	foster child
cum honōre	with honor
cum laude	with praise
ēmerita (pl., -*ae*) fem.	deserved by service; (retired)
ēmeritus (pl., -*ī*) masc.	deserved by service; (retired)
ex officiō	(arising) from one's office; by virtue of an office
honōris causā	for the sake of honor
in absentiā	absent (from an assembled group)
in locō parentis	in the place of a parent
locus sigillī	place for (lit. of) the seal (as on an official transcript or document)
magnā cum laude	with great praise
summā cum laude	with the highest praise

Exercise

Among the mottoes on the preceding pages find as many examples as you can of the "inspirational words" noted below. Give the word quoted and, if possible, the original ultimate word form that you first encountered earlier in the text. E.g., faith: *semper fidelis* (*fidelis* - faithful) from (*fides* - faith)

1. truth
2. light
3. hope

4. virtue
5. wisdom/knowledge
6. faith

Chapter Thirty-Two
Expressions of Time

References to various aspects of TIME have been assembled in this lesson. Most deal with time "when" or "how long." A few however specify time only in reference to some other fixed moment such as birth, death, or a war. Some of these phrases are used in English as adverbs as when we say "he talked *ad infinitum*." Others occur as adjectives; for example, "She was given a *per diem* allowance while attending the conference."

Time Expression	Meaning
ab incūnābulīs	from the beginning (lit. "from the cradle")
ab initiō	from the beginning
ab ōvō	from the beginning (lit. "from the egg")
ad fīnem	to the end
ad infinītum	to infinity
ad interim	for the meantime
ad nauseam	to a sickening degree (or point)
annō Doiminī (A. D.)	in the year of the Lord
annō mundī	in the year of the universe
ante bellum	before the war
ante merīdiem (a. m.)	before noon
ante mortem	before death
ex tempore	out of time; impromptu; with no time for preparation
impromptū	not ready; without preparation
in aeternum	into eternity
in futūrō	in the future

in perpetuum	into perpetuity
in praeteritō	in the past
in praesenti	in the present
interim	in the meantime
per annum	by the year
per diem	by the day
per mensem	by the month
post bellum	after the war
post mēridiem (p. m.)	after noon
post mortem	after death
post partum	after birth
prō tempore (prō tem.)	for the time being
sĭcut ante	as before
statim (stat)	at once
status quo ante	standing where it was before
tempus fugit	time flies

Exercise

Write *ten* brief sentences in which you employ properly a different Latin expression of time found in this lesson. E.g., "I so enjoyed this subject that I could study these classical languages *ad infinitum!*"

Ave atque vale! Catullus
(Hail and farewell!)